Directors' Choice
The Greatest Film Scenes of All Time and Why

Directors' Choice
The Greatest Film Scenes of All Time and Why

Robert D. McCracken

FILM AESTHETICS

Marion Street Publishing Co.

Copyright © 1999 by Robert D. McCracken
All rights reserved. No part of this book may be reproduced or
transmitted in any form or by any means, electronic or mechanical,
including photocopying, recording, or by any information storage and
retrieval system, without permission in writing by the Publisher.

Library of Congress Catalog Card Number 98-83163
ISBN 0-9639119-4-5

MARION STREET PUBLISHING CO.
3930 South Swenson, Suite 810
Las Vegas, Nevada 89119

Printed in the United States of America

For my brother, Mike,

whose lifelong love of art helped inspire

my romance with that world.

Contents

List of Tables and Figures	ix
Acknowledgments	xi
Overview	1
Part 1: Great Scenes in the Movies	**7**
Introduction	7
About Art	8
About Science	10
Measuring the Subjective	11
The Scientific Study of Film	12
Research Methods	12
Results Part 1: The Greatest Scenes, Shots, Films, and Directors	17

The Greatest Shots in Film, 19
The Greatest Movies, 19
The Greatest Directors, 22

Results Part 2: What Makes a Great Scene Great?	25

Craft Statements, 27
Emotion Statements, 29
Intellectual Statements, 34

Part 2: The Magnificent Ten: Greatest Scenes from Movies	**39**

Lawrence of Arabia, 40
The Player, 41

Contents

On the Waterfront, 43
Citizen Kane, 45
The French Connection, 47
The Battleship Potemkin, 48
Singin' in the Rain, 50
Apocalypse Now, 52
Psycho, 53
Casablanca, 56

Part 3:	Directors' Greatest Film Scene Choices and Reasons	59
Part 4:	Art Defined and Its Origins	165

What Is Art? 165
Where Does Artistic Merit Exist? 169
Film: A Pinnacle of Art 171
The Human Mind and the Origins of Art 172
    Consilience and Art, 172
    Dualistic Thinking, 173
    Bonobos Watch Movies, 174
    In the Beginning, 175
    The Human Family Lineage, 176
    Emotions and Their Function, 187
    Origins of Art and Religion, 194
    The Biology of Emotions, 197
What Is Beauty and Why Are We Attracted to It? 201
    Beauty: What Is It? 201
    On the Innate Attraction to Beauty, 207
    Watching Emotions of Others, 208

Afterword: Commercial Applications		211
Bibliography		213
Appendix A:	The Questionnaire and Letter	217
Appendix B:	List of Great Directors	221
Appendix C:	Terms Participants Used to Connote Emotions, Feelings, and Sensations	229
Index		235

Tables and Figures

Tables

1	Ten greatest scenes in movies	3
2	Movies with the largest number of greatest scene nominations	3
3	Top ten greatest directors	4
4	Summary of data collection	15
5	Paid versus nonpaid participants	16
6	Greatest scenes in movies	20
7	Greatest shots in movies	21
8	Movies with the largest number of greatest scene nominations	23
9	Greatest directors	24
10	Distribution of craft, emotion, and intellectual statements	26
11	Crafts mentioned by directors in their justifications of great scene selections	28
12	Frequently used terms denoting emotions	31
13	Ten most frequently used terms denoting high affect emotions and feelings	32
14	Summary of abstract concepts used by directors	37
15	Human family lineage	178

Figures

1	Two dimensions of art	168
2	Scheme illustrating the human lineage	180

Acknowledgments

Susan Kay performed most of the many clerical tasks involved in our survey of the members of the Directors Guild of America. Jean Charney transcribed all the directors' responses and did most of the word processing of the manuscript. Cynthia Tremblay proofread the transcriptions of the directors' responses and Bobette Host proofread the entire manuscript. Michelle Asakawa edited our manuscript and prepared it for typesetting. Sandra Rush did the typesetting, indexing, and final proofreading.

Two of my colleagues at Film Aesthetics, Michael McCracken and Theodore D. Graves, were a constant source of stimulation in developing the ideas contained in this book, and Dr. Graves assisted in the data analysis. The directors who gave so generously of their time and effort in responding to our survey made this book possible. My deeply felt thanks to all these people.

Robert D. McCracken
November 1998

Overview

The question we wanted to answer is this: "What is it that makes a good movie?" Or, "Why are some films so enjoyable, even memorable, and others so boring and uninteresting?" We know there are many opinions on these questions. Such opinions span a wide variety of ideas and theories, and it is difficult to make sense out of it all.

In trying to understand what distinguishes good films from bad ones, we decided to look at the question scientifically. By using the best methods available to the social sciences, we hoped to rise above the level of personal opinion and say something we could back up with scientific research. By better understanding film quality, we hoped by implication to be able to answer these questions, "What is art? How did it originate?" We began our research with as open a mind as possible so as not to bias our results. We deliberately avoided commitment to any particular theory about film or its viewing. We were unaware of any preference for one method for making films over another. We chose to conduct our research with a group of filmmaking experts, and we were determined to let our conclusions emerge out of what these experts told us.

The experts we chose to "speak" to were film and television directors. We assumed they know as much, probably more, about actually making movies as any other group. Because a whole film is a very complex work of art and would be difficult to deal with in detail, we narrowed our focus to single scenes in movies to make our research more manageable. In 1993–1994 we mailed questionnaires to most of the directors who were members of the Directors Guild of America, the largest and most important professional organization for film and television directors. We kept our questionnaire simple. After defining what we meant by a film scene, we asked the directors to make a list of up to ten selections that they considered to be the "greatest," "most memorable," "most distinguished" scenes in the history of movies. No restrictions on possible choices were imposed. Then the directors were asked to cite their reasons for making each selection.

One hundred and seventeen directors responded to our questionnaire. By counting the directors' selections we assembled a table of film scenes in order of the frequency mentioned. The scene that landed at the top of our "greatest" or "most memorable" list was the farewell scene from *Casablanca*. It was followed by the shower scene from *Psycho*. Table 1 lists the top ten scenes. [Because the last of our questionnaires were mailed in February 1994, any film released after that date was not considered. Given the fact that new great scenes are continually being made, some directors no doubt might wish to amend their lists if given the chance. For example, *Leaving Las Vegas* (1995), *LA Confidential* (1997), *Titanic* (1997), *Saving Private Ryan* (1998), and many other critically hailed recent films were not considered.]

By adding up the number of times scenes from a particular film were chosen, we constructed a list of the greatest films. A list of the ten films with the largest number of greatest scene nominations is found in Table 2. The top film was, not unexpectedly, *Citizen Kane*, followed closely by *Casablanca*. We also used our great scenes data to compile a list of top directors. By combining data for number of films with great scenes listed and total scenes nominated, Alfred Hitchcock ended up at the top, followed by Stephen Spielberg. The list of the ten greatest directors, according to our data, is found in Table 3.

Making the lists in Tables 1–3 was the easy part. Next we analyzed and reanalyzed the directors' reasons for making their selections. (The directors' selections and their justifications are re-

Table 1. TEN GREATEST SCENES IN MOVIES

Rank	Film	Scene	Date
1	Casablanca	Farewell at end	1942
2	Psycho	Shower scene	1960
3–4	Apocalypse Now	Ride of the Valkyries	1979
	Singin' in the Rain	Dance to title song	1952
5	The Battleship Potemkin	The Odessa steps	1925
6	The French Connection	Car chase	1971
7–8	Citizen Kane	Rosebud sled burns	1941
	On the Waterfront	"I coulda been a contender"	1954
9	The Player	Opening scene	1992
10	Lawrence of Arabia	Sharif rides out of mirage	1962

Table 2. MOVIES WITH THE LARGEST NUMBER OF GREATEST SCENE NOMINATIONS

Rank	Film	Date
1	Citizen Kane	1941
2	Casablanca	1942
3	Apocalypse Now	1979
4	Psycho	1960
5–7	Gone with the Wind	1939
	2001: A Space Odyssey	1968
	Singin' in the Rain	1952
8	Schindler's List	1993
9	Lawrence of Arabia	1962
10–11	The Battleship Potemkin	1925
	The Godfather	1972

printed in Part 3 of this book.) Using a technique called *content analysis*, we counted the number of times different words and concepts were used in the directors' justifications for their selections, and we organized the results under different topics, or headings, that seemed appropriate.

Table 3. TOP TEN GREATEST DIRECTORS

Rank order	Name	Rank order by number of films with great scenes listed		Rank order by total number of scenes nominated		Combined score
1	A. Hitchcock	1	+	1	=	2
2	S. Spielberg	2	+	2	=	4
3	S. Kubrick	6	+	5	=	11
4–6	F. F. Coppola	10	+	3	=	13
	O. Welles	10	+	3	=	13
	W. Wyler	2	+	11	=	13
7	D. Lean	6	+	8	=	14
8–9	C. Chaplin	8	+	7	=	15
	J. Ford	2	+	13	=	15
10	W. Allen	2	+	15	=	17

No one was surprised to find that words and concepts relating to *craft* or techniques of making films were the most frequently listed rationales for choosing a scene. Craft terms refer to such things as the use of the camera or visual qualities of a film, the writing or story's plot, the actors' performances, film editing and directions, and so on. What really surprised us—and perhaps some would argue it shouldn't have—was the extensive use directors made of words and concepts having to do with human *emotions* in their justifications. The list of different emotion-related terms the directors used looks like a thesaurus of emotions; more than 400 different terms connoting emotions were used. Moreover, the greater the length in words of the directors' justifications, the more likely they were to use emotion words; this was not true for craft terms. (From a scientific point of view, greater use of emotion terms coinciding with more lengthy responses strengthens our confidence in the validity of our findings on emotions and film quality.) When you ask a director why a scene is great, there is a powerful tendency, after he or she mentions craft and technique, to praise the emotional content of the scene and its power to evoke emotion in viewers. We also found

Overview

directors justify a scene's selection in terms of what we call its intellectual qualities, such as the film's theme—for example, the battle between good and evil—and the use of metaphor, symbolism, abstract values, and the like. But the intellectual factor was not mentioned nearly as often as either craft or emotion.

From our results we concluded that the key to making great scenes in film is the skillful use of craft to evoke emotion in viewers. With this in mind, we concluded that at rock bottom *all* art can be defined as *craft plus emotion*. The level of craft and the emotion evoked in viewers can, of course, vary in works of art, but these are the key elements. There are other factors important to art, such as its intellectual content, social context, personal relevance, and participation by the viewer, but in the end art boils down to the craft of the artist and the emotion of the viewer.

We believe these results can be used to develop methods to better predict scientifically the economic and artistic success of a film as it is being made and marketed. (For more on this, see the Afterword.)

Given the powerful role that emotions play in art appreciation, we have attempted in Part 4 to outline a theory of the origin of art in human society and the role that the evolution of the capacity to experience a sense of beauty, awe, ecstasy, and the sublime played in those beginnings. We suggest that it was the appearance of these higher emotions in our ancestors, perhaps some 50,000 or 60,000 years ago, that made the first true art and religion possible. An effort is made to show how the origins of art can help explain our capacity to appreciate it. The past 5 million years of human evolution are briefly outlined with an eye toward the supposition that the ever-increasing capacity for emotional complexity in our ancestors, along with an increased ability for rational thought, is the basis for the origin of both art and religion in modern humans. Scientists now believe they are beginning to understand the molecular basis of the panoply of emotions we all experience.

Art and the emotions it evokes are central to what we are as human beings. Film is arguably the pinnacle of art forms, and great films are among the most sublime of human achievements.

PART 1

Great Scenes in the Movies

Introduction

The art of filmmaking is only one hundred years old. The first motion picture wasn't shown to an audience until 1895. Yet, despite its youth—compared to painting, sculpture, drama, and other traditional art forms—movies are by far the most important art form of the twentieth century.

In this little book we are going to take a very special tour of the cinema, one like none ever presented. We are going on a tour of a gallery, the Louvre of great cinema. At this gallery, we are going to look at some of the greatest scenes ever to appear in films. In addition, we are going to determine, from the perspective of our research, what are the greatest films in history, and who are the greatest film directors.

Lists of great movies come and go, but one thing is different about our lists. They have been constructed as objectively and scientifically as possible, by asking directors themselves to nominate what they believe are the greatest scenes in the movies and state what it is that makes them great. We want to know more about that special something we all recognize but find so hard to put our fingers on that separates a great scene or a great film from ones that are not so good. What is more, because movies are an art form, in learning more about what makes movies great, we hope to gain some insight into what makes for great art in general. Because we will be studying movies using systematic procedures from the social sciences, we need to say a few words about art and science.

About Art

The term *art* has many definitions. The fact that it has been defined in many ways for over 2,500 years that we know of, and continues to be redefined (Menand, 1998: 39–41), suggests that it is a category of some diffuseness (Firth, 1995: 15). Aristotle (384–322 B.C.) distinguished between *techné*, which referred to anything deliberately created by humans, and *physis*, which referred to nature, or whatever exists outside humankind. In English, *techné* is found in such words as *technology*, *technique*, and *technical*; *physis*, of course, is the root of the word *physics*, perhaps the most fundamental of the physical sciences.

Many meanings exist for the word *techné*. Included under the ancient Greek usages of *techné* were such things as houses, clothing, carts, and tools; excluded were things of nature such as stars, mountains, waterfalls, and seashores. Also included under *techné* were a variety of sciences and arts, and knowledge, and rules of procedure on how to do or make things, including what we would call the *fine arts*. Plato (427?–347? B.C.), Aristotle's teacher, divided the arts into musical arts (songs, dances, instrumental performances, and combinations of these), visual arts (painting, architecture, sculpture, pottery making), and literary arts (poetry, drama, dialogue) (Angeles, 1981: 212; 289–290).

Fine arts have been represented as a separate subject of study since at least the origins of English universities in the twelfth century. In Western society, when we speak of art, we are usually talking about the fine arts, including painting, sculpture, architecture, music, dance, and literature. The newest of the major art forms, film—as we propose, by far the most important art form of the twentieth century—would also have to be considered a fine art; it is a synthesis of the elements in Plato's three subdivisions, with the additions of photography, cinematography, and film editing, which of course did not exist in Plato's time. As a historic culmination, film is arguably the highest, most complex, most evolved of all the art forms to this point in history.

Much of what is called art from non-Western cultures—for instance, sculpture from Papua New Guinea or Central Africa, dry or "sand" paintings from the Navajo Indians, or mythic tales from people such as the Hopi Indians—is closely linked to religious beliefs and observances, and has little real meaning for people outside local religious contexts. It was not until the early part of the seventeenth century, about the time of Dutch painter Jan Vermeer (1632–1675), that art in Western society began to separate from religion, a transition made possible by the rising wealth of a merchant class who replaced the church as the primary source for funding artists. He who has the wealth calls the tune.

The word *aesthetics* is important when considering art. Like the word *techné*, it comes from the Greek: *Aisthétikos* means "one who is perceptive of things through his sensations, feelings, and intuitions." Aesthetics typically involves the study of beauty and related concepts such as the sublime, the tragic, the ugly, the humorous, the drab, and the pretty by means of feelings, sensations, and emotions. Aesthetics also involves "the analysis of the values, tastes, attitudes, and standards involved in our experience of and judgements about things made by humans or found in nature which we call beautiful" (Angeles, 1981: 4). The aesthetic response is a subjective reaction to the observed, inseparable from and grounded in the emotions. Although objects and phenomena from the natural world, such as waterfalls and sunsets, are capable of stimulating in us feelings and emotions that can only be described as aesthetic, for something to be art in our terms, it must be, as the Greeks would say, *techné* or man-made, not *physis* or from nature. Art requires a human agency.

About Science

Whereas art is fundamentally subjective, science is the opposite. Science involves a systematic effort to view the world objectively. Science goes to great ends and does all that it can to rule out the subjective element in experience. Science involves the construction of theories about the nature of the world, and the careful testing and refinement of those theories through experiments and measurements. Measurements are taken, and using the principles of logic, the results are then checked against what the theory would lead us to expect; the theory is then modified or replaced as necessary so as to account for the measurements. A new set of measurements is then taken and again compared with the theory. In this stepwise fashion an ever-evolving edifice of theory and measurement is constructed. This edifice is what we call scientific knowledge, and we treasure it because it works. Because measurements are taken in the real world, and theories must work there, science is said to be empirical, derived from observations and experiments as opposed to the nonempirical or nonscientific, which derive from subjective opinion.

Because science is based on objective measurement, it is possible for others to agree on how measurements are to be taken and on their results. Because agreement on the results of measurement is possible, scientists can repeat each other's experiments. When one scientist repeats another's experiment and gets the same or similar results, the experiment is said to have been replicated. Repeatability gives us what is called *interobserver agreement*. When two or more observers agree that an experiment was or could be repeated under comparable conditions and that essentially the same results were or could be obtained, interobserver agreement is said to exist. Science proceeds and scientists work on the basis of interobserver agreement. Interobserver agreement concerning the results of measurement is relatively easily obtained in the study of the natural world, the world we can all see. But scientists run into big problems when they try to study the subjective world, the world within the human mind. Because art and aesthetics by definition involve subjectivity, scientists are often thwarted when they try to study art and aesthetics objectively.

The problem is that we are trying to look at and measure what is going on inside someone's head. We all know how difficult that can be. No way has been found to say with any confidence what another person is thinking and experiencing. An engineer can take a reading on a voltage meter, a biologist can count the number of fish in a stream, and everyone can agree with their measurements, but there is no way to reliably measure a person's aesthetic experience when viewing a film or listening to music. They can *tell* us what they are experiencing, but we cannot measure it directly.

Measuring the Subjective

Social scientists have struggled with this problem and have arrived at strategies based on inferences about shared experiences as noted in self-reports. Instead of trying to look inside the head of one person, a number of individuals are asked to report on their subjective experiences, for example while looking at a picture. Then the scientist takes all the reports and looks for patterns in the data. Although the patterns are really for a group, they tell us by inference something about individual experience. We call such findings *patterns of intersubjectivity*, *inter* meaning *between* or *among*. Such patterns of intersubjectivity exist because members of the group have certain things in common—the human nervous system, a culture or society, and a history of experience within that society. Thus, although we cannot know the exact experience of any one individual in a group, we do know something about the patterning of group experience, and then, by inference, something about the average individual's subjective state. In this way, we obtain interobserver agreement. Other researchers can agree with how we collected and analyzed our data, obtained these patterns of intersubjectivity, and inferred subjective states. In a manner of speaking, we looked "inside" people's heads without really doing so.

Paradoxical though it may be, we solve this same problem all the time in everyday life. For example, when members of American culture talk about "being in love," there is considerable agreement among people about the subjective feelings they experience when they fall in love, even though we cannot look inside each other's heads to assess how others "really" feel. We have interobserver agreements about love, a subjective experience that cannot be observed.

The Scientific Study of Film

The subjective experiences of film viewing can be studied scientifically in the same way. By studying the patterns of intersubjectivity in a group of filmgoers, we can determine what it is about films that pleases people and elevates some of the films to the level of great art while other films leave viewers disappointed.

The individual with the most authority on a film set is the *director*. He or she is most responsible for integrating the many crafts and skills needed to make a movie, from writing and rewriting of the script to the cinematography, lighting, instruction to the actors, composition of the shot, makeup, wardrobe, set design and construction, editing, and so on. More than anyone else involved in moviemaking, the director is faced with creatively translating a host of arts and crafts into a completed product. A painting is signed by its artist, a novel by its author; a film is released under the signature of its director. Given directors' central role in filmmaking, they are uniquely qualified to speak on issues of quality and aesthetics in film.

Research Methods

When we began this research we had no particular theory of film aesthetics in mind. Rather than start with a theory and test various hypotheses—the usual approach in science—we started with an open mind and tried to let a theory of aesthetics emerge out of the data we collected. This approach to *theory generating* is called *grounded theory*" (Glaser and Strauss, 1967) and is a preferred strategy at the beginning of an investigation, or when the researcher wants to take a fresh look at a research topic rather than to test and refine a previously existing viewpoint.

To provide us with a relatively large number of expert opinions about what constitutes great filmmaking, we decided to conduct a survey among the members of the Directors Guild of America, the

Part 1: Great Scenes in the Movies

preeminent professional association for film and television directors in the United States. Of the guild's more than 9,700 members, which besides directors includes assistant directors, unit production managers, and stage managers, 5,050, or roughly 90 percent of all those listed as "directors," were invited to participate.[1] Names were obtained from the guild's publicly available *Directory of Members* (1993).

Because a film is a lengthy and complex work of art, we also decided to simplify our task, and that of our participating directors, by focusing our attention on film scenes, the basic unit from which films are assembled.

Let us briefly define what we mean by a scene in a movie. A movie is made up of individual *camera shots* all carefully spliced together, one after the other. To make a shot, the camera is loaded with film, pointed at something, and turned on for anywhere from a fraction of a second to several minutes, then turned off. The result is a shot—the exposed film produced from a single camera setup. A *scene* is a segment of a movie made up of one or more related shots unified by a central concern—a location, an incident, perhaps a minor dramatic climax. A scene can last from less than a minute to up to ten minutes or more. A scene in a movie is a little bit like a building block. When the blocks are carefully stacked atop one another, a completed figure—in this case, a movie—results. On average, a ninety-minute movie contains between 90 and 120 scenes, with sometimes as many as 260 (Hubbert, 1998).

A one-page cover letter on formal letterhead stationery accompanied by our questionnaire and a postage-paid return envelope were mailed to each director in an individually addressed business-size envelope featuring our name and logo, using a first-class stamp. The letter explained that our research group, Film Aesthetics, was made up of a small assortment of film and social science professionals interested in better understanding the art of filmmaking. It then invited them as members of the Directors Guild of America to help

---

[1] Among those not included in our survey were the small number of directors without listed addresses and those with addresses outside the United States.

us compile a list of great scenes from the movies by nominating up to ten scenes they considered to be "the greatest," "most memorable," or "most distinguished" in film, together with a brief statement of the reasons for each of their selections. To avoid confusion, three short definitions of the word *scene* were included in the cover letter.[2] On the back of this one-page questionnaire directors were also invited to select one or two candidates for "the greatest single shot (a single camera setup) in the history of film" and reasons for their choices. That was all that was asked of them.

In order to provide substantial interobserver subjectivity and a basis for statistical analysis our goal was to obtain at least one hundred completed questionnaires. Experience with mailed surveys of this type has shown that the response rate is typically below 3 percent. We hoped that by making the questionnaire short and simple and the task professionally interesting to respondents we could obtain a higher response rate. However, because our research subjects were unusually busy, creative, and highly paid professionals, we were not sure what return rate to expect. Given the high cost of conducting a survey of this kind, we therefore decided to determine response rates (and therefore how many directors we would need to contact) through an initial mailing to a carefully selected random sample of 1,000 members of our subject population. This first mailing went out in late spring 1993. Eleven completed questionnaires were sent back, for a disastrously disappointing return rate of 1.1 percent.

A second mailing of 1,000 questionnaires was scheduled for fall 1993. By this time we were resigned to sending questionnaires to essentially all eligible directors. Even then we might not obtain sufficient responses to permit stable statistical results. So we also decided to conduct a small experiment. We wondered what effect an offer to *pay* participants might have on return rates and on data quality. Not knowing what to expect, we randomly selected one hun-

---

[2]The definitions came from Ephraim Katz's *The Film Encyclopedia* (1979), Ira Konigsberg's *The Complete Film Dictionary* (1987), and Louis Giannetti's *Understanding Movies* (1990). Copies of this cover letter and accompanying questionnaire are presented in Appendix A.

dred directors' names that had not previously been contacted and mailed them the identical questionnaire and cover letter. The only difference was that we included a short note promising to send them a $20 bill by return mail upon receipt of a completed questionnaire. To our pleasant surprise, the return rate jumped to 4 percent, whereas the return rate for the parallel mailing of 1,000 without an offer of payment was only 1.3 percent (see Table 4). A fourth and fifth mailing sent out simultaneously in early 1994 confirmed this finding: Those directors offered a token payment of $20 returned their completed questionnaires at more than triple the rate of those who were not offered payment.

In this manner a total of 117 completed questionnaires were obtained, containing a total of 1,016 great scene nominations, most with accompanying justifications for each choice, for an average of 8.7 great scenes per director. Though we consider the data on all returned questionnaires to be of high quality, directors who were paid seemed to be more committed to the task, generally giving more time and thought to preparing their answers. One director who was paid wrote the following comment on his questionnaire, illustrating how seriously some participants took making their selections.

> Over the past month your questionnaire has taken up more of my time than I ever intended it to. I found myself talking about scenes at work, at lunch, at home. There were heated discussions.

Table 4. SUMMARY OF DATA COLLECTION

Mailing & date	Number of questionnaires mailed	Payment	Number of questionnaires returned	Percent returned
I Spring 1993	1,000	none	11	1.1
II Fall 1993	1,000	none	13	1.3
III Fall 1993	100	$20	4	4.0
IV Early 1994	2,000	none	34	1.7
V Early 1994	950	$20	55	5.7

Relationships were formed and severed based on what scenes certain friends liked and other friends didn't. Often I found that there were scenes I remembered as being great, but I couldn't remember why. And I had to rent and fast-forward through *Touch of Evil, Miller's Crossing,* and *Chinatown* to pick the best scenes. (*Chinatown* didn't make the cut, nor did close runner-ups: *The Godfather I & II, The Conversation,* or *Five Easy Pieces.*) And only 10?! I could have listed a top 40, or 100. (And it was just cruel to limit shot choices to two.) In any case, it was a stimulating exercise, but there came a point when I just had to get it out—each day I thought of a new great scene that simply had to be included, but then I'd have to take one off. The horror, the horror. Thanks for the exquisite torture.

For example, 13 of the 59 directors who were paid typed their responses; only two of the 58 unpaid respondents did so. And their responses were over 40 percent longer, an average of 249 words versus 176 words for the unpaid respondents. On the average, they nominated more scenes (8.9 vs. 8.4), and their reasons for selecting these scenes were richer in content (see Table 5).

There were significant cost differences per returned questionnaire between paid and nonpaid participants as well. When total postage, clerical, and stationery costs were computed, the cost for paid respondents, including their $20 payment, was about $45 per completed questionnaire; the cost per completed questionnaire for unpaid participants was about $95, or over double. Paying participants therefore resulted in significant savings with the bonus of an

Table 5. PAID VERSUS NONPAID PARTICIPANTS

	Number of questionnaires mailed	Number of questionnaires returned	Percent returned
Not paid	4,000	58	1.5
Paid $20	1,050	59	5.6
Combined total	5,050	117	2.3

increase in data quality. The money itself probably did not account for this difference. Twenty dollars is not a lot of money for a film director in the 1990s. But when an offer is made to pay someone to fill out a survey questionnaire, the request seems to be taken more seriously.

Results Part 1: The Greatest Scenes, Shots, Films, and Directors

Many people compile lists of the best films of the year, the best performances, and similar items. Sometimes listmakers adopt a longer view and include films from a decade or more. Most of the time these lists are based on no more than one person's subjective opinion. The best known example is the annual listing by the Academy of Motion Picture Art and Sciences. Although the Academy Award nominations and awards are based on assessments by film professionals, they are highly sensitive to promotion, sentimentality, and box office receipts, and voters provide no justification for their choices. Recently the American Film Institute compiled a list of the top 100 American films by asking a group of 1,500 well-connected people in the film industry as well as others, including the president and vice-president of the United States, to pick the 100 top films from a ballot of 400 movies selected by the Film Institute. No word was given on who the participants were or what the return rate was, and participants were not asked to justify their selections (*Newsweek Extra: The 100 Best Movies*, 1998).

Between 1913 and 1970 the *New York Times* published about 19,000 film reviews. That sum is thought to represent only a fraction of the films produced worldwide during those years (Amberg, 1971). One can only guess at how many films have been produced since 1970. When we began this project, some suggested that with so many films involving so many scenes we could never hope to find agreement among directors on "the greatest" or "most distinguished" ones. The universe of possible choices was simply too large and people's preferences too idiosyncratic. Luckily for the sake of this study, these predictions proved wrong.

Directors' Choice

For the top fifteen scenes a remarkable core of agreement was found. Each received at least seven nominations, and the top five received double or triple that number. The farewell scene in *Casablanca* was the most frequently mentioned great scene in the movies, followed closely by the murder in the shower in *Psycho*. Eighteen percent of the directors included the *Casablanca* good-bye scene in their list of great scenes; 15 percent included the shower scene from *Psycho*. Tied for third and fourth on our list are the helicopter ballet to Wagner's "Ride of the Valkyries" in *Apocalypse Now* and Gene Kelly's dance to the title song in *Singin' in the Rain*. Both were selected by just under 15 percent of the directors. The slaughter on the Odessa steps in *The Battleship Potemkin* comes next, followed by the car chase in *The French Connection*, listed by 12 and 9 percent of the directors in our study, respectively. The "I coulda been a contender" scene featuring Marlon Brando and Rod Steiger in the backseat of a taxi in *On the Waterfront* and the final scene from *Citizen Kane*, where the Rosebud sled burns, tied for seventh and eighth place, with just under 9 percent each. The technically masterful opening scene from *The Player* (8 percent) was the ninth most frequently mentioned, and Omar Sharif riding out of the desert mirage in *Lawrence of Arabia* (7 percent) was tenth. The scene featuring the edit from the bone tossed into the air by an ape man to a space station in *2001: A Space Odyssey*, the breakfast scene in *Citizen Kane*, the slow-motion fight scene from *Raging Bull*, the train wreck in *The Fugitive*, and Charlie Chaplin eating his shoe in *The Gold Rush* round off the top fifteen scenes, with about 6 percent of the directors listing each of them. All fifty-four scenes receiving three or more nominations are included in Table 6.

The top fifteen scenes are well distributed in time. Two are silent films from the 1920s, three are from the 1940s, two from the 1950s, three from the 1960s, two from the 1970s, one from the 1980s, and two from the 1990s.

The scenes run the gamut in terms of content, from one of the most romantic movie scenes ever produced *(Casablanca)* to one of the most terrifying *(Psycho)*. They include one of the best chase scenes ever *(The French Connection)*; a scene with outstanding special effects *(The Fugitive)*; scenes exhibiting superlative techniques, such as *The Battleship Potemkin* for editing and *The Player* for camera movement and staging; *Singin' in the Rain* for dance and choreography; and seldom matched acting with its revelation of character in *On the Waterfront*.

Although another group of film directors, or a different sampling of film crafts, might produce some different nominations or rank orderings, most people knowledgeable about film would agree that all these scenes represent distinguished examples of the craft, worthy of appearing in a Louvre of twentieth-century filmmaking. (For interested readers, particularly film buffs and students of cinema, a description of the top ten scenes and the circumstances under which they were produced is presented in Part 2 of this volume.)

The Greatest Shots in Film

In addition to indicating their favorite movie scenes, most of our respondents also nominated one or two "greatest shots" from a single camera setup. Sixteen listed the long opening shot, really a scene, from *The Player*. It is probably the most complex shot ever undertaken in film, involving almost unimaginable coordination between camera and actors and lasting eight minutes and six seconds. The number two shot on our list, which helped inspire the one from *The Player*, is the famous and complex opening shot from *Touch of Evil*, which lasted three minutes and twenty seconds. It was nominated by fifteen directors. Tied for third and fourth on our list are the pullback shot of the rail yard in Atlanta in *Gone with the Wind* and Omar Sharif riding out of the desert mirage in *Lawrence of Arabia*. The long steadicam tracking shot of Ray Liotta's character entering the Copacabana in *Good Fellas* is number five, nominated by nine directors (see Table 7).

The Greatest Movies

One way to compile a list of "the greatest movies" is to simply count the number of times scenes from a single film were nominated as among the greatest. By using this method, *Citizen Kane* tops our list: Thirty-one directors included scenes from this film in their top ten

Directors' Choice

Table 6. GREATEST SCENES IN MOVIES

Rank	Number of nominations	Film	Scene	Date
1	21	Casablanca	Farewell at end	1942
2	18	Psycho	Shower scene	1960
3–4	17	Apocalypse Now	Ride of the Valkyries	1979
		Singin' in the Rain	Dance to title song	1952
5	14	The Battleship Potemkin	The Odessa Steps	1925
6	11	The French Connection	Car chase	1971
7–8	10	Citizen Kane	Rosebud	1941
		On the Waterfront	"I coulda been a contender"	1954
9	9	The Player	Opening scene	1992
10	8	Lawrence of Arabia	Sharif rides out of mirage	1962
11–15	7	Citizen Kane	Breakfast over the years	1941
		Raging Bull	Fight scene	1980
		The Fugitive	Train wreck	1993
		The Gold Rush	Chaplin eating his shoe	1925
		2001: A Space Odyssey	Cut from bone to spaceship	1968
16–19	6	E.T., the Extra-Terrestrial	Kids riding bikes against the moon	1982
		Ben-Hur	Chariot race	1959
		Gone with the Wind	"Frankly, my dear . . ."	1939
		The Great Dictator	Playing with the globe	1940
20–24	5	Casablanca	Singing of national anthems	1942
		Five Easy Pieces	Toast scene	1970
		Gone with the Wind	War dead at railroad station	1939
		City Lights	Chaplin seen as benefactor	1931
		Close Encounters of the Third Kind	Landing of the mother ship	1977
25–34	4	Dr. Strangelove	Pickens rides H-bomb	1964
		Hiroshima Mon Amour	Love scene in bed at opening	1959

Part 1: Great Scenes in the Movies

Table 6. GREATEST SCENES IN MOVIES—continued

Rank	Number of nominations	Film	Scene	Date
25–34 (continued)	4	A Night at the Opera	Stateroom scene	1935
		A Place in the Sun	Clift & Taylor's kiss	1951
		The Silence of the Lambs	First meeting with Hopkins	1991
		Butch Cassidy and the Sundance Kid	The big jump	1969
		Casablanca	Bogart & Bergman meet again	1939
		Citizen Kane	Opening shot	1941
		Taxi Driver	De Niro practicing in front of mirror	1976
		The Piano	Piano plunges into sea & Hunter decides to live	1993
35–54	3	Touch of Evil	Opening shot	1958
		The Bridge on the River Kwai	Guinness blows up bridge	1957
		Citizen Kane	Thatcher library	1941
		The Godfather	The horse's head	1972
		The Godfather	The garden scene	1972
		The Gold Rush	Chaplin & the potato	1925
		The Gold Rush	The teetering cabin	1925
		Gone with the Wind	The burning of Atlanta	1939
		Henry V (Olivier version)	Battle of Agincourt	1944
		High Noon	Waiting for the train	1952
		Jaws	Shaw describing the U-boat experience	1975
		Lawrence of Arabia	Battle at the train	1962
		On the Waterfront	Final scene	1954
		Schindler's List	Girl in the red dress	2993
		Schindler's List	Clearing of the ghetto	1993
		2001: A Space Odyssey	The "Blue Danube" planet dance	1968
		The Treasure of the Sierra Madre	Gold dust flies away	1948
		Manhattan	Final scene	1979
		The Ten Commandments	Parting of Red Sea	1956
		Dr. Strangelove	Sellers calls Russia	1964

Table 7. GREATEST SHOTS IN MOVIES

Rank	Number of nominations	Film	Shot
1	16	*The Player*	Opening shot
2	15	*Touch of Evil*	Opening shot
3–4	11	*Gone with the Wind*	Crane shot of Atlanta railroad station
		Lawrence of Arabia	Sharif rides out of mirage
5	9	*Good Fellas*	Entering the Copacabana

list. *Casablanca* is a close second with 30 nominations. These are followed by *Apocalypse Now* and *Psycho* with 23 and 22 nominations, respectively. *Gone with the Wind, 2001: A Space Odyssey,* and *Singin' in the Rain* round off the top seven with 19 nominations. *Schindler's List* with 16, *Lawrence of Arabia* with 15, *The Battleship Potemkin* and *The Godfather*, each with 14 nominations, *On the Waterfront* and *The Gold Rush* with 13, and *The Treasure of the Sierra Madre* with 12 nominations follow close behind. Table 8 lists all thirty-one films that received six or more nominations. Again, this list is only from the perspective of our data, but most people knowledgeable about film would probably agree that all are worthy of inclusion in our Louvre of twentieth-century filmmaking.

The Greatest Directors

A similar method can be used to compile a list of the greatest film directors. A few directors may get a high ranking because of great scenes in one or two films (e.g., Francis Ford Coppola for *Apocalypse Now* and *The Godfather*), whereas others get a high ranking because scenes from many of their films each receive a few nominations (Woody Allen). Each is a path to high ranking on our list. Only a few directors—Alfred Hitchcock, Stephen Spielberg, and Stanley Kubrick—receive high ratings by either approach. Using our data, directors can be ranked either by the number of their movies from which great scenes were nominated or by the total number of great scene nominations received. Either method produces similar results; the Spearman rank order correlation between these two approaches

Part 1: Great Scenes in the Movies

Table 8. MOVIES WITH THE LARGEST NUMBER OF GREATEST SCENE NOMINATIONS

Rank	Number of nominations	Film
1	31	*Citizen Kane*
2	30	*Casablanca*
3	23	*Apocalypse Now*
4	22	*Psycho*
5–7	19	*Gone with the Wind*
		2001: A Space Odyssey
		Singin' in the Rain
8	16	*Schindler's List*
9	15	*Lawrence of Arabia*
10–11	14	*The Battleship Potemkin*
		The Godfather
12–13	13	*On the Waterfront*
		The Gold Rush
14	12	*Treasure of the Sierra Madre*
15–16	10	*The Player*
		The French Connection
17	9	*Raging Bull*
18	8	*Star Wars*
19–23	7	*Ben-Hur*
		Butch Cassidy and the Sundance Kid
		E.T., the Extra-Terrestrial
		Dr. Strangelove
		The Fugitive
24–31	6	*Bridge on the River Kwai*
		City Lights
		Close Encounters
		Grand Illusion
		The Great Dictator
		High Noon
		Jaws
		Shane

is .69 (see Table 9). These two approaches can be combined by adding the two rankings and reranking their sums. This is the approach we used to produce Table 9. (See Appendix B for a list of the directors and their films from which Table 9 was compiled.) After the top three come Francis Ford Coppola, Orson Welles, and William Wyler, closely followed by David Lean, Charlie Chaplin, John Ford, and

Table 9. GREATEST DIRECTORS

Rank order	Name	Rank order by number of films with great scenes listed		Rank order by total number of scenes with great scenes listed		Combined score
1	A. Hitchcock	1	+	1	=	2
2	S. Spielberg	2	+	2	=	4
3	S. Kubrick	6	+	5	=	11
4–6	F. F. Coppola	10	+	3	=	13
	O. Welles	10	+	3	=	13
	W. Wyler	2	+	11	=	13
7	D. Lean	6	+	8	=	14
8–9	C. Chaplin	8	+	7	=	15
	J. Ford	2	+	13	=	15
10	W. Allen	2	+	15	=	17
11	M. Scorsese	10	+	9	=	19
12	J. Huston	10	+	10	=	20
13	F. Fellini	6	+	18	=	24
14	G. Stevens	10	+	15	=	25
15–16	M. Curtiz	24	+	5	=	29
	F. Capra	10	+	19	=	29
17	R. Altman	17	+	14	=	31
18	A. Kurosawa	10	+	21	=	31
19	S. Eisenstein	24	+	11	=	35
20	B. Wilder	17	+	19	=	36
21	R. Wise	10	+	27	=	37
22	E. Kazan	24	+	15	=	39
23	F. Truffaut	17	+	23	=	40
24	J. Renoir	24	+	19	=	43
25	V. De Sica	17	+	27	=	44
26	W. Wellman	24	+	29	=	46
27–28	W. Disney	24	+	23	=	47
	R. Reiner	24	+	23	=	47
	A. Resnais	17	+	23	=	47
30	B. Edwards	24	+	31	=	48
31	R. Scott	17	+	29	=	53
32–34	S. Lumet	24	+	31	=	55
	R. Polanski	24	+	35	=	55
	B. Bertolucci	24	+	31	=	55
35–38	R. Attenborough	24	+	35	=	59
	I. Bergman	24	+	35	=	59
	H. Hawks	24	+	35	=	59
	L. McCarey	24	+	35	=	59

Note: Data in table were obtained by combining (totaling) rank order of number of films with great scene nominations with rank order of total number of scenes nominated.

Woody Allen to make up the top ten. But all the directors listed in Table 9 are worthy of a place in our Louvre of great cinema.[3]

Results Part 2: What Makes a Great Scene Great?

The reasons directors gave for making their selections of great scenes is the heart of this study. Analysis of these data is less straightforward. We wanted to know what it is about a great scene that makes it great and, by implication, a movie great, and perhaps by further implication, what makes for great art in general. Because we did not begin our study with some existing theory in mind, we designed our research to provide as much room for discovery as possible. In an open-ended format, directors were simply asked to give us *their* reasons for choosing a great scene.

Because these explanations consisted of phrases and sentences of various length rather than easily codable yes/no or multiple choice answers, a technique known as *content analysis* was used. Content analysis is a somewhat subjective analytic tool and must be approached with care and an open mind if objectivity and replicability are to be achieved. The researcher must avoid imposing his or her preconceptions or biases on what is being analyzed and must try as much as possible to let the data speak for themselves and go where they may. Content analysis is a lot like a nondirective psychotherapist letting the patient express his or her own needs and arrive at his or her own solutions rather than the therapist deciding all the answers. Content analysis can be made more objective and replicable by having two or more researchers perform the task independently and compare their results. If this is properly done, interobserver agreement can be achieved and the same or very similar interpreta-

---

[3]Though the majority of the directors in our survey are Americans, some of their selections are for foreign films. Even so, the survey is admittedly biased toward American and English-language films. A different list of great films scenes likely would have been obtained if European, Indian, or Asian directors had been surveyed. Many of the choices would have been different, but presumably the reasons for selecting those scenes would not change appreciably. They, we suggest, are universal.

tions arrived at. If approached with an open mind, interesting and surprising results often can emerge.

As a first step in our content analysis, the directors' written justifications for the great scenes they selected were closely scrutinized, and a basic unit of analysis was defined: any meaningful descriptive word or phrase other than simple superlatives such as "brilliant," "classic," or "the best." (Use of such superlatives by directors in their justifications is circular and carries no useful meaning: A scene is great because it is "the best.") This task was performed independently by two researchers, with about 85 percent agreement.

As a second step in our content analysis, these descriptors were then categorized and tallied. When the directors' written comments about these top movie scenes were analyzed in this way, the results almost "jumped" off the data sheets. Three basic themes emerged as important in the directors' determining their choices: *craft* statements, *emotion* statements, and *intellectual* statements. (Each of these is further discussed below.) Each director's comments about each scene nominated were then independently scored by two researchers for whether *craft*, *emotion*, and/or *intellectual* reasons were included for nominating that scene. Interobserver reliability on these more global ratings was in the high 80s, and all differences were discussed and resolved. (For the benefit of those interested, particularly students of film, the directors' comments are reproduced in Part 3 of this book. Readers are invited to try their own hand at content analysis.) Table 10 presents the distribution of these three variables in the 1,016 scenes listed by the directors.

Table 10. DISTRIBUTION OF CRAFT, EMOTION, AND INTELLECTUAL STATEMENTS

Proportion of 1,016 scenes rated in which each category of reasons for greatness appeared

Craft statements	Emotion statements	Intellectual statements
66%	56%	33%

Part 1: Great Scenes in the Movies

Craft Statements

Not surprisingly from a group of film directors, the most commonly mentioned reasons for selecting a scene as "great"—comprising more than 1,350 statements for all 1,016 scenes—centered on the technical crafts used in making film, everything from the script to casting, costumes, performances, camera work, lighting, sound, editing, and strategies in their use. Directors mentioned one or more of these technical reasons about two-thirds of the time when saying why they selected a "great" scene. Given the central role craft plays in film production and the fact that filmmaking is a highly technical and collaborative art form—certainly the most technical and collaborative art form since the construction of Gothic cathedrals—this is not unexpected. It is obvious, but bears repeating: Craft lies at the heart of filmmaking, and this shows up in our research. Alfred Hitchcock emphasized the importance of craft in filmmaking, or any art form, when he said, "You've got to know your craft in order to express the art" (Bogdanovich, 1997: 554). Director Sidney Pollack expressed a similar view to film and theater students when he said that one is "best off to know as much as you can about the art form" (Pollack, 1998).

Most frequently mentioned of the filmmaking crafts was the quality of the cinematography, lighting, and other visual properties of a scene (298 comments), followed by a high-quality script (including plot and dialogue; 179 comments). The skill of the performers was the next most commonly mentioned aspect of the filmmaker's craft (156 comments). These directors also frequently noted with admiration the quality of another's direction (121 comments). Editing came next (89), followed by the quality of the sound track (55). These were the major elements noted, but nearly all the crafts and skills needed to make a film were mentioned at least once (see Table 11).

The following quotes will give the reader some of the flavor of the many comments the directors made regarding craft in the great scenes they selected:

Table 11. CRAFTS MENTIONED BY DIRECTORS IN THEIR JUSTIFICATIONS OF GREAT SCENE SELECTIONS

Elements in directors' evaluations of great film scenes	Total	Elements in directors' evaluations of great film scenes (continued)	Total
Camera/Visual	298	Animation	7
Story/Plot/Writing	179	Casting	8
Performance (acting/dancing)	157	Makeup	2
Director/Direction	121	Set design	3
Editing	89	Setup	5
Miscellaneous technical	64	Stunts	3
Music	55	Computer work	2
Combination/Synthesis	42	Big/Panoramic	23
Sound/Silent	28	Other Production Aspects	
Lighting	18	Character	62
Staging	17	Action	35
Timing	16	Concept	16
Special effects	14	Audience (reference to)	16
Setting	12	Simple (done simply)	37
Costumes	4	Creative /Inventive	39
Execution	4	Total	1,376

Camera: *Citizen Kane:* "First effective use of the foreground and background wide-angle deep-focus shots. Heating up the set focusing on the light to increase the depth of field." Also from *Citizen Kane:* Scene where parents are discussing young Kane's future while boy plays outside in the snow: "All in deep focus—it visually relates to the action occurring inside determining the boy's future." *Singin' in the Rain:* Title song dance: "When the camera sweeps up and around it takes the audience with it."

Camera and Direction: *The Player:* Opening scene: "Just a technological masterpiece. One continuous 8½-minute shot. (I've tried it. It can't be done. But Altman did it.)"

Performance: *On the Waterfront:* "I coulda been a contender" scene in taxi: "The most influential piece of acting technique in postwar American cinema." "Beyond all the hype of this scene, Brando proves

Part 1: Great Scenes in the Movies

he is one of our best actors." *City Lights:* Final scene: "The devastating beauty of the concept and Mr. Chaplin's performance." "Chaplin's face and expression. Perfection." "Shamelessly manipulative, yet it works."

Music and Dance: *Singin' in the Rain:* Gene Kelly dancing the title number. "This is one of the most charming and memorable musical numbers in cinema history. Perhaps its simplicity combined with a great piece of music and a great dancer is what makes this scene stand above all others in musicals." "[His dancing] has lifted my spirits for 44 years." "All the elements—performer, camera, set design in perfect harmony."

Direction: *2001: A Space Odyssey:* Flying bone turns into floating spaceship. "The greatest transition in the history of film. Kubrick is the only director who could make a single cut span millions of years—and have it make sense." *The Fugitive:* Train wreck scene. "Andrew Davis' exciting analysis of a single action—into many physical aspects—intensifying the experience and lifting it physiologically and emotionally off the screen and into the audience. Awesome. Sets the stage for the nonstop running conflict between Ford and Jones." *The Treasure of the Sierra Madre:* "The 3-way dialogue between the trio—Bogart, Huston, Holt—where Huston literally tells the entire movie we're to see! John Huston economically settled the audience in for a walloping good ride...."

Script: *Tootsie:* The scene when Dustin Hoffman (as Michael Dorsey) is doing the live soap and tears off his wig to let the whole world know who he is. "Again, the structure of this *brilliant* script—that takes us to this moment."

Editing: *Psycho:* The shower scene. "Use of quick cuts along with music made for great suspense." "The terror, and how it's created by editing." "Amazing editing of image and sound."

Emotion Statements

Alfred Hitchcock once said, "I want to cause the audience to emote." He said he was much more interested in emotion than thought; he wanted an audience to feel, not think (Bogdanovich, 1997: 476, 480).

Directors' Choice

Perhaps we should not have been surprised, but we were, by the strength of the second theme that emerged from this content analysis. In giving their reasons for selecting great scenes, directors used emotion statements in over half of the scenes discussed. And these directors employed a veritable thesaurus of emotional language: over 1,100 words or phrases involving human emotions, feelings, and sensations. (A list of over 400 different emotional terms used by the directors in this study is presented in Appendix C.)

Any term used three or more times was categorized and placed in Table 12, arranged in a continuum from positive to negative in feeling tone. Interestingly, these terms are quite evenly distributed in number along this emotional continuum. Thirty-five percent are clearly positive in affect: love, sex, beauty, and comedy. Thirty-one percent are clearly negative: fear, violence, sadness, and tragedy. The remaining 34 percent are more ambiguous in affect and probably fall somewhere in between.

Table 13 lists the ten most frequently used terms denoting emotion, those cited eight or more times. The word *powerful* was used 25 different times. *Suspense* was used 22 times, and *comedy* 21 times.

A primary goal in filmmaking, and perhaps in all art, is to evoke an emotional response in the viewer. All the craft skills discussed in the previous section are used for this purpose. Directors' comments about four great film scenes illustrate this point:

The helicopter assault to the music of Richard Wagner's "The Ride of the Valkyries" in *Apocalypse Now*: "With the Wagnerian hero music blaring [and] the automatic weapons blasting, this scene is deservedly an all-time classic of moviemaking; it manages to stimulate almost every emotional response from an audience: laughter, horror, fascination, disgust, embarrassment, sympathy, admiration, resentment, glee, and bewilderment." "Music and helicopters coming over the landscape sends chills down spine."

The shower scene in *Psycho*: "A horrific, terrifying scene.... Horrible images created without really seeing anything." "Tension and horror set up perfectly with various angles...." "Use of quick cuts along with music made for great suspense." "The terror, and how it's created by editing."

Table 12. FREQUENTLY USED TERMS DENOTING EMOTIONS (used 3 or more times; N = 652)

Positive affect (35 total terms)			Mid-range affect (33 total terms)			Negative affect (33 total terms)	
Love/Sex	**Beauty/Moving**	**Humor**	**Feelings**	**Power**	**No label**	**Fear/Violence**	
charm 4	amazing 3	comedy 21	excitement 3	impact 4	pathos 3	brutality 3	pain 6
erotic 4	awe 3	comic 7	exciting 9	intense 3	poignant 6	chilling 9	rage 3
love 12	ballet 4	funniest 5	feel 11	power 19	sad 7	claustro-	savage 3
passion 6	beautiful 18	funny 8	feeling 7	powerful 25	sadness 3	phobic 3	scared 4
romance 7	beauty 10	hilarious 6	feelings 5	powerfully 3	tears 3	danger 5	shock 7
romantic 9	feel good 3	humor 11	felt 8	**Total 54**	tragedy 4	dangerous 4	shocking 5
sex 5	hope 6	laughter 3	**Total 43**	**= 8%**	**Total 26**	desperate 3	suspense 22
sexiest 3	joy 5	wit 3	**= 6%**		**= 4%**	desperation 3	suspenseful 4
sexual 6	magic 6	**Total 64**				devastating 3	surprise 8
sexy 4	magical 4	**= 10%**	**Other emotion terms**			eerie 3	tense 3
tender 3	moving 13		atmosphere 3	fantasy 7		fear 11	tension 17
Total 63	poetic 6		drama 5	frustration 3		fears 3	terrifying 4
= 10%	poetry 3		dramatic 11	haunting 4		frightening 7	terror 10
	satisfying 5		emotion 6	memorable 14		horrifying 4	violence 10
	spectacular 4		emotional 18	mood 8		horror 13	violent 6
	touching 4		emotionally 5	riveting 3		insanity 5	vulnerable 3
	Total 97		emotions 6	unforgettable 3		intense 3	**Total 200**
	= 15%		experience 6	**Total 105**		madness 3	**= 31%**
			fantasies 3	**= 16%**			

35% OF TOTAL USAGE   **34% OF TOTAL USAGE**   **31% OF TOTAL USAGE**

Table 13. TEN MOST FREQUENTLY USED TERMS DENOTING HIGH AFFECT EMOTIONS AND FEELINGS

Term	Number of times used in directors' justifications	Term	Number of times used in directors' justifications (continued)
Powerful	25	Beautiful	18
Suspense	22	Tension	17
Comedy	21	Memorable	14
Power	19	Moving	13
Emotional	18	Horror	13

Other frequently used terms: love (12), dramatic (11), fear (11), feel (11), humor (11), beauty (10), terror (10), violence (10), chilling (9), exciting (9), romantic (9), felt (8), funny (8), mood (8), surprise (8).

The scene where the supplicants approach the Godfather in his dark study to ask for favors: "Astonishing scene that sums up the entire world of the film. Incredibly efficient and full character portrayal. Godfather character believable, honorable, terrifying, powerful, sympathetic. The scene is so full of qualities—graciousness, revenge, honor, compassion, pain. It is a powerful scene-setter for the entire film."

The final scene in *Casablanca:* "There's no question that the lovers' separation and final lines bring everything together in a totally satisfying, memorable, and gratifying way." "Mood; emotional impact...." "Emotional & aesthetic masterpiece...." "Michael Curtiz skillfully left to the last *instant* most of what would be an ultimately satisfying/glorious/enriching and sad end that would *continue* in the minds of audiences forever."

Fear is an emotion that can make a scene from the movies memorable for life. The Pods take on human features in *Invasion of the Body Snatchers:* "Scared the piss out of me at 14; still does." When the chandelier falls in *Phantom of the Opera:* "Scared me to death when I was seven, and still does." The shower scene from *Psycho:* "Strikes a chord of fear that everyone can relate to. It stays with you." End of

Part 1: Great Scenes in the Movies

the film *The Public Enemy*, where Jimmy Cagney's mother opens the door and his propped-up body falls into the camera: "I can hear the audience gasp after some 70 years." When Judy Garland as Dorothy finally meets the Wizard of Oz: "Scaring the shit out of kids for over 50 years!"

But positive emotions can also produce memorable scenes, such as Dr. Zhivago's reunion with Laura: "Lean was a master of the moments which stick in your mind *forever* . . . filled with passion, love, longing, hope, and celebration, all in one!" Or, in the initial kiss between Elizabeth Taylor and Montgomery Clift in *A Place in the Sun*, where "There is a dissolve in the middle of it that stops the heart. It is the height of romance between these gorgeous young people."

When they discussed the emotional content of a scene, these directors frequently mentioned the effective *portrayal* of emotions by the actors: In *The Elephant Man*, "Dr. Treeves [Anthony Hopkins] listens to Merrick [John Hurt] recite a psalm and go beyond the point he has been taught. With Merrick's voice in the BG [background], the camera slowly pans in to a closeup on Treeves. And right when it stops—a single tear. This is not a special effect. It's magic between Lynch, Hopkins, and Hurt."

Good actors are particularly effective at evoking emotional responses in the audience through portrayal of emotion. Human beings are programmed to respond to the emotions exhibited by others around them. (A baby cries, and the whole nursery begins to wail.) We as audience share the emotions portrayed by actors, and in doing so we bond with them as human beings—perhaps this is why many become culture heroes, almost like good friends.

But many other techniques can also effectively evoke an emotional response, such as the lighting in *film noir*. Or, in *Wolfen*, "The speeded up, low travel shot across deserted empty lots in N.Y.C. It terrified me. I had never seen anything like it. The point of view of a predator, but who or what kind baffled me . . . so fast, so low, so out of control."

Finally, sometimes various cinematic techniques are used to *heighten* the emotions evoked by a scene, as where Hawk Quinlan

[Orson Welles] kills Uncle Joe Grand [Akim Tamiroff] in *Touch of Evil:* "The cinematography, quick cuts, and eerie lighting from a swinging lightbulb perfectly complement this chilling assault—Quinlan's first truly evil deed."

The directors who responded to our questionnaire were, as would be expected, well aware of their craft in the service of emotional arousal; a lay audience might rate "great scenes" far more heavily in terms of their own emotional response and far less in terms of the filmmaking skills that gave rise to that response. A successful film modulates and sustains a powerful symphony of emotions, feelings, and sensations in the viewer from beginning to end; an unsuccessful film either fails to elicit emotions or does not modulate them effectively.

Interestingly, those directors who were paid for completing questionnaires used significantly more emotion terms than those directors who were not paid, even when the greater length of their responses is taken into account. This was not true for craft and intellectual statements. One explanation for this difference may be that raters relatively quickly exhaust their potential for justifying a scene's selection with technical terms and must delve deeper. And the deeper one goes, the more one may rely on terms denoting emotions and affect, the true wellspring of cinematic greatness.

Intellectual Statements

The third theme found through our content analysis provides further insight into what underlies a film scene's greatness. We call this theme the *intellectual* factor. Comments within this theme frequently cited the presence of some abstract concept within the film's story or structure such as symbolism, metaphor, paradox, and irony, as reasons for a scene's greatness:

First scene in *8½:* "Fellini uses symbolism in the opening traffic jam to ensnare us in a film about his foibles, his visions, his dreams." Charlie Chaplin playing with the globe in *The Great Dictator:* "Nothing could better symbolize the power-hungry desire of Hitler to rule the world." Final scene in *The African Queen:* "The heroics of the odd English couple conceiving and plotting the destruction of [a] Ger-

Part 1: Great Scenes in the Movies

man boat is a metaphor for the resolve of Britain's overcoming great odds."

The accuracy or absurdity of a scene's portrayal of reality was also noted. In *Dr. Strangelove or, How I Learned to Stop Worrying and Love the Bomb*, Slim Pickens rides the bomb to Armageddon, waving his hat like a cowboy: "Who else [but Stanley Kubrick] could make a joke of our most universal fear?" "It captured in a single image the insanity of the midcentury madness in America."

Frequently statements about an intellectual dimension of a scene note the juxtaposition of opposites: When Humphrey Bogart confronts Sydney Greenstreet and friends in the hotel room in the *The Maltese Falcon*, it's "the combination of wit and menace." In the first conversation between Diane Keaton's Annie Hall and Woody Allen, with subtitles of their thoughts, "Two constant dialogues [were] happening simultaneously—our thoughts vs. our words." Regarding the air cavalry attack in *Apocalypse Now*, "Was Vietnam a game? Or war? Depended on what your role was. This scene captures this perfectly." And, "This scene manages to capture the absurdity of war in a fascinating combination of humor and violence." These intellectual contrasts heighten the emotional impact of the scene. Intellectual contrasts can serve other purposes. For example, in the christening scene crosscut by the mob's bloodletting from *The Godfather:* "By combining innocence with depravity, Coppola creates the metaphor for the film."

Sometimes these comments involve the way a scene tells a story. For example, in the opening scene from *Midnight Express* where Billy [Brad Davis] tapes the drugs to his body and tries to board the airliner: "In one scene without dialogue, only with the SFX [sound effects] of his nervously beating heart, Billy establishes his character, snared in bonds of *his own making*. Great visual metaphor of the life he's made for himself." Or the famous back-of-the-taxi scene in *On the Waterfront:* "In one short scene we learn all about Terry Malloy [Marlon Brando] and how he got sold out."

Sometimes these directors simply noted a social or philosophical commentary conveyed by the scene, such as "the redeeming power of love" (in the death of Dustin Hoffman as Ratzo on the bus to Florida in *Midnight Cowboy*). *Pascali's Island* shows how "jealousy can cloud judgment," and in the Brazilian film *Pixote*, the scene where Pixote suckles at the breast of a prostitute "makes a statement about the cause of sociopathic behavior—the deprivation of love, and the futile search for intimacy. [It is] a humanizing note in a savage world." In the final scene from *All Quiet on the Western Front*, when Lew Ayres reaches out to touch a butterfly and is shot by the sniper, neither knows that the war is over: "This one scene epitomizes the futility and heartlessness of war—more than any book, poem, or speech."

The intellectual component can often heighten the emotional component of a scene: Call it mind in the service of emotion. The above-mentioned scene from *All Quiet on the Western Front* is noteworthy because it is "simple, moving, & so much [is] said in a brief sequence." It has "sheer simplicity," "immortal memory," and it "shows the heartbreak of war in a most poetic way." The final scene from another war film, *The Bridge on the River Kwai*, is also memorable: "Because it sums up the complex moral situation the film examines, the destruction of the bridge has enormous emotional impact."

A summary of the major abstract concepts and values used by directors when discussing this intellectual component of great scenes is contained in Table 14. But this component frequently could not be scored simply on the basis of a key word or phrase, requiring instead a more complex and global evaluation. For example, the corpse in the pool in *Sunset Boulevard* "says so much about Hollywood and his lips don't move!!!"

These intellectual statements often have to do with the sociocultural embeddedness of a film. This embeddedness refers to the meanings of symbols, language, concepts, visual and mental images, and storytelling modes shared by both viewer and filmmaker. Without embeddedness the viewer "doesn't get it." There are two types of embeddedness: One appeals to more localized group values and thinking, and the other is more universal. The ability of a filmmaker to transcend a local sociocultural context and tap these universal themes probably increases a film's chances of achieving greatness.

Table 14. SUMMARY OF ABSTRACT CONCEPTS USED BY DIRECTORS

Concept	Total times used in directors' justifications
unreality/reality	27
metaphor	10
symbolism	10
irony	8

Other abstract concept terms used: absurdity (5), stylized (5), expressionism (3), surreal (3), abstract (2), analogy (2), patriotism (2), idealism (1), naturalism (1), realism (1), sarcasm (1), satire (1) **TOTAL = 82**

Abstract values and states: amoral, bravado, bravery, corrupt, courage, darkness, death, dehumanization, evil, folly, foolhardiness, futility, glory, graciousness, honesty, honor, honorable, imaginative, inhumanity, intelligent, innocent, irreverence, life, loyalty, morality, redemptive, truth, truthful, understand. **TOTAL = 33**

Scene summarizes the film: TOTAL = 15

Statements involving abstract thoughts or concepts: "Self-love needs an audience, even a deaf audience" (*And the Ship Sails On*, singing competition in boiler room). "Encapsulates the whole Woody Allen persona" (*Manhattan*, Woody Allen on couch talking into his tape recorder on why life is worth living). "Simplicity of the acting contrasted with the ornate cathedral setting" (*Juarez*, Muni's walk to Maximillian's coffin and leaving it). "It is O. Henry's *The Gift of the Magi*" (*Casablanca*, final scene). "A seductress at odds with her environment" (*Double Indemnity*, introduction of Barbara Stanwyck). "The last American leftist to be memorialized" (*For Whom the Bell Tolls*, when Roberto chooses to be left behind). **TOTAL STATEMENTS = 171**

Almost all of the top scenes noted in this study, especially those that have stood the test of time, have a transcendent quality about them that explores in an important way, or makes a statement about, what it means to be a human being. In doing so they are deeply satisfying to vast numbers of filmgoers from a variety of backgrounds.

In summary, great film art, and we suspect, *all* great art, can be judged by the extent to which it displays three critical components: superb craftsmanship, an emotional response in the audience, and the power to engage the mind. Many of the greatest scenes in film tend to involve all of these dimensions, though appeal may be obtained on the basis of only one or two components. Gene Kelly's performance of the title song and dance routine in *Singin' in the Rain*, for example, received no comments concerning an intellectual dimension from any of our raters; its greatness appears to stem purely from superb craftsmanship and our emotional response to it. As is clear from our research, the intellectual component is far less important for determining great filmic art than either the emotions experienced by the audience or the cinematic crafts by which these emotions are evoked. But when the intellectual dimension is present, it adds an interesting ingredient.

PART 2

The Magnificent Ten: Greatest Scenes from Movies

Our list of great scenes in the movies was determined through a survey of the members of the Directors Guild of America, the principal professional organization of most American film and television directors. We asked the directors to make a short list of what each considered the greatest scenes from the movies. We defined a scene as "a portion of a motion picture made up of a series of shots of varying angles normally unified by location, time, and a story." We tabulated the results and found that a few scenes were mentioned often and a large number of scenes were mentioned just once. The scene mentioned the most often went to the top of our list, the second most often mentioned was ranked second, and so on down the list. This is how we ended up with our list of great movie scenes.

In this section we will briefly discuss the ten scenes that topped our list. These scenes are the peak of cinematic achievement, great art in the movies, comparable in many ways to other great works of art: Leonardo da Vinci's *Mona Lisa*, William Shakespeare's *Hamlet*, or one of Michelangelo's three *Pietàs*. Most of these scenes are immediately recognizable to American filmgoers—they are a part of our culture, a part of our artistic heritage. And like all great art, the more you see them, the more you love them; and the deeper your appreciation. That, by the way, is one definition of great art: "The more you see it, the better it looks." One tends to tire of repeated viewing of inferior art.

Lawrence of Arabia

Number ten on our list of great scenes comes from *Lawrence of Arabia*. An Arab chief, played by Omar Sharif, rides out of a mirage and first meets Lawrence, played by Peter O'Toole. The film's director, Englishman Sir David Lean, was a genius at combining exotic locales with absorbing drama. He had a remarkable eye for capturing on film the spectacularly beautiful. Who, for example, can forget the stunning beauty of Lean's "ice palace" in *Doctor Zhivago*, or the pounding surf in *Ryan's Daughter*?

In none of David Lean's films is this ability more evident than in *Lawrence of Arabia*, considered by many to be his magnum opus. *Lawrence of Arabia* has been called "the ultimate epic—cinema at the apex of its ambition and intelligence." In *Lawrence of Arabia* the desert, with its vastness, mystery, and menace, is the star, where the simile of the Arabian sea of sand is translated into screen poetry. Martin Scorsese has called it "one of the most beautiful films ever made" (Corliss, 1989: 62).

When the film opened on December 9, 1962, it was 222 minutes long. Afterwards, at the behest of exhibitors, producer Sam Spiegel had it cut to 202 minutes, and in 1971 it was again cut, to 187 minutes (Gold, 1988: 2). The restored version, released in 1989 as 217 minutes, follows Lean's original master plan. It is said that *Lawrence of Arabia* was the first motion picture to go before the camera without a budget. Columbia Pictures, which released the film nationally, agreed that the cost would be whatever was necessary to complete the project.

The story in *Lawrence of Arabia* concerns the exploits of T. E. Lawrence, a young Oxford-bred English lieutenant who led the Arab tribes in a revolt against the Turks, an ally of Germany in World War I.

In this famous scene Lawrence (O'Toole) is introduced to Sherif Ali, the Arab chieftain (Sharif). Lawrence and a guide have stopped

Part 2: The Magnificent Ten: Greatest Scenes from Movies

at a desert well belonging to Sherif Ali's people. A speck, an imperceptible dot, appears on the playa in the far distance, then moves, seemingly endlessly, toward the thirsty travelers. Slowly the rider metamorphoses out of a mirage.

Marlon Brando was originally slated to play Lawrence, but he had a commitment to play Fletcher Christian in *Mutiny on the Bounty*, and the producer couldn't wait for him. Albert Finney turned the part down. Instead, the producers cast a relative unknown in the part, a young Irish Shakespearean actor named Peter O'Toole. O'Toole's six-foot, two-inch height and flax-blue eyes were in sharp contrast to the real Lawrence, who was five feet, four inches tall, and was described by author Lawrence Durrell as "a disgusting little thing."

The part of the Bedouin leader Sherif Ali ibn el Karish also went to a name unknown to American and European filmgoers. A French actor was signed for the part, but in screen tests shot on the desert, he looked, as producer Sam Spiegel put it, like a European in disguise. In frustration, David Lean asked his assistants to bring him pictures of every Arab actor they could find. From a stack of 2,000 photos, Lean picked the picture of a relatively unknown young Egyptian actor named Omar Sharif. Spiegel flew to Cairo to give him a screen test. Sharif spent the next twenty months working on the film. The rest is, as they say, history.

Director Stephen Spielberg was fifteen years old when he first saw *Lawrence of Arabia*. "The day before I saw it," he says, "I thought I wanted to be a surgeon. The day after, I knew I wanted to be a director. Whenever I want to see what great films used to be like, I watch *Lawrence*" (Corliss, 1989). In 1988, Spielberg said he had seen the film at least thirty times.

Lawrence of Arabia received ten Academy Award nominations and won seven, including Oscars for best picture, best director, cinematography, and editing.

The Player

Number nine on our list of the Magnificent Ten consists only of a single shot, a single camera setup. And what a shot it is. Many authorities call it the most virtuoso shot ever made for a movie.

Directors' Choice

Several of the directors who participated in our research referred to it as a "technical masterpiece." One said, "I've tried it. It can't be done. But [director Robert] Altman did it."

This scene has an interesting pedigree—a history, as it were, that is worth noting. In 1958 Orson Welles directed and starred in a film titled *Touch of Evil*. The picture is set in a squalid, decadent border town, and the story centers on police efforts to solve a car bombing. In it, Welles is at his best as both director and actor, playing an obese, slovenly police detective who, though corrupt, has the ability to intuitively finger a guilty suspect.

The opening shot of *Touch of Evil* is a single complex take made from a crane showing a bomb being planted in the trunk of a car, which then drives through the streets of the border town, crosses the border checkpoint, and blows up. Charlton Heston and Janet Leigh, who star in the film with Welles, are present in much of the shot: We see them going unsuspectingly about their business. The shot lasts three minutes and twenty seconds and stood for more than thirty years as the pinnacle of great shots in film.

Welles's shot in *Touch of Evil* was brilliantly superseded by Robert Altman in the opening shot to his 1992 film, *The Player*. In this marvelously complex setup, the camera moves about and pans in and out of sets as though it were connected to the eye of God. In this single shot, which lasts more than eight minutes, the film's mood, characters, and environment are established.

In the jargon of Hollywood, "players" are the people who are most deeply into the moviemaking game—film producers, agents, movie stars, studio executives—the folks who get the movies made. Based on the 1988 novel of the same name, *The Player* is a movie about moviemaking, an acerbic and witty look at the Hollywood psyche. It is the ultimate insider's look at moviemaking, and it features cameo roles by sixty big-name stars such as Julia Roberts, Angelica Huston, Cher, Nick Nolte, and Bruce Willis. These cameos gave the film a sense of reality, but they also make it surreal. The multilayered story has a little something for everyone—psychological drama, exposé, an offbeat love story, satire . . . even a thriller. It portrays the soulless world of Griffin Mill, a young studio executive played by Tim Robbins who is about to take a fall in a world where no principle is precious enough to uphold. Even committing murder can be just another career move. Although the story deals with the players in Hollywood, in the film Tinseltown is really a metaphor for modern society.

The story in *The Player* is circular, told as a movie within a movie. The opening scene begins as director Altman shouts, "Quiet on the set!" Also, about halfway through the shot a conversation between two of the characters plays homage to Welles in *Touch of Evil*. The scene is technically a masterpiece. For full appreciation, the viewer must not blink. *The Player* received nominations for three Academy Awards, but came home empty handed.

On the Waterfront

The script for *On the Waterfront* grew out of a Pulitzer Prize winning series of articles in a New York newspaper on labor corruption on the local loading docks. Budd Schulberg, the script's author, worked two and one-half years on the script before it went in front of the cameras; much of that time he spent observing dock workers and listening to their complaints about the mob's influence and their fears about dealing with it. At one point a priest who was leading the effort to clean up the corruption, the character played by Karl Malden in the film, told Schulberg, "You'd be a helluva lot safer just stayin' home and makin' it up" (Schulberg, 1994: 241).

On the Waterfront was released in 1954 and is the story of Terry Malloy, an amoral and illiterate small-time thug played by Marlon Brando. Malloy allows himself to be used by his corrupt older brother, played by a newcomer to the screen, Rod Steiger. The young thug's actions lead to the death of an uncooperative dock worker. The dead man's sister, played by another newcomer to the screen, Eva Marie Saint, and a priest, played by Karl Malden, are determined to bring the murderers to justice. They spur Brando's character, whose inner core is one of decency, to his conscience. Until the last scene of the movie, Malloy tries not to take a stand but attempts to remain loyal to his brother, his employer, and himself—all at the same time—a hopeless goal. In the film we see the evolution of a tough guy who, as critics put it, "couldn't resist the sensitive truth inside himself," the brute whose better instincts compel him toward a moment of greatness. At the end of the film, he testifies against the criminals. The film critic for the *New York Times* said, "Marlon Brando's Terry Malloy is a shatteringly poignant portrait of an amoral, confused, illiterate citizen of the lower depths who is goaded into decency by love, hate, and murder" (A. W., 1954).

The famous scene featuring the encounter in the taxi between the brothers ties for number seven on our list of great scenes. It shows the awakening of conscience in Brando's character. Some say the scene is the most influential piece of acting technique in postwar American cinema and illustrates the power of film—as the camera burns on Brando and Steiger's faces—to translate hidden emotion into an intensely moving audio-visual experience. *On the Waterfront* remains one of the best-acted films ever made. It still moves modern audiences because it deals with deep psychological truths.

Frank Sinatra was initially tagged for the lead role of Terry Malloy, but when director Elia Kazan found that Marlon Brando (his discovery in the Broadway production of *A Streetcar Named Desire*) was available, Sinatra was dropped, but only after considerable yelling and screaming by Sinatra's agent. Leonard Bernstein made his debut as a movie composer in this film.

Kazan said *On the Waterfront* was one of the three best scripts he had ever seen. The other two were *Death of a Salesman* and *A Streetcar Named Desire*—pretty good company.

Good as the script was, just about every major studio (20th Century Fox, Warner Brothers, Paramount, MGM, and Columbia) turned Kazan down. Producer Sam Spiegel finally saved the day and eventually convinced Columbia Pictures to finance it. The film was shot entirely on location in Hoboken, New Jersey, just across the river from New York City—in thirty-six days, for $900,000.

On the Waterfront received twelve Academy Award nominations and took home eight Oscars, including best picture, best director, best screenplay, best actor (Marlon Brando), and best supporting actress (Eva Marie Saint).

Part 2: The Magnificent Ten: Greatest Scenes from Movies

Citizen Kane

When we asked the directors in our research to make a short list of the greatest scenes from the movies, several replied, "Any scene from *Citizen Kane*." Those directors were not far off the mark. Almost any scene from that masterpiece of cinematic art would fit very comfortably into our Magnificent Ten.

François Truffaut, the outstanding French director, has called *Citizen Kane* "the film of films" (McBride, 1991: 6). Critics have said that it is a cinematic encyclopedia of almost everything that can be done in films. The famous final scene in the picture, in which the Rosebud sled is tossed into the furnace and the rosebud secret is revealed to the audience, tied for seventh place on our top ten list. (The time-lapse scene showing the deterioration of Kane's first marriage tied for eleventh on our list.)

Citizen Kane is the masterpiece of Orson Welles, the twenty-five-year-old wunderkind who had established a huge reputation on the New York stage and on national radio and was given carte blanche in Hollywood. "Never has a man been given so much power in the Hollywood system," he is quoted as saying in an interview. "An absolute power. And artistic control" ("Cashiers du Cinema," 1964).

Citizen Kane is a technical masterpiece. It makes use of the camera and microphone as though they had just been discovered. Although the dazzling techniques were not new, never had they been combined with such exuberance in a film: deep focus photography, sets with ceilings, actors stepping on each other's lines, rooms in the Xanadu castle so huge and cavernous that voices echo, camera movement, large numbers of process shots, scenes photographed half in shadow, and half a dozen characters that aged fifty years in the picture (Canby, 1991). In making *Citizen Kane*, Welles said he had "luck as no one had." He had Greg Toland, whom he called "the best director of photography that ever existed," as cinematographer; the two men shared top billing in the credits. Welles said, "I also had the luck to hit upon actors who had never worked in films before; not a single one of them had ever found himself before a camera until then. They all came from the theater. I could never have made

Citizen Kane with actors who were old hands at cinema" ("Cashiers du Cinema," 1964).

Welles did not start off with the idea of making *Citizen Kane*. He began with the idea of adapting Joseph Conrad's *Heart of Darkness* to the screen. When this proved too expensive, he eventually turned to a story of the life of a business tycoon and collaborated with Herman J. Mankiewicz on the script. The method of telling a story through questioning unreliable witnesses had been used by Joseph Conrad in *Lord Jim* and had been used in film.

Citizen Kane is an almost mythical tale of the great American dream of rags to riches gone sour, the dream of American materialism gone mad. Loosely based on the life of newspaper magnate William Randolph Hearst, it tells the story of Charles Foster Kane, who after inheriting great wealth as a child and being raised by a banker, becomes a newspaper tycoon. He falls in love and marries, then has an affair with a singer. The affair leads to the downfall of his political aspirations. He then divorces his wife and marries the singer, who eventually leaves him. He dies, old and alone, in his castle on a hill of his own creation after whispering his last word, "Rosebud."

The story is told through a series of flashbacks as reporters attempt to discover what Kane meant by "Rosebud." The reporters never learn the implications of the word, and viewers only learn in the last scene that "Rosebud" is something from Kane's childhood, from a time before he was rich and powerful.

Although *Citizen Kane* was released in 1941, most critics say it remains as fresh now as the day it opened. The final scene in *Citizen Kane* begins as reporters abandon their search for the meaning of "Rosebud"; the camera then pans across the belongings of the dead man to reveal his secret. The sled from his childhood is tossed into the furnace, and as it begins to burn, the paint blisters to reveal the image of a bloom and the word "Rosebud."

Citizen Kane is almost always at or near the top of most people's list of the greatest films ever made. It was number one in the American Film Institute's recent list of top 100 films, and it was number one on our list of the greatest films. *Citizen Kane* was nominated

Part 2: The Magnificent Ten: Greatest Scenes from Movies

for nine Oscars but received only one, for screenplay, shared between Orson Welles and Herman J. Mankiewicz. Welles said he had the best luck in making *Citizen Kane*; after that film, he said, he "had the worst bad luck in cinema. But," he added, "that is in the order of things" ("Cashiers du Cinema," 1964). Sadly, Welles's genius was never permitted to flower again as it had on his first film.

François Truffaut once said *Citizen Kane* probably "started the largest number of filmmakers on their careers." Young people see it and say, "I want to do that." William Friedkin, who directed the sixth greatest scene on our list, has said, "I had always thought of films just as entertainment. *Kane* made me want to be a filmmaker" (Canby, 1991:16).

The French Connection

Number six on our list of magnificent scenes comes from *The French Connection*, a 1971 film directed by William Friedkin. It is based on the real-life story of a pair of New York City narcotics squad detectives, Eddie Egan and Sunny Grosso, who play a hunch that eventually leads to the smashing of a $32 million dope-smuggling ring. Among the highlights of the film is a pulsating chase through the streets of Brooklyn—the niftiest such scene, one critic said, since silent movies. In his review of the film for the *New York Times*, Vincent Canby said, "*The French Connection* is a film of almost incredible suspense, and it includes, among a great many chilling delights, the most brilliantly executed chase scene I have ever seen" (Canby, 1971).

The French Connection was based on a best-selling book by Robin Moore. Shot almost entirely on location in New York City, it was at the time one of the most ambitious movie projects ever filmed in the Big Apple. Friedkin and the film's producer, Philip D'Antoni, got the idea for a chase involving a car and an elevated train while taking a walk one afternoon on the New York streets. The scene was shot in Brooklyn in the middle of the winter. Actor Gene Hackman did much of his own driving, often at speeds above 70 miles per hour. In the scene, Hackman's character, Detective Jimmy "Popeye" Doyle, is chasing the killer, Pierre Nicoli, played by Marcel Bozzuffi.

Directors' Choice

The killer is trying to escape on an elevated subway train. Hackman commandeers a motorist's car in order to follow the train. As he negotiates his way through traffic at high speed, the detective must drive with one eye on the streets and one eye on the train. The camera cuts constantly between the detective and his prey as the scene unfolds.

Several directors in our survey say this is still the chase scene by which all others are measured. *The French Connection* has been called "an astonishingly well-edited film" (*Hollywood Reporter*, October 29, 1971). The smooth flow of action in the chase scene is pure movie magic. The chase, William Friedkin recalled, "was filmed one shot at a time, with a great deal of rehearsal, an enormous amount of advance planning, and a good deal of luck." He said, "At least 50 percent of the effectiveness of the sequence comes from sound and editing." The sound was added after filming. "As I look back on it," Friedkin said, "the shooting was easy. The cutting and the mixing were enormously difficult" (Friedkin, 1972: 19). "I can't say too much about the importance of editing," Friedkin admitted. "When I looked at the first rough cut of the chase, it was terrible. It didn't play. It was formless in spite of the fact that I had a very special shooting plan which I followed in detail. It became a matter of removing a shot here or adding a shot there, or changing the sequence of shots, or dropping one frame, or adding one or two frames" (Friedkin, 1972: 19). He had enormous help from his editor, Jerry Greenberg.

The French Connection received nominations for eight Academy Awards and was a winner in five categories, including best editing, best writing, best picture, best director, and best actor, Gene Hackman.

The Battleship Potemkin

Number five on our list of magnificent scenes may not be familiar to many moviegoers, but it is well known to, and has been intensely studied by, three generations of filmmakers and film students. It comes from the Russian film *The Battleship Potemkin*, filmed in 1925.

Leaders of the Bolshevik Revolution recognized the power of film as a propaganda tool to shape people's opinions and emotions.

Part 2: The Magnificent Ten: Greatest Scenes from Movies

Upon taking power they instituted a state-funded program of filmmaking. They planned an important film to commemorate the twentieth anniversary of the failed 1905 revolution against the csar and selected a bright young student of the theater, Sergei Eisenstein, to direct it. Although only twenty-seven years old when filming began, Eisenstein—like Leonardo da Vinci, with whom he felt a close affinity—was an innovative creator and daring theoretician. Like his young counterpart Orson Welles in America fifteen years later, Eisenstein did not have a great deal of experience in filmmaking; he had made only one previous feature film, but he had lots of ideas, and he used them in making *The Battleship Potemkin*.

Though he took a few minor liberties with the historical facts (dramatic license, as they say), the story told in *The Battleship Potemkin* recounts an actual historical incident. In 1905, the czarist-armored cruiser *Potemkin* was lying off the port of Odessa in the Black Sea when her crew refused to eat worm-ridden meat brought on board. In punishment, the brutal commander ordered that ten sailors be shot by marines; the marines refused, and mutiny broke out on the *Potemkin*. News of the mutiny spread in Odessa, and the oppressed citizens, thinking the reign of the czarist government was about to end, gathered in a square to honor those sailors fallen in the mutiny. City officials loyal to the czar ordered Cossack troops to attack the citizens, and the *Potemkin* responded by opening fire on city hall. When the *Potemkin* got word that the Russian fleet was out to subdue them, the mutineers sailed out to challenge the fleet and die as heroes. The sailors of the fleet, however, sympathized with their comrades on the *Potemkin* and fired not a shot as the mutineers sailed on to safety in a Romanian harbor. The scene depicting the massacre of the citizens on the Odessa steps was the fifth most-mentioned scene on our list; it is one of the most memorable in film history.

Eisenstein turned out to be one of the great geniuses of filmmaking theory. He believed that montage, the careful cutting and splicing together of different shots into tightly constructed sequences, could be used to powerful effect. Rapid cuts and contrasting images could be used, like language, to convey ideas and stir strong emotions. He laid great stress on the meaning of small details and objects in his shots. Eisenstein's theories are evident throughout the scene on the Odessa steps. In film montage, Eisenstein believed that a single shot or filmstrip that was neutral in content or single in meaning could be transformed when placed next to a second shot, such that new and higher levels of intellectual and emotional meaning emerged from the associations or collisions. In montage the whole was greater than the sum of the parts. The principles of montage, he said, were imbedded in Chinese hieroglyphics, where "pictures" are combined to create a concept. New meaning could emerge from linking two unrelated concepts. The Chinese, for example, juxtapose a picture of an eye with a picture of water to produce the new idea "to weep" (Mayer, 1972: 7).

The Battleship Potemkin had a big impact on European filmgoers but was pretty much ignored in the United States. So gripping was Sergei Eisenstein's technique that riots broke out in Germany when viewers thought they were watching a newsreel. The French were so afraid of the film that it was banned by the state censor until 1952. The film lives on; its greatness endures. One critic has said, "*Potemkin* is not one of those ships that they will sink with torpedoes. It has weighed its anchors forever."

The Battleship Potemkin was made before Academy Awards were given out.

Singin' in the Rain

The next two films to be discussed tied for third place on our list of the Magnificent Ten. We'll look first at one of the most well-known dance scenes in cinematic history and then turn our attention to one of the most stunning scenes ever created for film.

Singin' in the Rain has been called the greatest musical film ever. There's no doubt that the 1952 film has a thoroughbred's pedigree. It was made by MGM Studios, the acknowledged home of the film musical; it was produced by Arthur Freed, who in addition to being an important lyricist, produced virtually every great Hollywood musical of the 1940s and 1950s; and, most important of all, it starred and was codirected by Gene Kelly, who with his incomparable grace

Part 2: The Magnificent Ten: Greatest Scenes from Movies

and charm, was a key figure in shaping the Hollywood musical during its golden age. Stanley Donen codirected.

Singin' in the Rain is the story of Don Lockwood, played by Gene Kelly, a swashbuckling Hollywood star of silent films at the time when sound was first being introduced into films. The switch, which could be tragic for those stars whose voices were unsuitable for talkies, is played for comic effect. The handsome Lockwood's leading lady in his silent films is beautiful, but her voice is the caterwaul of a hag. Since her voice makes her appear foolish in sound movies, the voice of an aspiring young actress—played by Debbie Reynolds—is dubbed in over the star's voice. Meanwhile, Lockwood has fallen in love with Reynolds's character, who is at first resistant to his charms. In the end she returns his love and receives her due recognition as the talent behind the voice.

Gene Kelly's dance to the title song, "Singin' in the Rain," is considered by many to be the greatest dance number in all film history. As one of the directors in our research wrote, the scene is "a seamless combination of performance, choreography, camera, editing, and music." With its charm and wit, all elements are in perfect harmony. Like all great art, it is timeless and cannot help but lift the spirit.

"I wanted to bring audiences back to their childhoods," Kelly later said, "when they could cavort in the rain even though their mothers would give them hell. . . . I wanted them to feel like they were in love. A fellow in love does silly things." Through Kelly's incomparable dance, we can experience once again the joy of singin' in the rain.

The scene was originally scripted to be danced by a trio consisting of the film's stars—Kelly, Reynolds, and Donald O'Connor. But Kelly knew that somewhere in the film he should have a featured solo dance, and he decided to make "Singin' in the Rain" it, with the main concept of the scene coming from the lyrics.

The *Singin' in the Rain* dance scene consists of only ten shots, begins and ends with a dissolve, and lasts a little under five minutes (Wollen, 1992: 25). The shooting of the dance scene was done outdoors on MGM's backlot, on its East Side Street. Complex engineering was needed to provide the proper flow of water through many pipes for the rain and downspouts. Holes were specially dug on the sidewalk and in the gutter and filled with water precisely where Kelly's choreography required it. Reflecting surfaces and complex camera movements and crane shots were carefully synchronized with the dance steps.

Singin' in the Rain received two Academy Award nominations and no winners.

Apocalypse Now

When *Apocalypse Now* opened in 1979, its director, Francis Ford Coppola, is quoted as saying, "My film is not about Vietnam; it is Vietnam" (Hunter, 1992: 18). *Apocalypse Now* is perhaps the most stunning film ever made—beautiful, even poetic, but at the same time grotesque, horrifying, and repulsive.

Apocalypse Now is loosely based on Joseph Conrad's 1902 novella *Heart of Darkness*. Coppola was also influenced by other favorites of his, including the philosopher Fredrich Nietzsche, folklorists James Frazer and Jessie Weston, and poet T. S. Eliot. It is the story of Captain Willard, played by Martin Sheen, a military assassin who has been ordered to track down and—as his orders say—"terminate with extreme prejudice" a fellow American named Colonel Kurtz. Marlon Brando plays Kurtz as a highly decorated officer who has gone mad and has become a megalomaniac leading Montagnard tribesmen on random genocide missions. We first meet Martin Sheen's character in a rundown Saigon hotel, where he is presumably recovering from an earlier mission. Upon receiving his new orders, his voice-over tells us, "I was going to the worst place in the world . . . and I didn't even know it." The assassin travels upriver to the area where the renegade colonel is believed to be and encounters a number of graphically portrayed, hallucinatory-like experiences along the way. He enters the mad colonel's kingdom, a surreal domain where the colonel explains his philosophy to the assassin: The victor must utilize man's primordial instinct to kill without compassion or moral dilemma. In the end Sheen's character kills the colonel, but he sails away haunted by guilt.

Of the film, Coppola said, "I took *Heart of Darkness* and dressed

Part 2: The Magnificent Ten: Greatest Scenes from Movies

it up in Vietnam, but it was mythical operatic style about war in any time period." Regarding his intentions in making the film, he has said, "The most important thing I wanted to do . . . was to create a film experience that would give its audience a sense of horror, of the madness, the sensuousness, and moral dilemma of the Vietnam War" (Cannon, 1979: 10).

The attack of the helicopters on a Vietnamese village accompanied by Wagner's "Ride of the Valkyries" tied for number three on our list. This one scene took six weeks to shoot, and one editor worked solely on it for a solid year. In the scene, we see Robert Duvall as the gung-ho surf-loving Lieutenant Colonel Kilgore (emphasize kill-gore), who lays waste to a village because the surfing nearby is said to be good.

The scene of the helicopters flying into battle to the music of Wagner is a keynote statement for the entire film—bravery, bravado, foolishness, moral ambiguity, beauty, and degeneracy. It is one of the most gut-wrenching scenes ever captured on film. It represents the highest use of film as art, where image and sound become linked in a dance, first clasping each other, then moving apart, then merging once again.

Filming *Apocalypse Now* was like a war in itself. Twice, sets in the Philippines, where the film was shot, were destroyed by typhoons and had to be rebuilt. The picture started out with a $12 million budget but ended up costing $31 million, much of it Coppola's own money. The planned seventeen weeks of shooting ballooned to nearly thirty-four, and the completed film premiered three years after filming began. A million and one-half feet of film were shot for the picture. The original edited version was six hours long.

Apocalypse Now was nominated for eight Academy Awards and received two Oscars, for cinematography and sound.

Psycho

Before it was made into a movie in 1960, *Psycho* was a moderately successful novel by Robert Block. Advance copies of the book were sent to several movie studios to garner interest; the script reader's opinion at Paramount Studios, which ended up producing the film,

Directors' Choice

was typical: "Too repulsive for films, and rather shocking even to a hardened reader.... Cleverly plotted, quite scary toward the end, and actually fairly believable. But impossible for films" (Rebello, 1991: 13). But director Alfred Hitchcock had been on the lookout for a good story, one with a lot of surprises. "I've never dealt with whodunits," he later explained. "They're simply clever puzzles, aren't they? They're intellectual rather than emotional, and emotion is the only thing that keeps my audience interested" (Rebello, 1991: 19). A tale with two horrifying murders, transvestism, incest, and necrophilia was bound to catch his eye.

When Hitchcock read the book, the shower scene—and the suddenness of the murder in the shower—appealed to him. That scene was what persuaded him to turn the book into a movie. Once he decided to make the film, he is said to have had his production assistant buy up as many copies of the novel from bookstores and the publisher as possible to preserve the suspense for his audience.

Psycho is the story of a boy's love for his mother gone bad. Marian Crane, played by Janet Leigh, is on the run after stealing $40,000 from her boss. Norman Bates, played by Anthony Perkins, checks her in to his Bates Motel, much to the displeasure of his mother. A little later, when Norman finds Marian stabbed to death in the shower, he blames his mother, then disposes of Marian's body. A detective hot on Marian's trail for the theft of the money shows up at the Bates Motel, and he, too, is stabbed to death. Marian's sister and another man arrive to investigate Marian's disappearance, and after a buildup of almost unbelievable tension, the sister finds Mrs. Bates's shriveled corpse, and Norman dressed as his mother.

Number two on our list of greatest scenes from the movies, the famous shower scene is something of a deviation from Hitchcock's preferred long, convoluted shots. The murder of Janet Leigh's character takes forty-five seconds on the screen and is the product of seventy shots coming in slashing, quick sequence. Leigh has said she was stunned when she saw the first edit of the scene, having had no idea the effect would be so powerful. The scene was not that difficult to film. As was his practice, Hitchcock had planned every setup in great detail, with every frame shot from story boards.

Part 2: The Magnificent Ten: Greatest Scenes from Movies

Hitchcock was very clear in his instructions to Leigh about the shower scene. She was not just getting the dirt off, she was cleansing herself of the wrong she had done. She was becoming a virgin again, a kind of rebirth, and the peacefulness the audience felt would make her terrible murder all the more shocking (Rebello, 1991: 109).

The shower scene involved many repetitive images, showing a lot of motion but very little activity: The victim is seen taking a shower, taking a shower, then sliding, sliding, sliding . . . stab, stab, stab—with screeching violins accenting the action on the soundtrack. Yet interestingly, the knife is never seen to break the skin—that was left to the viewer's imagination as the chocolate syrup from a plastic squeeze bottle (which had only just come on the market and was used for blood) flowed, flowed, flowed.

The shower scene in *Psycho* illustrates Hitchcock's theory of cinema. "Montage is the essential thing in a motion picture," he said. "Pure cinema is complementary pieces of film put together, like notes of music make a melody. . . . Cinema is montage—it's pieces of film, three frames long if you want it, placed next to other pieces of film" (Bogdanovich, 1997: 476, 522, 524).

The set for the shower scene was tiny, no more than a six-foot tub. The door to the filming was locked, and a guard was posted at the door. A stunt woman, not Anthony Perkins, played Ma Bates in the scene. Hitchcock considered Perkins to be "excessively shy around women," and because he was not needed for the scene, he excused Perkins to spare him unnecessary embarrassment and discomfort (Rebello, 1991: 109–110). The scene was not shot nude. Moleskin was sculpted, then glued over Janet Leigh's private parts. A knife with a retractable blade was held by Hitchcock himself, since he knew just where the knife needed to be in the frame.

Psycho was shot in forty-five days for the relatively small sum at that time of $800,000.[1] Paramount executives thought the film was a

---

[1]In fact, Paramount didn't want to make the picture and so would not approve the use of Technicolor or big stars, and the studio's executives were uncooperative about the budget for the film. Hitchcock chose to finance it personally (Bogdanovich, 1979: 29). Thus, Paramount gave Hitchcock a free hand to design a fantastic program of promotion.

potential bomb and put roadblocks in its path, but Hitchcock prevailed. To enhance the picture's frightening effects, Hitchcock requested that the theaters be kept dark after the picture ended, and partly as a publicity gimmick he suggested that "No one, but NO ONE," be admitted after the start of each performance. *Psycho* ranks as one of Hitchcock's masterpieces and is a landmark in film history.

Be honest now: To this day, can you take a shower in a strange motel without just a twinge of anxiety? Janet Leigh says she still does not take showers.

Psycho received four Academy Award nominations but no winners.

Casablanca

We come now to what our research found to be the greatest scene in the history of cinema. Hedy Lamar and Ann Sheridan were considered for the female lead. George Raft turned down the opportunity to play the hero. Ronald Reagan was even considered for the part. The film has resulted in more memorable lines than any movie in history: "We'll always have Paris." "Of all the gin joints in all the towns all over the world, she walks into mine." "Round up the usual suspects." Or how about, "Here's looking at you, kid." "Play it, Sam. Play 'As Time Goes By'." "I'm shocked! Shocked to find that gambling is going on here."

Casablanca is the most romantic film ever made, the wonderful tale of love, life's greatest treasure, found, then lost, then found again, only to be given up for a higher purpose. The story is set during World War II. It was adapted from an unproduced play called "Everybody Comes to Rick's." Humphrey Bogart, in his first role as a romantic lead, plays the part of Rick Blain, the cynical owner of Rick's Cafe in Casablanca, Morocco, frequented by an assortment of humanity, especially refugees from the Nazis. Rick comes to possess two stolen letters of transit that will permit unimpeded passage to freedom for anyone who carries them. Rick has previously been in love with, then was abandoned by, a beautiful woman in Paris—a woman named Ilsa, played to perfection by Ingrid Bergman. Still-

Part 2: The Magnificent Ten: Greatest Scenes from Movies

burning desire and anger born of rejection erupt in Rick when Ilsa, in the company of her husband, a renowned leader of the resistance to the Nazis, shows up in Casablanca. Ilsa and her husband need Rick's letters of transit or Ilsa's husband will be killed by the Nazis. Rick and Ilsa reaffirm their love for each other, and he agrees to give them the letters of transit. Then, in a climactic last scene, the lovers part forever.

Initial reviews for *Casablanca* were mixed. Notices in the trade papers were favorable regarding the box office potential. Critic Bosley Crowther's review in the *New York Times* said, "Yes, indeed, the Warners here have a picture which makes the spine tingle and the heart take a leap" (Crowther, 1942). Many reviewers dismissed it as "entertaining but empty" melodrama (Turner Publishing, 1992: 170).

Despite early critical ambivalence, *Casablanca* has been called a sublime accident. Bogart's character matched most Americans' image of themselves as tough on the outside and moral within. It was a perfect film for a country fighting the Nazis and later feeling beleaguered by the Communists. Unlike, say, *Citizen Kane* or *Apocalypse Now*, which were products of genius and inspiration, *Casablanca* was thoroughly a studio film, filmed on a production line, using the writers, craftsmen, and facilities available at the time. No one expected greatness, yet something happened in the film's production and everything came together perfectly. Magic was captured on celluloid forever.

The last scene in *Casablanca* cinches the picture's greatness. The whole story leads up to it, a classic scene of a man's deeper character finally expressing itself in dramatic opposition to his outward persona. In the film, what was ultimately satisfying, glorious, enriching, sad, and larger than life is left for expression to the last possible moment. And we remember it forever!

Humphrey Bogart wore five-inch high lifts so he could look Ingrid Bergman in the eye. Bergman was only available for the filming of *Casablanca* for a set period of time. If filming was going to be completed before she had to leave, shooting had to begin before the script was finished. Pages were written the night before they were shot. Three writers worked on the script; Bergman would sometimes pester them about how the story was going to end—which leading man was she going to end up with? "As soon as we know, you'll know," they would tell her. One scenario called for the film to end with Rick and Ilsa on a ship listening to a speech by President Roosevelt. Luckily for generations of moviegoers, that ending was tossed out. The film's producer, Hal B. Wallis, was unsatisfied with the original version's final fade-out. He wrote one last sentence of dialogue, and it became the film's famous tag line. Bogart reluctantly returned from a vacation to record the words spoken by Rick as he and Claude Rains's character walk into the Casablanca fog: "Louis, I think this is the beginning of a beautiful friendship" (Harmetz, 1992).

Like most of the scenes on our list, the farewell scene from *Casablanca* is now thoroughly grounded in our culture, embedded there by a kind of social selection analogous to natural selection in biology. Howard Koch, one of the three screenwriters who received an Academy Award for the *Casablanca* screenplay, tells how in 1982 an unemployed writer submitted a screenplay titled "Everybody Comes to Rick's" to 217 Hollywood agents. It was the screenplay for *Casablanca*; the original title had been retained. The thirty-one agents who did read it rejected it outright, with comments such as "try something that really grabs you" (Koch, 1986: 31).

Casablanca received eight Academy Award nominations and won three, for best picture, best directing, and best screenplay.

PART 3

Directors' Greatest Film Scene Choices and Reasons

Directors' great scene selections and their justifications have been transcribed verbatim and appear without directors' names to ensure participants' privacy.

Note that though the responses are arranged alphabetically by film title—with comments about the same scene grouped together—the various comments are otherwise randomly ordered. A few responses refer to a combination of films or fail to identify a particular film by title; those entries appear at the end of this list under the subheading "Miscellaneous."

For readers' convenience, we have indicated within brackets the original release date and director(s) of each film. This information follows the first appearance of a film's title in the list. Respondents on occasion listed titles having one or more remakes but did not specify which version they were nominating; in that case, we did our best to correctly identify the version; any errors in release dates and director names are thus ours.

Here, now, are the descriptions of greatest scenes and their justifications as submitted by the directors.

Directors' Choice

Adventures of Robin Hood, The [1938, Michael Curtiz and William Keighley]—The duel between Robin and the Sheriff of Nottingham in the last reel. The triumph of good over evil in the best duel scene/sequence ever shot.

Adventures of Robin Hood, The—A long sword fight between Robin Hood (Errol Flynn) and the Sheriff of Nottingham. A perfectly shot and edited sequence that perfectly captured the swashbuckling atmosphere. Very skillful and rehearsed acting, camera, lighting, editing combination.

Affair to Remember, An [1957, Leo McCarey]—Where Cary Grant talks to Deborah Kerr at end, with her on couch. He ultimately discovers she bought his painting. Emotion well handled. That is, the audience is on the edge, knowing, wanting that he should discover how great her love . . . and he does. It's perfect!

African Queen, The [1951, John Huston] The final sequence, beginning with [Humphrey] Bogart and [Katherine] Hepburn sighting the German gunboat *The Louisa* until end. The heroics of the odd English couple conceiving and plotting the destruction of German boat is a metaphor for the resolve of Britain's overcoming great odds. Comic yet warm and endearing facing danger with great courage.

African Queen, The—Bogart and Hepburn in many of their downriver scenes. Because in each scene they would adroitly unveil something new—a danger, a growing love, a purpose—and Huston played it with blinding simplicity.

Aguirre, the Wrath of God [1972, Werner Herzog]—Klaus Kinski on bow of ship, staring at nothing. Camera angle, pose, rigidity, everything one needs to know about the interior state of Aguirre, his relationship to the environment and his fate.

Airplane! [1980, Jerry & David Zucker and Jim Abrahams]—Automatic pilot. Great idea, hilarious.

Alexander Nevsky [1938, Sergei Eisenstein]—Battle on ice. Endpoint of concept of formal ("dialectical") visual construction. After

Part 3: Directors' Greatest Film Scene Choices and Reasons

this, Eisenstein lost it—and nobody thereafter championed his theory.

Alexander Nevsky—Battle on the ice. The attack by the German wedge on the Russian army. . . . The powerful use of conflicting images—montage to put the viewer inside the battle. Eisenstein said the scene "passes through all the shades of an experience of increasing terror, where approaching danger makes the heart contract and the breathing irregular." (Shows how the creation of movement and image gives a film maker complete control over emotional content of the experience.)

Alexander Nevsky—Battle on the ice. Impeccable relationship of shot's composition & cutting.

Alexander Nevsky—Battle on the ice. Brilliantly planned angles & montages—and that Prokofiev score!

Alien [1979, Ridley Scott]—Sigourney Weaver, having put the cat out, is almost ready to put her bikini-clad self into cold storage in her sleep pod when she realizes the alien is also aboard her lifeboat. She eases into the carapace of her spacesuit and does battle. Remarkable scene. Transmogrification of beautiful, sexy, vulnerable woman into a kind of space monster herself. Transformed, sheathed in an exoskeletal protective layer—still vulnerable within. It permits us to value her as a desirable woman and as a warrior. As in many other woman-in-peril moments, this incident engages our fears. But here it also highlights the theme of alien-ness. Otherness. Jousting. Armor. Archetypal combat. (Also, I was convinced there was an alien fetus inside the cat. And that was what was going to jump out next!)

Alien—Sigourney fights the mother alien. Wearing a bulldozer suit, Sigourney Weaver has a fight to the death with the mother alien. Not only is the illusion perfect, but this sequence gets the adrenaline going! It has excitement, dazzle, and humor.

Alien—The scene in which Sigourney Weaver gets ready to go into hibernation and discovers she's not alone. As she begins to undress Sigourney discovers the sleeping alien. She is vulnerable, but she shows her strength and wits as she flings the creature out through the airlock.

All About Eve [1950, Joseph Mankiewicz]—The party where George Sanders sends Marilyn Monroe to meet Greg Ratoff. Sheer bristling sophisticated writing that sums up the B'way and Hollywood phoniness.

All Quiet on the Western Front [1930, Lewis Milestone]—Scene of actor in shell hole reaching out for butterfly. Shows the heartbreak of war in a most poetic way.

All Quiet on the Western Front—The end—culminating in reaching for the butterfly. Simple, moving & so much said in a brief sequence.

All Quiet on the Western Front—The final scene—when Lew Ayres reaches out to pick a flower [butterfly] and is shot by the sniper, neither knowing that the war is over. This one scene epitomizes the futility and the heartlessness of war—more than any book, poem or speech. Sheer simplicity. Immortal memory.

All Quiet on the Western Front—When . . . Lew Ayres is killed by a French sniper.

All Quiet on the Western Front—The ending, the butterfly. Symbolism at its best.

All That Jazz [1979, Bob Fosse]—The heart attack scene. Strong editing, great visual pacing. A true example of what great film making should be. A summary of a man's life.

All That Jazz—The audition scene. First times jump cuts were used that way so far as I know.

All That Money Can Buy (aka *The Devil and Daniel Webster*) [1941, William Dieterle]—Final scene—Mr. Scratch on the fence. The surprising breaking of the fourth wall, plus the essence of Mr. Huston's great performance.

Part 3: Directors' Greatest Film Scene Choices and Reasons

Amadeus [1984, Milos Forman]—Solieri writes down the requiem. Creation.

Amarcord [1973, Federico Fellini]—The boys masturbating in the parked car. A scene of pure comedy and nostalgia done shamelessly and gently, with his richest palette of actors and colors.

American in Paris, An [1951, Vincente Minnelli]—Gene Kelly's big dance number. Inventive, energized choreography and editing.

American in Paris, An—The Gene Kelly/Leslie Caron dance sequence on the quai to "Our Love is Here to Stay." The epitome of the musical technique of investing dance numbers with plot-furthering ability; also, a gentle and romantic love story, told in Technicolor-pretty pictures and balletically graceful movements.

American in Paris, An—The fountain sequence in the park. What more can be said. It has everything a film maker could dream of.

And the Ship Sails On [1983, Federico Fellini] Singing competition in the boiler room over the noise of the ship's engines. The apotheosis of artistic vanity, in fact all vanity: in which appearances replace substance. Self-love needs an audience, even a deaf audience.

Annie Hall [1977, Woody Allen]—McLuhan in movie line. What every director wants to do to a critic.

Annie Hall—Woody Allen & Diane Keaton in the movie line; Marshall McLuhan makes an appearance. This scene is a high point in this perfect comedy, but it also reminds us of how experimental this film was.

Annie Hall—Scene of the first date-like conversation between Annie Hall and Woody Allen—we hear the conversation w/subtitles of their thoughts. It is a conversation we have every day—all moments of two constant dialogues happening simultaneously—our thoughts vs. our words.

Apartment, The [1960, Billy Wilder]—Match dissolve from large

Directors' Choice

interior insurance office completely empty to same bubbling with humanity. Exquisite visualization of the dangers of the organization man—a popular scene of society politics at the time. Here Wilder shows awesome control of his art with a filmic brush stroke.

Apocalypse Now [1979, Francis Ford Coppola]—Robert Duvall on the beach. "I love the smell of napalm in the morning. . . ." Yet he further says with regret, "You know some day this war will be over!" Sometimes a scene is so powerful, so moving that it is not grasped in its entirety yet it becomes relentless in its memory ... giving way to the second half which I perceive to be the more terrifying, is hopeless, this one scene shall only be half remembered.

Apocalypse Now—The helicopter attack on the small Viet village. A beautiful ballet.

Apocalypse Now—Invasion scene. Great action; Duvall's napalm line memorable; no loss of visual scope; music.

Apocalypse Now—The "smell of napalm in the morning" scene, including the attack helicopter ballet. Extremely condensed story moment. Like a keynote address for the film. Bravery, foolishness, American bravado, incredible and almost abstract beauty of the flames. And the grim hint of reality in lines of bowed soldiers or prisoners dimly slogging in the distance. Outrageously funny dialogue by Duvall. Wonderfully clear demarcation line drawn between two views of the war.

Apocalypse Now—Air cavalry attack on hamlet to "Ride of the Valkyries." Best music video ever! Was Vietnam a game? Or war? Depended on what your role was. This scene captures this perfectly.

Apocalypse Now—Helicopter flight accompanied by "Ride of the Valkyries." Mega irony.

Apocalypse Now—Helicopter scene. Music and helicopters coming over the landscape sends chills down spine.

Part 3: Directors' Greatest Film Scene Choices and Reasons

Apocalypse Now—Helicopter attack on village scored to Wagner. Visual tour-de-force. Execution and editing unparalleled.

Apocalypse Now—Helicopter attacks beach. Scope & size.

Apocalypse Now—The helicopter sequence culminating on the shore front with Robert Duvall saying, "I love the smell of napalm in the morning (and Charlie don't surf)." The analogy to the contemporary America's sped up methadrine-like [sic] state of the mid-'60s to the mid-'70s says more about us in this movie away from America save for *The Wild Bunch*.

Apocalypse Now—Air cavalry attack on the village. Set to Wagner, this scene manages to capture the absurdity of war in a fascinating combination of humor & violence. Duvall is extraordinary.

Apocalypse Now—Surfing scene. The most outrageous and audacious behavior for men at war. Man going mad.

Apocalypse Now—The long sequence of the helicopter landing on the beach. From the "Ride of the Valkyries" music to surfing on the beach, nothing more perfectly captures both the horror and absurdity of war.

Apocalypse Now—The attack scene when Robert Duvall says, "I love the small of napalm in the morning." A perfect portrayal of the lunacy in Vietnam. The leader proves how safe he has made this place by ordering a soldier to surf on the beach.

Apocalypse Now—Helicopter attack [to the "Ride of the] Valkyries." Spectacular—action, setting, sound, dialogue.

Apocalypse Now—The helicopter assault over the beach (the "I love the smell of napalm in the morning" scene). With the Wagnerian hero music blaring [and] the automatic weapons blasting this scene is deservedly an all-time classic of movie-making; it manages to stimulate almost every emotional response from an audience: laughter, horror, fascination, disgust, embarrassment, sympathy, admiration, resentment, glee, and bewilderment.

Apocalypse Now—De Niro [sic: s/b Duvall] on the beach, "I love the smell of napalm . . . smells like victory." Sad irony of the situation.

Apocalypse Now—The arrival of the gunboat to the midway station at night. Just an incredible production setup of light, fireworks, etc., creating the ultimate fantasy, craziness of an unreal war and a river trek through craziness.

Apocalypse Now—Seq. on delta where they kill Vietnamese in boat. The best scene ever filmed showing the panic of soldiers in combat.

Apocalypse Now—Nighttime bridge attack. Mind-numbing depiction of the savage stupidity of war.

Apocalypse Now—The opening—Martin Sheen in his hotel room. The heat, the ceiling fan, the journey to come.

Apocalypse Now—Martin Sheen, drunk in hotel room. Pain & desperation at its rawest. The scene is still difficult to look at. Great jump cuts.

Apocalypse Now—End scene in Kurt[z]s' compound. Mood; photography; mystery; performance; sound; mix of naturalism, surrealism, expressionism.

Arsenic and Old Lace [1942, Frank Capra]—Cary Grant discovers body in window box & aunts reveal they've been poisoning old men. This showcases Cary Grant's offbeat & unique humor in a leading/romantic acting career. The timing is precise, the comedy dark yet still *funny*.

Auntie Mame [1958, Morton DaCosta]—Roz Russell at first party. All around, top drawer!

Au Revoir les Enfants [1988, Louis Malle]—The SS drag 3 boys into schoolyard after 3 girls "confess" Gestapo is fatherly—loving. Chilling performances. A moment that cannot be forgotten. So simply played—so horrifying.

Awful Truth, The [1937, Leo McCarey]—Cary Grant, Irene Dunne,

Part 3: Directors' Greatest Film Scene Choices and Reasons

dog & hat. The combination of dialogue and action—the essence of screwball romantic comedy.

Babette's Feast [1987, Gabriel Axel—When the meal is served and all who partake are affected. Poetic, subtle, intelligent, insightful, inspiring rendering of all main characters in the film in one room.

Bad Day at Black Rock [1955, John Sturges]—The restaurant (coffee shop) w/ [Ernest] Borgnine & [Spencer] Tracy that leads into the fight. The staging could not have been better. Sturges, one of the most underrated directors, was perfect here. Another great script and the *perfect* cast. Robt. Ryan as the faggot & Tracy as the hero worked so well.

Bad Day at Black Rock—Scene where Borgnine and [Lee] Marvin taunt Tracy in the diner. Great character portrayals. Tension stretched to the breaking point, then a very satisfying release when Tracy explodes.

Bad Lands [1939, Lew Landers]—Pick any scene. A movie full of brilliant scenes that uses irony as a key element in its original storytelling and dramatic construction.

Baghdad Cafe [1988, Percy Adlon]—Surprise magic trick. A turning point—truly surprising and engaging—in one of the slyest films ever.

Bambi [1942, David Hand, supervisor]—Bambi running away from hunters—realizes his mother isn't there. If you want to stir innate/primal feelings of fear & panic in any child, recall the scene where Bambi says, "Mother? Mother?" Not a dry eye.

Bambi—Bambi's mother dies. Shock & sadness.

Bambi—The forest fire/gets lost. It paralleled my own worse fears [at] age six. It still scares me. Writing/Animation.

Bang the Drum Slowly [1973, John Hancock]—Slow motion victory scene. If not the first, one of the best uses of slow motion for dramatic emphasis.

Directors' Choice

Battleship Potemkin, The [1925, Sergei Eisenstein]—Odessa steps. Not only the premier example of montage but a montage with emotion, theme, passion.

Battleship Potemkin, The—[Respondent calls this *Ten Days that Shook the World.*] The Czarist soldiers marching down the Odessa steps shooting the civilian populace. Brilliant use of cross-cutting to build tension and fear—a real pioneering use of cinema technique.

Battleship Potemkin, The—The Odessa steps sequence. Perhaps the finest scene in any movie. Though silent, you can hear the shots, screams, and footsteps.

Battleship Potemkin, The—The massacre on the steps. A lesson to all film makers—image & storytelling joined together.

Battleship Potemkin, The—Odessa Steps sequence (soldiers massacring a crowd of civilians). Metaphor, violent action, compositional brilliance are fused like the most complex symphonic music.

Battleship Potemkin, The—Baby carriage. Before it was a cliche, it was a scene.

Battleship Potemkin, The—Odessa steps mayhem. Brilliant inception of formal visual construction—and the realization of what could be created by the juxtaposition of individual shots.

Battleship Potemkin, The—The Odessa Steps scene. Much copied but still the best.

Battleship Potemkin, The—Odessa steps sequence. The brilliance of the editing.

Battleship Potemkin, The—Odessa steps. Another classic. The tension of the baby carriage rolling down the steps, and the woman's glasses breaking, tells a powerful story.

Battleship Potemkin, The—Carriage rolling down steps. Possibly most memorable visual image in films.

Part 3: Directors' Greatest Film Scene Choices and Reasons

Battleship Potemkin, The—Odessa steps. Extraordinary cinematography & editing.

Battleship Potemkin, The—Battle on Odessa steps. Editing, transposition, terror. It all stands up after decades.

Battleship Potemkin, The—Baby carriage on steps. Famous for all the many noted reasons.

Beauty and the Beast [1991, Kirk Wise and Gary Trousdale]—Dance scene between Beauty & the Beast. Great, moving animation and gorgeous music.

Being There [1979, Hal Ashby]—Peter Sellers' lecture to the President of the U.S. (Jack Warden) on how the garden grows. Simplicity vs. realism with double meanings and interesting characters.

Ben-Hur [1925, Fred Niblo]—Chariot race. Superb camera, stunt, and editing. Great pace and excitement.

Ben-Hur [1959, William Wyler and Andrew Marton]—Chariot chase. Its action and energy.

Ben-Hur—Chariot race. Brilliant action sequence.

Ben-Hur—Chariot race. Intensely involving epic action scene by Andrew Marton—great climax to film—that pits two brothers against each other. One of the greatest mano a mano sequences that have become a structural fixture in action adventure movies. Stars Charlton Heston. Directed by William Wyler.

Ben-Hur—Chariot race. Tense, violent, big spectacular.

Ben-Hur—Chariot race. Classic adventure & build of suspense.

Ben-Hur—Crowd scene—parade into Roman city. It was the first time I went to the movies at night. It was amazing.

Best Years of Our Lives, The [1946, William Wyler]—Frederick March returns from WW2—and enters the apt. for the first time—to see

Directors' Choice

Myrna Loy and the children. The staging—the ent. to the building—the doorman. The ent. to the hallway. The doorbell ringing. The daughter answers. Her "look." The cut to Loy as she says "Who is it?" The look from her & the realization that her husband's home from the war. THE BEST.

Best Years of Our Lives, The—Fred. March arrives home for 1st time. Sublime emotional moment.

Best Years of Our Lives, The—Dana Andrews in the aircraft graveyard. No dialogue—the camera telling the story.

Best Years of Our Lives, The—Harold Russell showing Cathy O'Donnell the workings of his artificial arms. William Wyler took a total amateur, Harold Russell, and brought forth a gentle, loving, startling scene, and it virtually brought all the horrors of war into the lives of every audience, everywhere, for all time.

Bicycle Thief [1948, Vittorio De Sica]—When father catches bicycle thief who turns out to be epileptic and has episode. Shock and surprise—tables turned. Great sense of humanity.

Bicycle Thief—The separation of the boy from his father. Poignant, sad, and real.

Big [1988, Penny Marshall]—The breast fondle scene. Concept and performances that were truthful, and innocent and tender.

Big Sleep, The [1946, Howard Hawks]—Bogie meets General Sternwood in hothouse. Hawks at his peak, Chandler's best scene, Bogie perfect, Wm. Faulkner smoothing out rough edges.

Billy Jack [1971, Tom Laughlin]—Billy realizes town bullies are going to get him. Slips out of his boots to fight them. Suspenseful, economically shot, excellent fight sequence.

Birds, The [1963, Alfred Hitchcock]—Tippi Hedron returns to her father's farmhouse to discover his eyes have been pecked out. Perfectly constructed . . . classic progression.

Part 3: Directors' Greatest Film Scene Choices and Reasons

Birth of a Nation [1915, D. W. Griffith]—The carpetbagger gets them freedom. The tide turns.

Black Orpheus [1958, Marcel Camus]—The carnival parade as Death chases Marpessa Dawn while Breno Mello tries to protect her. Virtually an opera of a film, this masterpiece of growing tension, fear, and suspense appeals on many levels: the exotic locale, the haunting music, the flamboyant costumes, the bewitching charm of the lovers, the grace and subtlety of their nemesis.

Black Stallion, The [1980, Carroll Ballard]—The scene on the beach when Alec and the stallion establish their bond. A story without words... told through the beauty of Caleb Deschanel's photography and Carroll Ballard's restrained editing. A beautiful movie scene.

Black Stallion, The—Boy meets horse. A tender scene of "love" contrasted with the previously violent scene of the shipwreck. An emotional high.

Black Stallion Returns [1983, Robert Dalva]—Race sequences. Wonderful combination of visuals.

Blockheads [1938, John Blystone]—Ollie picks Stan up at the hospital. Visual humor again. Stan is sitting in such a way that Ollie thinks he has lost a leg in the great war. The audience knows better. The fun is watching Ollie try to get Stan into the car without acknowledging in any way that Stan has lost a leg. Great Laurel & Hardy.

Blow-Up [1966, Michelangelo Antonioni]—Blow-up montage. Superb use of montage—metaphysical revelation of image leading to conclusion.

Blow-Up—David Hemmings trailing Vanessa Redgrave in park. Pure cinema. The whole film works without dialogue. So good that Francis Coppola remade it (*The Conversation*).

Blow-Up—Discovery of body in park. Montage & sound are eerily unsettling.

Directors' Choice

Blue Velvet [1986, David Lynch]—Scene where Dennis Hopper stalks & tortures Isabella Rossellini. Haunting ordinariness of violence—production design & music under Lynch's eye coordinated so effectively.

Body Heat [1981, Lawrence Kasdan]—Bill Hurt breaks down the glass door to fuck Kathleen Turner awaiting him inside her house. The most erotic scene in movie history. Rather than a "sex act" scene, this has elements of uncontrolled sexual passion, dangerous/forbidden seduction, the metaphor of "breaking" into her—all played against SFX of innocent wind chimes.

Body Heat—When Hurd [sic] breaks into house to fuck Turner. Great build.

Bold and the Brave, The [1956, Lewis Foster]—I couldn't resist. Nicole Maury . . . play[s] a love scene that soars with no explicit sex (WW II). . . . British Academy named it one of the best love scenes of all time.

Bonnie & Clyde [1967, Arthur Penn]—Final death sequence in slow motion. The use of slow motion & emphatic violence invented modern action films.

Bonnie & Clyde—Gene Hackman wounded. Getaway scene, his wife screaming as police shoot at car getting away. Most shooting scenes elicit little or no sympathetic reactions. I was moved by this woman screaming who had little or no idea of what she was involved in.

Bonnie & Clyde—In cinema after first kill watching *We're in the Money*. Grief.

Bound for Glory [1976, Hal Ashby]—The steadicam shot that goes through the train. [No reason given.]

Brazil [1985, Terry Gilliam]—Opening scene. New great stylized world.

Breaker Morant [1980, Bruce Beresford]—[Response illegible.]

Part 3: Directors' Greatest Film Scene Choices and Reasons

Breathless (A Bout de Souffle) [1960, Jean-Luc Goddard]—Belmondo steals the car and drives to Italy. Exhilarating movement and atmosphere.

Breathless [1983, James McBride]—The chase scenes. [No reason given.]

Bridge on the River Kwai, The [1957, David Lean]—Japanese troop train is crossing recently completed bridge. Multi-leveled conflict: Bridge is about to be blown up by commando force. Alec Guinness tries to save and then blows up the bridge. Tension, suspense, morality all in one.

Bridge on the River Kwai, The—Alec Guinness must help destroy the bridge. Because it sums up the complex moral situation the film examines, the destruction of the bridge has enormous emotional impact.

Bridge on the River Kwai, The—When the major realizes what he's done and hits the plunger. We've spent the whole film watching these men build the bridge—we're as caught up in it as he. Even in war nothing is cut and dried.

Bridge on the River Kwai, The—Last scene. Big, panoramic cast of thousands, fools the audience. Full of irony, idealism and truth.

Bridge on the River Kwai, The—British soldiers marching to tune under leadership of their colonel. Success in protecting patriotism and esprit of soldiers.

Bridge on the River Kwai, The—Wide shot of the completed English version of the bridge. The power (and folly) of British pomposity.

Bridges at Toko-Ri, The [1954, Mark Robson]—Ending—with Wm. Holden trying unsuccessfully to escape Japanese. Well shot & suspenseful. Feeling of dread & fear & hopelessness.

Bridge Too Far, A [1977, Richard Attenborough]—Closing. The general tells his surviving officers that this bridge was just too far.

Directors' Choice

The absurdity of war and those in command who send their men to battle not sure of the outcome.

Brief Encounter [1945, David Lean]—The couple parts at the train station for the last time. Love has power over all things—regardless of moral & social standards.

Broadway Danny Rose [1984, Woody Allen]—Warehouse chase when helium [is] being released. Combination of suspense and humor.

Broadway Melody of 1940, The [1939, Norman Taurog]—Eleanor Powell and Fred Astaire dance to Cole Porter ("Begin the Beguine"). Mostly one single camera shot using crane, dolly, C. U. to master. Timing was perfect. Toward the end of this number they made another cut.

Browning Version, The [1951, Anthony Asquith]—Michael Redgrave's farewell speech to his uncaring school. My personal discovery of a truly great actor—he moved me to tears.

Bull Durham [1988, Ron Shelton]—"I like long slow kisses" . . . etc. Concept/Writing/Performance. I wish I had said that to that girl.

Bull Durham—Kevin Costner: "I like cock, pussy . . . soft, long, wet kisses."

Bullitt [1968, Peter Yates]—Car chase scene over hills of S.F. The sense of urgency, movement & reckless abandon felt at every bump & hill throughout the audience.

Bullitt—The car chase. It's still one of the best action scenes . . . .

Bullitt—The car chase. To see it now almost is a cliche. But they did it first and best. The ultimate compliment—to steal from greatness!

Butch Cassidy and the Sundance Kid [1969, George Roy Hill]—The big dive. Best of breed.

Butch Cassidy and the Sundance Kid—From "Who *are* those guys?" to

Part 3: Directors' Greatest Film Scene Choices and Reasons

the leap off the cliff. A distillation of all the zaniness, pathos, humor, and misguidedness of these two utterly original screen characters; powerful example of good screen writing, acting, direction, and cinematography uniting to create an unforgettable moment.

Butch Cassidy and the Sundance Kid—Final scene. Made you laugh at death.

Butch Cassidy and the Sundance Kid—Butch & Sundance leap off a cliff into a distant river—seemingly suicidal. A model for many of the "buddy" films that followed, such as the "Lethal Weapon" series.

Butch Cassidy and the Sundance Kid—The bicycle musical interlude "Raindrops Keep Falling on My Head." Like a folk ballet; underscoring this odd ménage à trois, the scene (dreamlike) pulls one into the characters' love of life and one another.

Butch Cassidy and the Sundance Kid—"Raindrops" bike scene. Outstanding use of a song and activity to bring variety to a strong story.

Butch Cassidy and the Sundance Kid—When she [Katharine Ross] unbuttons blouse in front of [Robert] Redford. Sexy, suspense, surprise.

Bye, Bye, Birdie [1963, George Sidney]—Musical telephone sequence—perfect mix of live action & animation—creative use of split screen.

Cabaret [1972, Bob Fosse]—The introductory with Joel Grey & the chorus. Orchestra, ambience, music. An inspired visualization—using all the elements of film to get the tone and character of Germany of that time—giving the film a great jump start.

Cabeza de Vaca [1990, Nicolás Echevarria]—The moment where the captive/Cabeza is drawn into healing and the "other world" by the Indian shaman.... Seeing Cabeza, spirit broken and a

Directors' Choice

virtual pet, suddenly transform . . . with power he never dreamt possible, into a healer is an inspiration to mankind.

Caddyshack [1980, Harold Ramis]—Bill Murray & Chevy Chase in the greenskeeper's shack; they discuss Judge Smaylese and Carl's plan to become head greenskeeper. These two men are responsible for some great comedy and this scene shows them in true form.

Caesar and Cleopatra [1945, Gabriel Pascal]—Act I—Caesar at the Sphinx. George B. Shaw, Claude Rains, Vivian Leigh/the writing, the casting, the acting, the lighting.

Caine Mutiny, The [1954, Edward Dymtryk]—The final courtroom scene, the breakdown of Captain Queeg. This scene set the standard for all courtroom melodramas.

Cape Fear [1991, Martin Scorsese]—De Niro and Juliette Lewis in the theater, kiss. Scary, sexy, repellent, riveting. Great, great acting—Scorsese shoots it so simply, just short/reverse shot, and it's perfect. Any wild camera moves would have stolen the attention from the actors.

Cape Fear—De Niro's character seduces Juliette Lewis's character in a school auditorium. Even bad movies can have great scenes. Here Scorsese finally calms the camera down and lets two wonderful actors work. A chilling scene.

Carnal Knowledge [1971, Mike Nichols]—J. Nicholson & C. Bergen—"cunnilingus scene." It was the first time I ever saw this in a film and it was very exciting.

Casablanca [1942, Michael Curtiz]—The final scene w/Bogart & Ingrid as they say their farewells and she leaves. The structure of this wonderful screen play that leads us to this moment. The great performance by Bergman in the most romantic movie of all time.

Casablanca—Claude Rains, Bogart, Bergman, Henreid together in the

Part 3: Directors' Greatest Film Scene Choices and Reasons

tag of the film. May be the most romantic scene ever filmed. And the tag line may be the best ever.

Casablanca—Two scenes in equal measure: Bogart & Bergman in the explication of what really happened in Paris—and finally between Rains & Bogart. The most sublime Hollywood "accident," in which the exploitation of a "set" resulted in what is arguably commercial film making at its artistic best.

Casablanca—[Respondent said *The Maltese Falcon.*] Ending—Bogie & Claude Rains walking away. The lighting, the dialogue, the music all come together to create a memorable scene with a timeless quality & great ending.

Casablanca—"Round up the usual suspects." The end of this film is a true summation. It's been overanalyzed too many times. But there's no question that the lovers' separation and the final lines bring everything together in a totally satisfying, memorable, and gratifying way.

Casablanca—Airport goodbye. Emotional & aesthetic masterpiece.

Casablanca—Climactic last scene where Rick, a man who prides himself on not sticking his neck out, puts life on line and lets his woman go with another man. A classic scene of a man's deeper character finally expressing itself in dramatic opposition to his outward persona. He cared deeply, and we finally saw how much.

Casablanca—Closing scene. It couldn't have ended any other way.

Casablanca—Closing scene. Meaningful summation of the film's content—a statement.

Casablanca—Closing (last) scene of Claude Rains, Ingrid Bergman, Humphrey Bogart. The economy of shots and absence of clutter. The direction. Editing. Acting.

Casablanca—End scene: Bogart & Rains, "Louie, this is the begin-

Directors' Choice

ning. . . ." It blends the two conflicting factors together—for a possible sequel.

Casablanca—Farewell scene, where we realize Bogart will do the noble thing, let Bergman leave with her husband. In what is the penultimate romance story of the war, we see the inner nobility and self-sacrifice of a man in love "doing the right thing."

Casablanca—Final scene at the airstrip. It defined everything that was great about Hollywood—stars, lofty notions, dramatic moments, bigger than life.

Casablanca—Final scene at airport. Mood; emotional impact; photography; acting; writing.

Casablanca—Last scene at the airport. Writing.

Casablanca—Last sequence—plane taking off & Bogart & Rains walking off [with the words] ". . . beautiful friendship." [No reason given.]

Casablanca—The final scene where Bogart and Rains decide to join forces as they walk off into the fog. This is one of the greatest "feel-good" scenes ever filmed, and one of the best closing scenes of all time.

Casablanca—The goodbye scene at the airport. Everybody thinks this is good. How could I not include it.

Casablanca—The legendary wrap-up airport scene, of course, with Bogart and Rains walking away. Michael Curtiz skillfully left to the last *instant* most of what would be an ultimately satisfying/glorious/enriching and sad end that would *continue* in the minds of audiences forever.

Casablanca—The scene at the airport between Rick and Ilse. The consummate romantic ending to a perfect love story. It is O. Henry's "The Gift of the Magi." He gives her up for the war, she gives him up for her love for him.

Part 3: Directors' Greatest Film Scene Choices and Reasons

Casablanca—The famous ending. Shooting this scene on a sound stage and still gave the feeling of being outdoors (airport).

Casablanca—The singing of "Le Marseillaise." I can't help crying every time I see it.

Casablanca—The French and Germans vie to out-sing one another with their [national] anthems. Brilliant concept. A war without ammo. It's goosebump time every time I see it.

Casablanca—The singing of the French national anthem vs. the German national anthem. The scene begins w/ Rick nodding to the French band leader, which tells us about his character, then the scene is a mixture of drama, tension, pride, poignancy. It is a stirring scene of tears & national patriotism—the slow build of voices, the shots of the faces of the tyrants & patriots—the later tear-filled beaten but very much patriots and the one man Paul Henreid who pulls them together to stand up to the oppressors. Finally we see Ilse's fate & why she loves this man & will stand beside him.

Casablanca—Switching from singing of German anthem to "Marseillaise." Beautifully constructed, cut and the acting is superb—one of the most moving scenes I have watched.

Casablanca—The final scene will be on every list. I nominate the "Marseillaise" scene. Wonderful exploitation of the WW II mentality. A patriotic, manipulative feel-good scene.

Casablanca—When Rick first sees Ilse—again. So much much pain & back story is revealed in a simple moment.

Casablanca—Bogart and Bacall [sic s/b Bergman]—"looking at you" scene. Emotional payoff to movie.

Casablanca—Rick drinking—listening to Sam playing piano. He wants Sam to play "As Time Goes By," which takes us into the flashback to Paris when Rick & Ilse were lovers. Sets up the vulnerability of Rick and his love for Ilse, as we see in the flashback,

Directors' Choice

so when Ilse enters the saloon the audience has been brought up to speed on this relationship.

Casablanca—Bogart and Bergman rediscover each other at "Rick's Place." This scene is shot using mostly closeups and with barely any dialogue, yet the audience knows that these two characters had been deeply involved.

Chariots of Fire [1981, Hugh Hudson]—Opening scene, runners on beach. Beautiful photography combined with music set up the whole film.

Charley Varrick [1973, Don Siegel]—Joe Don Baker threatens sailor in brothel. Its simplicity and ability to show threat and violence without showing any.

Children of Paradise (Les Enfants du Paradis) [1945, Marcel Carné]—Mime reveals thru pantomime that his future wife is not a thief by acting out the crime. Through filmic language, the delineation of an era and all the characters are revealed in an entertaining, imaginative way.

Children of Paradise—J. C. [John-Louis] Barrault mimes the theft of wallet. Revelatory performance by Barrault.

Chinatown [1974, Roman Polanski]—"My sister my daughter." Nicholson & Dunaway.

Cinema Paradiso [1989, Guiseppe Tornatore]—The final scene... shots put together by old man. Emotional and powerful scene.

Citizen Kane [1941, Orson Welles]—The newlyweds' loving breakfast that pans to and fro to end in silence (years later). The loss of love in a few moves of a camera.

Citizen Kane—The breakfast scene. Great storytelling. Same people at same table over the years as their marriage dissolves.

Citizen Kane—Eating scene montage. Too many great scenes to single out any one, especially featuring those where Orson Welles confronts Joseph Cotten. Or any demonstrating his driving motiva-

Part 3: Directors' Greatest Film Scene Choices and Reasons

tion for power. Eating scene montage—in less than a minute—shows the relationship deteriorating between husband and wife. First effective use of the foreground and background wide angle deep focus shots. Heating up the set pouring on the light to increase the depth of field.

Citizen Kane—Breakfast scene montage that shows deterioration of Kane's relationship with wife. The most perfect economy in visual presentation of changes between two people over a period of time. No words spoken, just pictures worth a million words. Distilling what we all know all too well.

Citizen Kane—The time lapse scene at the dining table. The simplicity of set angles playing against the theatricality of changing makeup and wardrobe.

Citizen Kane—Orson (Kane) and wife sit at opposite ends of dining table. In three shots their marriage dissolves swiftly in front of your eyes. Brilliant use of camera.

Citizen Kane—The scene in which Rosebud is tossed into the furnace. I haven't seen anything that better illustrates the loss of innocence, esp. among the over-ambitious.

Citizen Kane—Rosebud scene. Step in film making evolution.

Citizen Kane—Rosebud scene. Remind[s] us that it's often the little things in life that shape our existence.

Citizen Kane—Last scene, sled going into fire, zoom in on "Rosebud." It is such a subtle yet powerful way to show what the character may have been reaching for throughout his entire life.

Citizen Kane—Final scene in house showing sled. Explains entire life of Kane.

Citizen Kane—The last scene, altho the whole picture is rife with imagery. Another wonderful payoff scene. Romantic, sentimental, fulfilling.

Citizen Kane—Closing sequence amongst enormous collection of

Directors' Choice

boxes ending with CU sled into furnace. Wonderful conclusion to an intriguing story. The audience now knows what everybody in the film never discovered.

Citizen Kane—Opening shot. Sheer power, evocation of mood, expressionism.

Citizen Kane—Opening titles. Just a really great shot, well planned.

Citizen Kane—Opening. Captures the tone and scope of the film. Sets the mood and introduces the brilliant use of effects, angles, and tones.

Citizen Kane—Open montage ending on stagehand. [No reason given.]

Citizen Kane—Visit to Thatcher Library. [No reason given.]

Citizen Kane—The Walter P. Thatcher library flashback sequence. Though not unified by time or place, the sequence is brief (around 3 minutes) and brilliantly, wittily compasses scenes of the character's rise & fall.

Citizen Kane—Kane confronts Thatcher w/critical article on establishment. Scene marks first real time the young dynamic Kane (and Welles) stated his passion and artistic commitment.

Citizen Kane—The scene [in] which the boy's future guardian is talking to the parent and young Kane is outside in the snow. All in deep focus—it visually relates to the action occurring inside determining the boy's future.

Citizen Kane—The scene where Kane fires Joseph Cotten (ending their friendship) and finishes Cotten's horrible review of his wife's performance. A simple but powerful scene that "cuts the cord" for Kane from his past life, sending him on the path to ruin.

Citizen Kane—Jump cut to rooster crowing loudly accompanied by screech on sound track. Shock in an appropriate place.

Citizen Kane—Pick any one. Best directed movie!!!

Part 3: Directors' Greatest Film Scene Choices and Reasons

Citizen Kane—Kane's walk through the mirrored hall. It captured the defeat of a man who had it all.

Citizen Kane—The opera sequence. Man's folly dramatized & visualized.

Citizen Kane—Kane & wife sitting before huge fireplace. Image of loneliness of material success.

Citizen Kane—Jigsaw puzzle scene in castle. A terrible indictment of misused power and useless love.

Citizen Kane—All scenes. [No reason given.]

Citizen Kane—Most scenes! Composition, lighting, perspective, foreground/background interest.

Citizen Kane—Every scene. Because... oh, all right, 2 scenes—Kane's speech & "Rosebud" revealed.

City Lights [1931, Charlie Chaplin]—Virginia Cherrill realizes at end of pic. [that] Chaplin is her benefactor. The consummate scene by the consummate artist.

City Lights—Final scene. The devastating beauty of the concept and Mr. Chaplin's performance.

City Lights—Blind girl now can see, recognized tramp as savior. Chaplin's face & expression. Perfection.

City Lights—Final scene of Chaplin and girl (Virginia Cherrill). She realizes he is her benefactor. Closeup of Chaplin with rose stem in his mouth probably greatest in history of films.

City Lights—Chaplin's exit. Shamelessly manipulative, yet it works.

City Lights—Pick any scene. I'll go with the suicide try by the millionaire. Just a near perfect movie. Chaplin directs, stars, composes the score. His directorial comedy timing is just as honed as his actors'.

Cleopatra [1963, Joseph Mankiewicz]—Cleopatra's entrance to the city. The size & scope of the shooting of this scene make it very memorable.

Cleopatra—Cleopatra enters Rome in gold splendor. Throw a blank check into any scene & they can all look like this.

Cliffhanger [1993, Renny Harlin]—Sky climbing/helo shot. Done without a double and just works.

Clockwork Orange, A [1971, Stanley Kubrick]—The fight scene (in old theater) between the 2 gangs. Violence to Puccini music. 1st approach to a violent scene treated as a beautiful visual ballet.

Clockwork Orange, A—Violent beating of man & preparation to rape his wife. A capella rendition of "Singin' in the Rain." Brilliant use of "happy" music makes violence especially ugly.

Close Encounters of the Third Kind [1977, Stephen Spielberg]—The landing of the mother ship. Thrilling.—Music, sound, visual image, story, imagination, and . . . whatever happened to awe?

Close Encounters of the Third Kind—The mother ship lands & we meet the aliens. Awe.

Close Encounters of the Third Kind—The landing of the mother ship. A tour de force of filmic inventiveness and creative bravura: animation techniques, musical scoring, and live action direction; the sequence works as the payoff to the suspense Spielberg has been building since the first scene of the movie—the audience just can't *wait* to see what's going to happen.

Close Encounters of the Third Kind—Encounter w/the alien at end. Mesmerizing—could it really happen—or has it already?

Close Encounters of the Third Kind—When spaceship lands. Visualization of humanity's greatest wish!

Close Encounters of the Third Kind—When the Bell X-1 and other planes are discovered in the desert. The opening gave me a frisson of anticipation that something oddly alien—maybe metaphysical—is about to begin.

Part 3: Directors' Greatest Film Scene Choices and Reasons

Color of Money, The [1986, Martin Scorsese]—The billiard contest. Well choreographed during the shooting of the billiard contest competition.

Color of Money, The—[Paul] Newman playing [Tom] Cruise at end of movie. Redemption of a down-and-out character.

Conformist, The [1969, Bernardo Bertolucci]—Jean-Louis Trintignant sees Pierre Clementi in Coliseum. The range of expressions on Trintignant's face convey more than script ever could.

Conversation, The [1974, Francis Ford Coppola]—360 degree pan w/Gene Hackman breaking the frame in the middle of shot. The shot opens as Gene Hackman's POV [point of view]. When the shot reveals the man whose POV it is, the grammar of the shot is broken. Brilliant representation of character disintegra[tion].

Cotton Club, The [1984, Francis Ford Coppola]—Fred Gwynne & [Bob] Hoskins argue over watch. Nearly perfect.

Court Jester, The [1955, Norman Panama and Melvin Frank]—Vestle with pestle scene with Danny Kaye et al. Side-splitting!

Crying Game, The [1992, Neil Jordan]—The love scene when Fergus discovers Dil to be male. Exquisite acting, cinematography, scoring & editing challenge us to ponder the meanings of love.

Cyrano de Bergerac [1990, Jean-Paul Rappeneau]—Gérard Depardieu recites poetry to his love on the balcony. Many levels. Nice editing structure. Huge range of emotions. A distillation of the theme of the story. Very moving.

Day for Night [1973, François Truffaut]—Both opening & closing scenes of this very "inside" film. Truffaut had fantastic eyes & ears for truth. The "goodbyes" at the end echo the plaints I have heard repeatedly during my career.

Day for Night—Entire movie company bids farewell to each other, making promises they will never keep. Perfect resolution of the shallow relationships among show people (e.g.) who are brought together in a momentary drama, and then separate forever.

Death in Venice [1971, Luchino Visconti]—Aschenbach's death scene. The futility of clinging to life, the inevitability of death. Brilliantly shot & staged.

Death in Venice—The protagonist dies as two boys play on the beach. The allure of the forbidden beautifully filmed.

Death in Venice—Ending scene; the death of the composer alone on the Venice beach. Gustav Mahler music combined to a wide shot of the beach. The man dying on a lounge chair. Young kids playing are not noticing the dye of his hair dripping on his forehead like blood.

Deer Hunter, The [1978, Michael Cimino]—Russian roulette scene when they're POWs and escape. One of the most powerful, gut-wrenching, claustrophobic scenes ever.

Deer Hunter, The—Robert De Niro plays Russian roulette to rescue his buddy. Forces him to take the gun & pull the trigger. It affected me strongly—I thought I'd have a heart attack—What a *friend* will do. "No greater love has a man that he would lay down his life...." *You are there*.

Deer Hunter, The—The Russian roulette sequence. The most tense sequence I believe ever filmed.

Deliverance [1972, John Boorman]—The redneck rape scene in the woods. For ultimate terror—the worst nightmare—brilliant direction, acting and script.

Deliverance—The rape scene. City boys get lost in the woods and are confronted with a nightmare.

Devil in the Flesh (Le Diable au Corps) [1947, Claude Autant-Lara]—The love scenes (noon to morning). Quite simply the most beautiful ever photographed.

Part 3: Directors' Greatest Film Scene Choices and Reasons

Diabolique (Les Diabolique) [1954, Henri-Georges Clouzot]—Body rising from bathtub. Vivid image of shock.

Dr. Strangelove or: How I Learned to Stop Worrying and Love the Bomb [1963, Stanley Kubrick]—Slim Pickens rides the bomb to Armageddon. Who else could make a joke of our most universal fear?

Dr. Strangelove . . .—Slim Pickens riding the atom bomb waving hat like a cowboy. It captured in a single image the insanity of the midcentury madness in America.

Dr. Strangelove . . .—Slim Pickens manually releasing his bomb and riding it to ground zero. A great image. The world is coming to an end, and Slim is off to the rodeo.

Dr. Strangelove . . .—Slim Pickens finds out that he really is going to bomb Russia. Major "King" Kong's patriotic speech "medals & citations" captures horror and glory of war insanity.

Dr. Strangelove . . .—President phones Soviet leader to explain attacking bombers. Simply shot, well lit, great comedic scene for Peter Sellers.

Dr. Strangelove . . .—Sellers, as the president, tells the Russian premiere about the erroneous bombing. Sellers is at his best in this "monologue" on the phone. The stakes could not possibly be higher and the scene is one of the funniest ever.

Dr. Strangelove . . .—President on phone w/ Russian premiere. Reasons? It's hilarious.

Doctor Zhivago [1965, David Lean]—Zhivago on a streetcar sees Lara on the street. He fights the crowd to get off and get to her. Zhivago has a heart attack and drops dead. Lara, not knowing this, turns the corner and is gone, not knowing Zhivago has returned to her and her love.

Doctor Zhivago—After being separated for so long, when Zhivago is finally reunited with Lara . . . Lean was a master of the moments which stick in your mind *forever*. . . . Filled with passion, love, longing, hope and celebration, all in one!

Doctor Zhivago—The ice castle scene where Omar Sharif sends Julie Christie off in a sled, then rushes upstairs to wave goodbye, shattering the ice that covers the window.

Dodsworth [1936, William Wyler]—Dodsworth's confrontation with wife at end & his leaving her. One of the most realistic performances. Director stayed with a scene and did not cut away needlessly.

Don't Look Now [1973, Nicholas Roeg]—When red doll turns around at end of alley. Some subconscious appeal, changes, different.

Don't Look Now—Donald Sutherland & Julie Christie having sex. Flash-forwards intercut reveal husband's haste and wife's poignant unfulfillment. Sex as an omen of doom.

Do the Right Thing [1989, Spike Lee]—Garbage can scene. It achieved its purpose: catharsis. Like the characters, you were stifled by the heat, the stupidity, everything, and the scene was a great release.

Double Indemnity [1944, Billy Wilder]—Edward G. Robinson enumerating the various ways of suicide. The brilliance of Robinson's monologue in which he captures the essence of the differences between one suicide & another—it simply elevates the film.

Double Indemnity—The intro. of Barbara Stanwyck in *Double Indemnity*. You see her feet walking down stairs. Her pumps & golden bracelet tell us everything about her. Well, almost . . . . We immediately know this is a seductress at odds with her environment who's on the prowl—i.e., "trouble."

Downhill Racer [1969, Michael Ritchie]—Last race down the hill. Through the use of the PA system it foretold the future, and the impersonalization of an unknown athlete—the next challenger—the future.

Part 3: Directors' Greatest Film Scene Choices and Reasons

Dresser, The [1983, Peter Yates]—Tom Courtney changes the book after [Albert] Finney's death. Love.

Dresser, The—"Hold that train!"—at the railway station. A most perfect example of the supernatural power of charisma. At the sound of Finney's voice, the train waits.

Duck Soup [1933, Leo McCarey]—"Mirror Scene"—where 2 & then 3 Marx Bros. duplicate each other's movements. Absurdity built on logic—again simply shot and incredibly well played.

East of Eden [1955, Elia Kazan]—Final scene. Beautifully acted, directed with insight & filmed w/love for each character.

East of Eden—Under the weeping willow: Cal tries to express his longing and Abra tries to resolve her conflicted attraction to him. Classic portrayal of youthful struggles toward maturity, self-realization; visualized with strangely appealing blend of romance and reality.

8½ [1963, Federico Fellini]—Finale. All passions resolved.

8½—Montage near end where all the characters come together. Final joyful conclusion to a wander thru someone's mind!

8½—Opening sequence. Fellini uses symbolisms in the opening traffic jam to ensnare us in a film about his foibles, his visions, his dreams.

8½—The "director" stands beneath looming construction while his asst. calls down, "Are you coming up?" It was the single shot that expressed the central idea of the film.

8½—In the baths. Exhilarating camera movement that perfect[ly] expresses the mood of the scene.

Electric Dreams [1984, Steven Barron]—Camera tracks from cello player, through heating system, to downstairs apartment. One of the first films to adopt an "MTV look," although a tame

Directors' Choice

version compared to today's MTV. Tasteful but extraordinary use of camera & movement.

Elephant Man, The [1980, David Lynch]—Dr. Treeves listens to Merrick recite a psalm and go beyond the point he has been taught. With [John] Merrick's voice in the BG [background], the camera slowly pans in to a closeup on Treeves. And right when it stops—a single tear. This is not a special effect. It's magic between Lynch, [Anthony] Hopkins, and [John] Hurt.

Elvira Madigan [1967, Bo Widerberg]—When the lovers eat strawberry & cream. Sensuous.

Elvira Madigan—The freeze frame (as I remember it) of the butterfly at the sound of shots off camera as the lovers commit suicide. If this shot seems familiar it is not unlike the final shot with the butterfly in *All Quiet on the Western Front*. Both are emotionally devastating. The irony of the butterfly when all is lost visually, wordlessly . . . in both films.

Empire of the Sun [1987, Stephen Spielberg]—Final reunion of mother & boy. Directed & edited to make audience feel both hope and fear of boy. Then at the moment of reunion the boy freezes. Powerful & human.

Empire Strikes Back, The [1980, Irvin Kershner]—Darth Vader tells Luke he is his father. Emotional zinger, and *huge* story surprise.

E.T., the Extra-Terrestrial [1982, Stephen Spielberg]—The children (on their bicycles) ascending to outer space. Suspended belief. A great example of film's transporting the audience beyond all reason!

E.T, the Extra-Terrestrial—The flying scene. For the sheer beauty of the matting and technological magic.

E.T., the Extra-Terrestrial—The bike ride across the moon. No other movie shot so successfully personifies film's ability to capture magical fantasy.

E.T., the Extra-Terrestrial—The kids, escaping on bikes, suddenly find

Part 3: Directors' Greatest Film Scene Choices and Reasons

themselves lifting off the street and flying through the air. The sequence begins by establishing the one-sidedness of the battle between the "bad" adults and the "good" kids, then, slowly but surely, nudges the balance toward the kids, until in the shot that takes the audience completely by surprise, E.T. enables them to fly, saving the kids and at the same time speaking directly to almost everyone's primal desire.

E.T., the Extra-Terrestrial—When the kids, about to be stopped, soar into the air on bicycles. The audience screams with delight, soars along with them.

E.T., the Extra-Terrestrial—Where the kids are cut off by a police blockade and E.T. lifts them and bike above. Pure magical emotional cheer moment. Visually, strategically, perfectly placed in film.

E.T., the Extra-Terrestrial—The death of E.T. and his resurrection—perfectly played and staged by one of the best directors ever. This fairy tale will live forever. All the children were wonderful. A great script—and it leads the audience to that wonderful ending—and there was *no* sequel.

Fantasia [1940, Walt Disney; Ben Sharpsteen, supervisor]—"Night on Bald Mountain." The best integration of music and abstract image. Most beautiful forerunner of all music videos.

Fantasia—"The Rite of Spring" sequence in which the violent beginning of the world is depicted. Landmark was a combination of animated visuals and classical music to dramatically convey a massive and significant historical period—in but a handful of minutes. Great for kids and adults.

Fantasia—The dance of the mushrooms from the Nutcracker Suite (actually, "Dance Chinoise"). This film was Disney's magnificent effort to perfectly marry the animated cartoon to classical movie themes. The scene is, to me, the most memorable for its simplicity, charm, and humor.

Feet First [1930, Clyde Bruckman]—Harold hanging from hands of

Directors' Choice

the clock. Suspense builds with every edit of brilliantly conceived pictures—it gets scarier and funnier each time something else breaks on the clock.

Fellini's Roma (aka *Roma*) [1972, Federico Fellini]—The Vatican fashion show. Vintage Fellini. The faces, the angles, the outrageous costumes, the irreverence.

Few Good Men, A [1992, Rob Reiner]—The court martial confrontation between Jack Nicholson and Tom Cruise. In the history of cinema there have been many great scenes of courtroom confrontations. The power of this one between a general and an ensign rates high because of the masterful performances of the two fine actors.

Few Good Men, A—Nicholson on the witness stand. Powerful indictment of military mentality.

Field of Dreams [1989, Phil Alden Robinson]—Final scene showing father & son playing catch, then cars arriving. Emotionally draining. Can't see how anyone would fail to be moved by that scene.

Field of Dreams—Kevin Costner and Ray Liotta playing catch at end of movie. Father and son reunited. Demonstrates the purity and power of sports.

Field of Dreams—The scene when Kevin [Costner] plays catch with his father. Fulfills the fantasy of every son—to have your father back, albeit briefly, to tell him what you never could.

Fisher King, The [1991, Terry Gilliam]—The great waltz in Grand Central Station. The ultimate fantasy wish of the deracinated; magnificently executed tableau describing the very soft heart of the story in this so-so film.

Fitzcarraldo [1982, Werner Herzog]—Hauling boat up mountain. Several levels of symbolism concerning human conflict in a mad mad nonsense of the task at hand—moving the boat!

Five Easy Pieces [1970, Bob Rafaelson]—Jack Nicholson orders toast

Part 3: Directors' Greatest Film Scene Choices and Reasons

in the diner. Performance, timing of editorial. Pure comic writing.

Five Easy Pieces—The tuna salad scene. Concept/writing/performance. I wish I had said that to that girl.

Five Easy Pieces—Jack Nicholson ordering in a diner. Universal frustration—acting.

Five Easy Pieces—Jack Nicholson ordering toast scene. Cause it's great! Great comedy—great acting.

Five Easy Pieces—Where Jack Nicholson loses it at a restaurant because he cannot get the order as he wants it. Jack Nicholson embodying a universal moment where bureaucracy reigns over flexibility . . . unnecessarily so. He challenges the bullshit.

Footlight Parade [1933, Lloyd Bacon]—"By a Waterfall" musical sequence. Busby Berkeley, at the height of his career, turned this musical number into one of the most elaborately staged dance (& swim) numbers ever filmed.

Forbidden Games (Jeux Interdits) [1952, René Clément]—The last scene in the railroad station. The children separated forever in this only shot in the entire film that is not intimate.

Forbidden Games—Mock funeral of small animal at her parents' grave. Unsurpassed depiction of how the brutality of war is swept away by the ritual sentimentality of children (acting like adults).

Forbidden Planet [1956, Fred Wilcox]—The ID attacking the space ship. This was a scene of science fiction (without modern technology) that horrified its audience.

Foreign Correspondent [1940, Alfred Hitchcock]—The great crowd of people with umbrellas as the assassin escapes. A brilliant concept—shot from overhead. A sea of umbrellas that move like the sea. Hitchcock at his best.

For Whom the Bell Tolls [1943, Sam Wood]—The love scene in the

Directors' Choice

sleeping bag/the final separation when Roberto chooses to be left behind. The last American leftist to be memorialized in a mainstream commercial film.

400 Blows, The [1959, François Truffaut]—Final scene—boy at shore. Freeze frame influenced picture making for all time.

400 Blows, The—Final scene—Doinel running to the sea. The scene is absolute poetry, from the long tracking shots to the final freeze frame. It's what's great about film: Tells a story w/pictures.

400 Blows, The—The ten-year-old kid is carted away in a police wagon trying to hold back tears. Heart wrenching zenith, again w/o dialogue. Contrast the lonely devastation of the kid with the "happy" lights of Pigalle, toward which the policeman drives & the "happy" music score of the Modern Jazz Quartet.

Frankenstein [1931, James Whale]—Raising the manmade body into the electric storm. Complete welding of design, lighting, movement, and performance to a climax.

Frankenstein—"It's alive" (when the monster comes to life). Complete premise for the film—the creation of man's greatest mystery: life.

Frankenstein—Monster comes to life. It chilled me. I was 11 years old.

Frankenstein—The lighting sequence when the monster is given life. Movie making of a camera, story, editing, direction into one eerie moment; to be copied in film after film.

French Can-Can [1955, Jean Renoir]—Final can-can scene. Totally incongruously moving. Pure joy in the creation of a popular art—can-can/cinema.

French Connection, The [1971, William Friedkin]—The car chase. Still the car chase by which all others are measured.

French Connection, The—Car chase. Breathlessly exciting and inherently dramatic; use of POV [point of view].

Part 3: Directors' Greatest Film Scene Choices and Reasons

French Connection, The—Car chase through Bronx. Needed a tranquilizer after viewing. Finest setup of a chase and editing to create feeling of being in the car.

French Connection, The—Scene where [Gene] Hackman pursues elevated subway in car. One of first scenes to employ the quick editing style so much in vogue today. Highest number of cuts per minutes at its time (I think).

French Connection, The—Car chase scene. First of its kind. Still the best.

French Connection, The—The chase scene. It had a kind of balletic beauty.

French Connection, The—Chase scene. The most exciting and awe-inspiring chase scene ever filmed.

French Connection, The—Car chase scene. Another standard [against] which others are compared.

French Connection, The—Car chase. The best chase ever.

French Connection, The—Car chase scene. Probably the all-time best car chase scene in any movie. It boggles the mind to think how that scene was set up & shot.

From Here to Eternity [1953, Fred Zinnemann]—Wide shot raid of Schofield barracks. [No reason given.]

From Here to Eternity—Burt Lancaster and Deborah Kerr in sandy beach embrace as the waves relentlessly break on shore. . . . The climax of the scene is as sexual as the '50s allowed it to be. The whole movie is tightly wound up in America's mores of the early 1950s. Zinneman pecks away at it and we root along as he does. . . . Kerr's last lines "I never knew it could be like this" is THE clarion call of the times.

Front Page [1931, Lewis Milestone]—During course of critical scene Adolph Menjou opens desk roll top, shovels air to Geo. E. Stone. The piece of business—giving the man they are hiding in the

Directors' Choice

desk a breath of fresh air—as much as any I can remember epitomized a whole film.

Fugitive, The [1993, Andrew Davis]—Train wreck scene. Keeps upping ante.

Fugitive, The—The train wreck. Most incredible stunt I've ever seen filmed.

Fugitive, The—Bus/train crash. Great stuff, action wise . . . unexpected clarity of action.

Fugitive, The—Train wreck. Andrew Davis's exciting analysis of a single action—into many physical aspects—intensifying the experience and lifting it physiologically and emotionally off the screen and into the audience. Awesome. Sets the stage for the nonstop running conflict between [Harrison] Ford and [Tommy Lee] Jones.

Fugitive, The—The scene of the train crashing into the bus. Of all the "cliffhangers" and last-minute rescues, this scene is tops. It is the spectacular and fiery aftermath that makes this scene so powerful. Harrison Ford, the fugitive, is indeed lucky to be alive.

Fugitive, The—Train wreck. A new standard in action. The mixture of live action & effects is seamless & electrifying.

Fugitive, The—The bus/train wreck. Absolutely seamless in composition.

Gallipoli [1981, Peter Weir]—The charge scene. One of the best war scenes ever filmed. It's surreal, haunting, & frightening & sad. Brilliant use of Albinoni's "Adagio."

Gandhi [1982, Richard Attenborough]— . . . Gandhi encourages the people of India to lie down in front of the oncoming British cavalry. One of the most powerful scenes of nonviolent resistance—proving that the power of the people "resisting" but "nonviolently" can turn away the imperial armed force of the greatest nation in the world at that time.

Part 3: Directors' Greatest Film Scene Choices and Reasons

General, The [1926, Buster Keaton and Clyde Bruckman]—Final chase sequence. Keaton and girlfriend take their train apart as they escape [from the] soldiers. Best comedy stunts ever, combining suspense, comedy, character.

General, The—Buster Keaton's frantic stoking of the train boiler with wood. Excellent pace and process camera work. Hilarious!

General, The—Scene where Keaton attempts to destroy pursuing train with cannonball. Perfectly timed, staged, and shot, it is also one of the funniest scenes ever filmed.

Gettysburg [1993, Ronald Maxwell]—Jeff Daniels gives a long, patriotic speech to his treasonous Maine troops. . . . Few movies have captured the rhyme and meaning of the Civil War, and fewer still have so encapsulated the humanitarian motives behind their struggle for union by the North.

Giant [1956, George Stevens]—James Dean character strikes oil. A perfect explosion of an individual character against a panoramic background.

Gilda [1946, Charles Vidor]—"Who Put the Blame on Mame?" Cinema's sexiest moment.

Gilda—The older man and Gilda on their bed as he asked about the other man. Tightly framed shot of two people as they move & rearrange while building the sequence of his closing in on her. Claustrophobic.

Glory [1989, Edward Zwick]—The pre-battle campfire spiritual scene. A passionate and heartbreaking scene of men doomed to die—but not without their dignity and cultural identity.

Go-Between, The [1970, Joseph Losey]—Opening title sequence—carriage arrives at the estate. The opening voice-over sequence written by Harold Pinter as perfectly as words in the English language can be.

Godfather, The [1972, Francis Ford Coppola]—The horse's head scene.

Directors' Choice

A shocking and powerful evocation of the Godfather's creative ruthlessness.

Godfather, The—Scene of horse's head in bed. Projected true horror of the milieu.

Godfather, The—Horse head in bed scene. Shocking, especially for its time. Extremely effective in carrying impact of idea.

Godfather, The—The Brando–Pacino scene in the garden. . . . Acting at its finest. A whole lifetime, two lifetimes, in one scene, a few simple angles, great dialogue, brilliant performance.

Godfather, The—Garden scene/godfather death. Father/son/grandson relationship; performance; truth; poignance; great death scene.

Godfather, The—Scene in garden w/ Brando. Lie at film's ending. [No reason given.]

Godfather, The—First scene with Brando. Defined the movie.

Godfather, The—Godfather "holding court" while daughter's wedding goes on outside. Beautifully acted, beautifully photographed, marvelously written.

Godfather, The—Wedding party. Scene-setter for entire movie. Excellent ethnic scene.

Godfather, The—The christening of a baby with crosscutting bloodletting of the mob. By combining innocence with depravity, Coppola creates the metaphor for the film.

Godfather, The—Baptism scene. [No reason given.]

Godfather, The—Execution scene. Excellent use of contrapuntal music and pictures.

Godfather, The—The final scene in the film. Michael is now godfather and the office door closes on Kay, his wife. At this pint Kay Corleone realizes the enormity of what she is up against. Michael

Part 3: Directors' Greatest Film Scene Choices and Reasons

is the new godfather, and she learns for sure that her husband is a monster.

Godfather, The—Scene where the first of the supplicants approaches the Godfather in his dark study to ask a favor of him. Astonishing scene that sums up the entire world of the film. Incredibly efficient and full character portrayal. Godfather character [is] believable, honorable, terrifying, powerful, sympathetic. The scene is so full of qualities—graciousness, revenge, honor, compassion, pain. It is a powerful scene-setter for the entire film.

Godfather II [1974, Francis Ford Coppola]—Robert De Niro walking along tops [of] buildings ready to kill Don. Sets up the first kill and catalyst for rest of his life.

Godfather II—Corleone & cohorts cut up cake of Cuba. Best political statement in movies.

Godfather I [1972], *II* [1974], *III* [1990]—All scenes. [No reason given.]

Gold Rush, The [1925, Charlie Chaplin]—Chaplin cooking and eating his shoe. The essence of his comic genius is revealed in the detail . . . picking out the nails, savoring the laces, etc.

Gold Rush, The—Turning into "chicken"; eating the shoe. Dramatization of hunger.

Gold Rush, The—Chaplin eating his shoes. Comedy at its most inventive.

Gold Rush, The—Classic Chaplin shoe-eating scene. The simple, clean camera and editing to project comic inventiveness.

Gold Rush, The—Chaplin's shoe-eating scene. In pantomime, Chaplin cooks & eats his shoe as if it were a gourmet meal. The humor & delicacy of this scene is beautiful. It is all silent.

Gold Rush, The—Charlie Chaplin eating his shoes. The acting. The inventiveness.

Directors' Choice

Gold Rush, The—Charlie & the dinner rolls [potatoes?]. An early great moment—of wonderful and touching characterization.

Gold Rush, The—Charlie Chaplin with two potatoes on ends of fork makes a dance. A ballet of Chaplin's facial expression set against the most brilliant dance number executed without the dancer using his legs but rather puppeting two potatoes.

Gold Rush, The—The tramp and the dance with the rolls [potatoes?]. The simplicity of the composition and Mr. Chaplin's magical performance.

Gold Rush, The—The cabin teeters back & forth on the edge of a crevasse as Charlie and his menacing opponent waltz to and fro. The wildness of the scene, the boldness of the concept.

Gold Rush, The—The cabin teetering on the edge of the cliff. Staged with people moving back and forth, gradually putting cabin out of balance. Builds and builds in constantly fresh ways.

Gold Rush, The—Charlie and thug in cabin chasing one another after cabin has been blown to edge of cliff. Combination of comedy & fear & audience having different info. than characters.

Gold Rush, The—Chaplin sets up for New Year's dinner; he is expecting the girls to show. The tenderness, the romance, the humor of Chaplin.

Gone with the Wind [1939, Victor Fleming (and George Cukor and Sam Wood)]—"Frankly, my dear . . ." Payoff to movie.

Gone with the Wind—"This land . . ."/"Frankly, my dear . . ." Writing and performance.

Gone with the Wind—End: Rhett and Scarlett: "Frankly my dear, I don't give a damn!" Classic romance! A great ending to a great film. Incredible timing.

Gone with the Wind—"Frankly . . . I don't give a damn." Dramatic impact; glamour; casting; setting; whole greater than sum of parts.

Part 3: Directors' Greatest Film Scene Choices and Reasons

Gone with the Wind—Final scene—"Frankly, my dear, I don't give a damn." Plot twist at the dead *end* of the story.

Gone with the Wind—End scene: "Frankly, my dear...." The melting point of a great drama; the only way it could logically end.

Gone with the Wind—The railroad yard—the crane shot. It defines big, powerful, motion pictures. Emblematic. It's *Hollywood*.

Gone with the Wind—Atlanta dead are laid out in the streets. In one single shot—by simply pulling back & up from a closeup to an extreme wide shot—the audience is struck by the enormity of the tragedy.

Gone with the Wind—Scarlett discovers the war dead at the station. Single shot serves as significant unit of the film's content & form to achieve epic proportions.

Gone with the Wind—When the camera travels back & climbs to reveal all the dead & suffering. We see *revealed* in an ever-widening shot the horror & hopelessness of war & Scarlett's need to escape from it.

Gone with the Wind—Atlanta depot scene. Tremendous scope filled with intimate specifics.

Gone with the Wind—The siege and burning of Atlanta. For pure spectacle, better than the *Ben-Hur* chariot race. Not as good, but longer than the dead horse or baby carriage in *Battleship Potemkin*.

Gone with the Wind—Burning of Atlanta. [No reason given.]

Gone with the Wind—Burning of Atlanta. Years ahead of its time production-wise.

Gone with the Wind—Exterior, Scarlett hungry, eats a turnip, and says she will never be hungry again. Scarlett O'Hara at this point has overcome everything, but she vows to rebuild Tara and by doing so will rebuild her own life.

Directors' Choice

Gone with the Wind—"I'll never be poor again." [No reason given.]

Gone with the Wind—Burning of Atlanta, & Rhett & Scarlett in "Frankly, my dear, I don't give a damn!" [No reason given.]

Gone with the Wind—Rhett carries Scarlett up the stairs, saying, "You won't turn me out tonight." Perhaps the most sexual tension in this scene than any other film from the '30s. One of several classic scenes from this landmark film.

Gone with the Wind—Melanie's death scene—Scarlett *finally* realizes it may be Rhett whom she really loves. Excellent action & direction—after almost four hours of the audience pulling for Scarlett to "wake up," she does—satisfying payoff.

Goodbye Mr. Chips [1939, Sam Wood]—On deathbed, Robert Donat hears a voice say he never had children—to which he counters: "But I had hundreds. . . ." Inside exploits of a London boys' school. Excellent sacrifices/characterizations.

Good Fellas [1990, Martin Scorsese]—Long steadicam shot down hall—through doors into restaurant. The ultimate use of a new technology which economically introduces new settings, new characters and reveals so much about the lead character.

Good Fellas—The long single camera move through the Copacabana following the lead & his date. This scene, with its series of small bits, the entry to the night club, the kitchen, the maitre d', etc., shows how the young woman is overwhelmed by power & romance tho' amoral.

Good Fellas—Being followed by the helicopter. [No reason given.]

Good Fellas—Joe Pesci: "Funny? You think I'm funny? Funny like a clown." [No reason given.]

Graduate, The [1967, Mike Nichols]—Seduction of Benjamin in hotel room. Camera angles and music set up the tension.

Graduate, The—Dustin Hoffman & Anne Bancroft seduction scene. Unusual relationship.

Part 3: Directors' Greatest Film Scene Choices and Reasons

Graduate, The—Technically a montage set to "Sounds of Silence" and "April Come She Will." Notable for inspired jump cuts, including one in which Benjamin leaps onto an inflatable raft and lands on Mrs. Robinson.

Graduate, The—Final scene showing Dustin Hoffman screaming "Elaine." Excellent summary of the relationships in the film. Extremely well shot in long shot.

Graduate, The—Underwater scene. Wonderfully comic irony in POV [point of view].

Grand Illusion [1937, Jean Renoir]—First meeting between Jean Gabin and Erich Von Stroheim. Two great actors in a great moment of confrontation.

Grand Illusion—Erich Von Stroheim, in neck brace & gloves, soothes French Lieutenant De Boeldieu [played by Pierre Fresnay]. First glimpse of this ramrod-straight Prussian's soft inner core.

Grand Illusion—Von Stroheim entertains the escapees at his fortress. It is a brilliant movie and [this] is the most poignant moment in it.

Grand Illusion—Any of the fight sequences. They redefined cinematography, action, slow motion, and light.

Grand Illusion—Final scene—[Jean] Gabin and [Marcel] Dalio escaping. Concept, writing, & acting. Shows brotherhood of men in time of war.

Grand Illusion—Soldier tries on woman's dress as others stare. Been done since but never better—moment of epiphany—in one moment you sense all the prisoners' loneliness. A total filmic moment.

Grapes of Wrath, The [1940, John Ford]—Henry Fonda as Tom Joad saying goodbye to his mother, Jane Darwell—an epiphany to all goodbyes & endings. With simplicity at its most powerful Ford keeps the brakes on the scene lest it run away and amp out.... The power of the scene threatens to bust open; Ford/Fonda get

Directors' Choice

more power without forcing it and the audience takes it with them.

Grapes of Wrath, The—The son's speech of farewell to his mother. It's incomparable emotional power.

Grapes of Wrath, The—Tom & Ma Joad riding in their flivver at night—talking—everyone else asleep. I'll never forget this heartrending talk—most of it seen as Tom & Ma's reflection in the windshield lit only by the lights of the dashboard on their faces.

Great Dictator, The [1940, Charlie Chaplin]—Chaplin's ballet with a giant global balloon. Sheer genius concept—the idea of Hitler playing with the fate of the universe was a brilliant satire.

Great Dictator, The—Chaplin juggles the [globe]. The perfect visual metaphor.

Great Dictator, The—Dance with globe. [No reason given.]

Great Dictator, The—Plays with globe. Again, nothing could better symbolize the power-hungry desire of Hitler to rule the world.

Great Dictator, The—Chaplin playing (tossing) with globe. The acting. The direction. The symbolism.

Great Dictator, The—"Hitler" playing with balloon world. Incredible image of tyrant and world.

Great Expectations [1946, David Lean]—Pip in graveyard, tree bending to howling wind; Pip scared—rushes into arms of convict. Classic, wonderful David Lean. Home, where Pip has come to the graveyard from, is screen left. Pip is so scared of the graveyard (screen right) that he races home, only to be shocked (and the audience too) by the appearance of the convict.

Great Gatsby, The [1974, Jack Clayton]—The final scene in the Plaza when the rich friends leave for Europe. We feel the frustration and despair of those who watch the clearly fatuous wealthy gloss over their blunders & let detritus fall for others.

Part 3: Directors' Greatest Film Scene Choices and Reasons

Greed [1924, Erich von Stroheim]—McTeague kills his partner in the middle of Death Valley while still handcuffed to him. In one dramatic moment, the power, intoxication, & tragic consequences of greed are summed up in one of the all-time great silent films.

Grifters, The [1990, Stephen Frears]—A guilty Angelica Huston visits her boss. Boss explains the "punishment of oranges-in-a-towel," an incredibly horrifying and chilling deterrence to disloyalty.

Gunga Din [1939, George Stevens]—Transporting elephants across a flimsy bridge high above the canyon far below. Personifies the danger and comedy of this marvelous translation of the Kipling classic.

Gunga Din—When Doug Fairbanks tells his love, Joan Fontaine, he must go with [Victor] McLaglen to rescue their captured comrade, Cary Grant. In one crackling and simple exposition scene, George Stevens encapsulates the man/woman love situation, *and* the duty of a man to himself, his comrades, his loyalties.

Hamlet [1948, Laurence Olivier]—Beginning of soliloquy, "To be or not to be. . . ." Brilliant use of in-focus and out-of-focus imagery of water to convey the momentous indecision as Hamlet weighs his choices—brilliantly acted and directed by Olivier. Filmic expression.

Hanussen [1988, István Szabó]—Hanussen predicts Hitler's election as chancellor. A very chilling scene. It makes one think of the possibilities of fate, chance, & the power of suggestion.

Haunting, The [1963, Robert Wise]—Two women sharing room—lying in separate beds—hold hands for comfort as booming sound surrounds room. Then they realize beds are 10 feet apart. Scared me more than anything I've seen. Director Robert Wise forced me to *imagine* whose hand was holding *what*? What was it like? And you never saw a "ghoul"—just the reactions of the "victims." It made my imagination scare me. The goal.

Directors' Choice

Henry V [1944, Laurence Olivier]—Battle of Agincourt. Stylized & real all at once. Magnificently staged & shot by Olivier.

Henry V—The battle of Agincourt. A very long tracking shot that followed the French cavalry into the arrows of the English. The climax of the movie's gradual change from theatrical to realistic images.

Henry V—Battle of Agincourt. Best battle scene ever made. Utterly convincing.

Henry V—Opening sequence in the Globe. The superb style and imagination of *everything*.

High Noon [1952, Fred Zinnemann]—Waiting for the train. Perfect choice and sequence of shots to show the loneliness and suspense. Textbook directorial technique.

High Noon—Clock countdown (real time) to train arrival. Dramatically sets scene for "showdown" in real time.

High Noon—Train arrival scene. Fantastic build thru use of pictures, music, sound, action. Extreme suspense.

High Noon—The final confrontation of Gary Cooper shooting it out with the bad guys. Much of this film is devoted to building up to this scene, the inevitable confrontation between good and evil. In the cowboy genre where that is a necessary ingredient, this scene is the best.

High Noon—The concluding gunfight. A classic statement of a classic movie moment—a cliché reanimated.

High Noon—Will Kane tries to enlist deputies at the church service. Beautifully written examination of blacklisting and our responsibilities as citizens.

High Sierra [1941, Raoul Walsh]—End. Ida Lupino at *her* best.

Hiroshima Mon Amour [1959, Alain Resnais]—The opening sequence—lovers intercut with the introduction of the city of

Part 3: Directors' Greatest Film Scene Choices and Reasons

Hiroshima. Modern erotic imagery and nonlinear cutting—a new experimental way of juxtaposing sound and image.

Hiroshima Mon Amour—The love scene. Incredibly erotic and composed and shot with a languorous beauty.

Hiroshima Mon Amour—The long scene in bed at the opening when they discuss love and the atomic aftermath. The viewer is drawn, via sexual love, into an examination of the destruction of Hiroshima and the many questions it opened.

Hiroshima Mon Amour—The love scene of naked bodies embracing as dust falls to cover them. Love, life, and death—all in one!

How Green Was My Valley [1941, John Ford]—The mine disaster sequence. Great personal drama fully realized.

Hurricane, The [1937, John Ford]—Storm sequence. Although shot in the forties in black and white in a tank, this action sequence rivals any shot today. The humanity of the characters comes through in the midst of the exciting typhoon.

Husbands and Wives [1992, Woody Allen]—Sydney Pollack's character tries to get his young girlfriend in his car. More violent than the goriest war scene, it's nearly impossible to watch—but you peek and watch it. The blackest of misanthropic comedies.

I Am a Fugitive from a Chain Gang [1932, Mervyn Le Roy]—Final scene in movie, fugitive Paul Muni, in dark shadows of night & his last "human" goodnight and goodbye from what he once was. The bone chilling reality that this moment is felt by both the actor and the audience—a last goodbye and farewell as human being ... His former love hears from Muni how he'll now live: "I steal...."

Imitation of Life [1934, John Stahl]—Freda Washington's grief and regret over mother's coffin at funeral. First time I heard an audience crying *out loud*. I was just a young boy at the time, but I knew I wanted to make audiences react out loud.

Directors' Choice

In Cold Blood [1967, Richard Brooks]—Execution scene when Blake character is put to death. He is both loathsome and pitiable, frightening and sad. To kill one is to kill the other. Viewers' emotions are at cross purposes. Conflict at its best.

Indiana Jones and the Last Crusade [1989, Stephen Spielberg]—Indy saves Dad from kidnapping in a tank. Great action directing/editing.

Indiana Jones and the Temple of Doom [1984, Stephen Spielberg]—Opening scene where diamonds & ice are mixed up—beautifully shot—terrific premise.

Informer, The [1935, John Ford]—The kangaroo court scene—where [Victor] McLaglen is interrogated by the IRA men. John Ford's simple staging—McLaglen's inspired (probably drunk) performance still stands up.

Informer, The—Gypo's examination by the IRA. The reality of it! Ford at his best.

Informer, The—Vic McLaglen's confession when he is exposed of how he killed his friend. Intimate study of Irish rebellion, great characterization under direction of John Ford.

In the Line of Fire [1993, Wolfgang Petersen]—Phone call scene between [Clint] Eastwood and [John] Malkovich. Terrifying performances—terrific lighting—*extremely* spooky & effective.

In the Name of the Father [1993, Jim Sheridan]—Opening riot. Jim Sheridan's brilliant use of filmic techniques to build the increasing degrees of intensity of a riot. It set up the environment and the character of the conflict to come—eventually reduced to human terms.

Invasion of the Body Snatchers [1955, Don Siegel]—Pods take on human features. Scared the piss out of me at 14, still does.

In Which We Serve [1942, Noel Coward and David Lean]—Final debarkation sequence. The brilliant understatement of that very emotional farewell.

Part 3: Directors' Greatest Film Scene Choices and Reasons

Isabel [1968, Paul Almond]—Opening on train (Genevieve Bujold). Broke new ground ('68) telling the story with flash cuts, increasing train rhythms, etc.

It Happened One Night [1934, Frank Capra]—The bedroom scene with blankets serving as "the walls of Jericho." This sweet love scene has a glorious combination of virtue and passion; comedy and sadness; hope and despair. Different values then, but just as much lust/heat!

It's a Gift [1934, Norman McLeod]—W. C. Fields tries to get to sleep on porch. Best comedy of 1930s, best scene.

It's a Mad, Mad, Mad, Mad World [1963, Stanley Kramer]—Opening scene, "Did you see the way it went just *sailing* right out there?" Perfect setup for the craziness to follow. Defines each major character, the plot, in one kooky scene. Love it when [Jimmy] Durante kicks the bucket. [Shelly] Winters: "That guy is *dead*."

It's a Wonderful Life [1946, Frank Capra]—Last scene—George Bailey comes home. What can I say? It always gets to me.

It's a Wonderful Life—The final scene where George's family, friends, and especially his brother come to his aid. A deeply emotional moment allowing the viewer to believe that all is not lost in spite of seemingly insurmountable odds. Everyone's life has meaning and will be rewarded.

It's a Wonderful Life—When he stops the drunk druggist from prescribing bad drugs. Pathos.

It's a Wonderful Life—The scene on the bridge between George Bailey & Clarence the Angel. A wonderful notion. Everyone who has ever wanted a guardian angel can relish this.

Ivan the Terrible [1942–1946, Sergei Eisenstein]—The charge of the Teutonic knights across the ice. What editing, what terror, what spectacle—all edited to the great Shostakovich music. This sequence could only be done on film—the ultimate charge.

Directors' Choice

Ivan the Terrible—All scenes. [No reason given.]

I Walked With a Zombie [1943, Jacques Tourneur]—Frances Dee travels by night to voodoo ritual. Val Lewton's greatest movie's most assured scene—poetry on a low-budget sound stage.

I Want to Live [1958, Robert Wise]—Death scene in gas chamber. "Take a couple of deep breaths . . . it'll be easier." If this isn't as strong a deterrent to crime as death itself, I don't know what is. Frighteningly real. (California death penalty [was] revoked after this film, by the way.)

Jailhouse Rock [1957, Richard Thorpe] / *The Girl Can't Help It* [1956, Frank Tashlin][tie]—Elvis Presley in prison blues choreographing the big production number and title of the movie. Little Richard in full color w/ Jayne Mansfield strutting by. Can't put any exact reason on both titles except that both pictures stirred up Americans & taught them how to [. . .]—And Presley's "J. R." and Richard's "Ready Teddy" made me happy.

Jaws [1975, Stephen Spielberg]—Robert Shaw's U-Boat monologue. Great performance. Breaks the cardinal rule "Show, don't tell," and does so brilliantly.

Jaws—Robert Shaw's description of sinking of the *Indianapolis*. The quiet terror of dying and fear of death told but not seen.

Jaws—Scene in boat's cabin, listening to description of the loss of life in the Pacific in sinking of the cruiser *Cleveland* [sic]. A fine, claustrophobic and chilling scene, with an almost academic description of the horrible danger of sharks. We feel the sea just beyond the fragile hull. A particularly effective building of fear in the on-screen listeners and in the film audience.

Jaws—The worried father's gestures copied silently by his young son at table. A "silent" scene that speaks volumes.

Jaws—Opening sequence—swimmer is attacked at night. Gruesome, affecting in its carefully manipulated *lack* of graphic gore. Lets our imaginations run rampant—brilliant!

Part 3: Directors' Greatest Film Scene Choices and Reasons

Jaws—The attack on the fishing boat finale. You are there! Ferocity unmatched in the cinema. Affected millions of ocean swimmers. Scared *everyone*.

Jezebel [1938, William Wyler]—The red dress. Forget *Gone with the Wind*. Wyler had it hands down.

Jezebel—The ball. Wonderful symbolism—a stunning moment.

Juarez [1939, William Dieterle]—Paul Muni's walk to the coffin of Maximilian and his leaving it. The character of Juarez & the acting of Muni were brilliant. The simplicity of the acting contrasted with the ornate cathedral setting.

Jules and Jim [1962, François Truffaut]—The cafe table after-love conversation—Le "joie de vie" of the 3 actors.

Jurassic Park [1993, Stephen Spielberg]—The scene where the herd animals run past the principals and are attacked by the Rex. The wonder of lifelike animals, generated by computer graphics—a true breakthrough.

Kagemusha [1990, Akira Kurosawa]—After the battle. He didn't show the battle; only the aftermath.

Key Largo [1948, John Huston]—Lauren Bacall in cabin with storm shutters with . . . from Humphrey Bogart. [Rest of response illegible.]

Key Largo—The first reveal of Edward G. Robinson as he sits in the bathtub. Full of mystery & foreboding and so simple.

Kid, The [1921, Charlie Chaplin]—Chaplin runs across the rooftops, gets [Jackie] Coogan, kisses him. It's so melodramatic, but there is such genuine emotion, it's so honest somehow, that anyone who's ever had or been a dad is moved greatly by it.

Kid, The—Next to last scene, where he is kissing the "saved" kid. Very touching, tender, scene of fatherhood.

Killing, The [1956, Stanley Kubrick]—The suitcase of stolen money

Directors' Choice

falls from the baggage cart and the airliner's propellers blow the bills all over the runway & away. A great climactic scene combining surprise and irony. The intricate robbery plan so well set up in the plot goes awry because of a trivial accident in which the protagonist's mega treasure is blown away. Great visual.

Killing Fields, The [1984, Roland Joffe]—The airlift from Saigon. Phenomenally staged—like the entire film—and the *feel* of "you are there" documentary.

Kind Hearts and Coronets [1949, Robert Hamer]—Whole movie. The funniest movie I ever saw.

King and I, The [1956, Walter Lang]—The king is dying. This scene is the culmination of everything that went before. You feel for the king, for Anna, the family, and especially the young prince. A very emotional scene, and perfectly in character.

King Kong [1933, Merian Cooper and Ernest Schoedsack]—Kong arrives at the gates of Kong. Faye Wray screams, the jungle music and the chanting of the natives built high suspense.

King of Hearts [1966, Philippe de Broca]—Genevieve Bujold walks the tightrope. In one scene, the meaning of the film was capsulized. The freedom of the insane, the insanity of war, the balance of life.

King of Kings [1927, Cecil B. de Mille]—The [crucifixion??]. Memorable. I was 5.

King Solomon's Mines [1937, Robert Stevenson]—The Watusi dance. Well shot & covered. Awesome in its ability to top some of the greatest scenery put on film.

Kurosawa's Dreams [1990, Akira Kurosawa]—The "waterwheel" sequence. Mr. Kurosawa's superb, funny, and moving tribute to death and living.

La Dolce Vita [1960, Federico Fellini]—A statue of Christ is being transported by helicopter. In the opening scene of the film Fellini cre-

Part 3: Directors' Greatest Film Scene Choices and Reasons

ates a powerful visual metaphor of the decadence of modern Rome.

La Dolce Vita—The statue of Jesus flying to St. Peters. The symbolism here is intense—old-time religion meets modern technology. One of Fellini's most inspired images.

Lady and the Tramp [1955, Hamilton Luske, Clyde Geronimi, and Wilfred Jackson]—Tramp takes Lady out on the town. They share a plate of spaghetti. Possibly the best love scene ever. Though the balcony scene from *Cyrano* is a close 2nd.

Lady Eve, The [1941, Preston Sturges]—Henry Fonda being tripped by Barbara Stanwyck & brought to her cabin, changing her slippers. About as sexy as it gets, full of understated & seductive tension peppered with great dialogue & beautiful gams.

Lady from Shanghai [1948, Orson Welles]—Funhouse mirrors. It's just plain brilliant. And *Citizen Kane* is *all* genius, so I couldn't find one scene [to choose].

Lady from Shanghai—The mirror scene! [No reason given.]

Lady from Shanghai—Shootout in hall of mirrors. Technical & artistic tour de force. Pure kinetic, abstract cinema in narrative form.

Lady Vanishes, The [1938, Alfred Hitchcock]—So many Hitchcock effects linger in the mind, but none more than Dame May Whitty's silent scream as the train whistle pierces the air. This scene still startles & the audience braces itself for a rough ride full of dangerous surprises.

La Femme Nikita [1990, Luc Besson]—Opening robbery. After years of evolution of cinematography, a stylistic revolution is still possible. May there be more! Good reason to go to the movies.

Last Emperor, The [1987, Bernardo Bertolucci]—The child emperor walks outside the palace door & looks over the cheering crowd. The juxtaposition of a 2-yr.-old ruling millions.

Last of the Mohicans, The [1992, Michael Mann]—Chase sequence, war

Directors' Choice

canoes on the river. Magua and his band chase Hawkeye. These are bloodthirsty savages. Hawkeye knows that if he is stopped and caught, he and his people will die. They hide under a waterfall.

Last Tango in Paris [1972, Bernardo Bertolucci]—First sex scene. Erotic.

Last Tango in Paris—Sex scene. Broke all traditional rules for sex scenes in mainstream movies.

Lavender Hill Mob, The [1951, Charles Crichton]—The run down the winding stairs of the Eiffel Tower. Starting slowly, it builds and builds as it spins into giddy hysteria.

Lawrence of Arabia [1962, David Lean]—Down in the desert and Omar Sharif coming to us out of a mirage. The cut from the blowing out of a match to the sun in the desert—classic.

Lawrence of Arabia—Lawrence & prince ride to each other. Perfect montage.

Lawrence of Arabia—Omar Sharif riding up to [Peter] O'Toole at the waterhole. In this very suspenseful scene the 19th century meets the 20th century.

Lawrence of Arabia—Ali approaches Lawrence on camel—from a tiny speck on a mirage to full frame. Extremely effective use of long lens—never seen anything to rival its power since this scene.

Lawrence of Arabia—Lawrence's camel approaching thru the heat haze. A remarkable visual experience.

Lawrence of Arabia—The scene at the well with the approaching camel rider and the killing of Lawrence's assistant. A brave edit choice, to allow the approaching rider to take so long. Dramatic conclusion. A strong lesson to Lawrence of the mentality of the Arab he would learn to deal with.

Lawrence of Arabia—O'Toole meets Sharif. Scope, size, intimacy of character.

Lawrence of Arabia—The sequence in the desert—Omar Sharif arrives

Part 3: Directors' Greatest Film Scene Choices and Reasons

on horseback (mirage-like) to meet Peter O'Toole. Introduction of a character into the picture with a bang.

Lawrence of Arabia—First train hijack. Exquisite setting of desert with modern-day conflict of war issues.

Lawrence of Arabia—Where Lawrence & co. blow up the train. He [climbs to] the top and faces death w/o fear, is shot and survives ... After the heights of his glory over the Turks, Lawrence faces another test of courage as he's nearly killed by a wounded Turk—a moment of surprise which exemplifies the complexity of his character.

Lawrence of Arabia—Battle at the train. Epic. Portrait of Lawrence as one of the few action adventure pictures with an intelligent hero. Strategic brilliance of Lawrence.

Lawrence of Arabia—At movie's end, Lawrence, again wearing his British Army uniform, sadly watches a group of Arab Bedouins and their camels as his Army car speeds him away from the Arab culture he loves. A great moment of desperate farewell sadness conveyed without dialog. Scene works powerfully because of the strong Arab visual imagery built up in the film—the leitmotif music cue that reminds us that Lawrence is leaving the sights and sounds he loves.

Lawrence of Arabia—First vista shot of desert. A vision of the infinite.

Lawrence of Arabia—Lawrence brings his Arab guide into officers' bar after taking Aqaba & crossing Sinai. The crucial scene in distancing Lawrence's heroism & vision from the British military establishment—done with elegant, moving brevity.

Lawrence of Arabia—Sunrise over the desert with dissolve to dunes. [No reason given.]

Le Mans [1971, Lee Katzin]—The start of the race. Its ability to show atmosphere and fervor at the start of [the] event.

Lethal Weapon [1987, Richard Donner]—The shootout in the Christmas tree lot. Fantastic action sequence.

Directors' Choice

Lethal Weapon 2 [1989, Richard Donner]—Chase scene from the "stilt house." This starts out as an ordinary run-of-the-mill chase scene but the ending is one of the best choreographed and edited pieces I have seen in a long time. It sticks in my mind like a surfboard through a windshield.

Letter, The [1940, William Wyler]—When Bette Davis finally breaks. James Stephenson's great performance as the lawyer leads Davis into this chilling scene. Wm. Wyler's marvelous direction and [Howard] Koch's great script. Certainly my favorite Davis film. The entire cast works well. Another perfect film.

Like Water for Chocolate [1991, Alfonso Arau]—Match-eating scene. Surreal resolution; perfect image of interior state.

Listen to Britain [1941 short, Humphrey Jennings]—Dame Myra Hess playing piano mixed with workers singing. My personal discovery of the power of a cut prompted only by music.

Little Big Man [1970, Arthur Penn]—The U.S. Cavalry wipes out the Indian village. Counterpoint of music and images evokes razor-sharp observation about brutality of U.S. soldiers.

Little Big Man—Chief dying on mountain. Rain (at end of film). Acting. Direction.

Little Foxes, The [1941, William Wyler]—Bette Davis (in foreground) *not* helping her husband as he collapses on stairs. So powerful with so much going on but done so simply.

Lonesome Cowboys [1968, Paul Morrissey]—Cowgirl flirting with disinterested cowboys redefined Hollywood film—redefined western genre.

Love and Death [1975, Woody Allen]—Woody Allen walking and talking with "death." A great concept.

M. [1931, Fritz Lang]—Peter Lorre's confession to the "court of criminals" at the film's end. Unsurpassed acting of a monologue that synthesizes all the themes of the film.

Part 3: Directors' Greatest Film Scene Choices and Reasons

Magnificent Ambersons, The [1942, Orson Welles]—The Last Great Ball scene. Here all the characters in the movie are united. The scene starts outside, goes in, goes into several rooms upstairs. The characters and their relationships mark the gradual industrialization of America in 1910.

Magnificent Ambersons, The—[Tim] Holt and [Agnes] Moorehead in dire, whispered exchange on stairway. Acting, writing, cinematography and direction at its best, singularly and collaboratively.

Magnificent Ambersons, The—Most scenes! Composition, lighting, perspective, foreground/background interest.

Male Animal, The [1942, Elliott Nugent]—Jack Carson demonstrating how he threw the TD [touchdown] pass with a sugar bowl which [Henry] Fonda takes away. I have always thought this one of the funniest scenes I can remember. Carson was the master of the double-take and never better at it than when he finds sugar bowl missing.

Maltese Falcon, The [1941, John Huston]—Humphrey Bogart tells Mary Astor he's "sending her over." When was the last time 2 people talked alone for 5 minutes!!!

Maltese Falcon, The—Bogart confronts Greenstreet and friends in hotel room. The combination of wit and menace.

Maltese Falcon, The—Any scene. The camera rarely moves, which makes this the best "cut" film I know of. You do not feel the camera!

Man and a Woman, A [1966, Claude Lelouch]—Setting up auto and auto racing scene. No dialogue. Just use of images and sound. Best portrayal of auto racing ever seen in a film.

Man and a Woman, A—The "man" drives across France to be with the "woman." His reasoning and anticipation through voice-over technique says everything about being in love. Timeless scene.

Manhattan [1979, Woody Allen]—Last scene. Tremendous emotional

Directors' Choice

impact. Closeups and Gershwin music make it one of screen's most memorable farewells.

Manhattan—Woody Allen running to see his old girlfriend before she leaves for Europe. Desire and relationship conflict, brought to a "regular folks" level.

Manhattan—Sitting in front of the 59th St. Bridge. [No reason given.]

Manhattan—Woody Allen on the couch speaks into his tape recorder about why life is worth living. Beautiful writing & the [scene] encapsulates the whole Woody Allen persona.

Man Who Shot Liberty Valance, The [1962, John Ford]—Liberty trips Jimmy Stewart, who's carrying John Wayne's steak. Wayne advises Liberty not to draw and to "pick it up".... "Great depiction of good vs. evil & value of someone guarding your "back door." Wayne was fearless. Tonti was a faithful friend. We all need this. I cheered when I first saw this—and still do.

Man Who Would Be King, The [1975, John Huston]—Michael Caine's return with [Sean] Connery's head to Kipling, who hears the story. End of a great adventure spoiled by a female-loving rogue (Connery).

Man Who Would Be King, The—Sean Connery on the bridge moments before being killed. This is such a proud, dignified death; he still acts as the king.

Mare Nostrum [1925, Rex Ingram]—Mermaid in the aquarium sequence. My first exposure to trick photography.

McCabe and Mrs. Miller [1971, Robert Altman]—Final manhunt sequence leading up to [Warren] Beatty's death. Visually breathtaking, suspenseful and painfully sad. Entire sequence is tremendously moving and primal.

McCabe and Mrs. Miller—The final shootout. A great climax to a great film—riveting, dramatic, ironic, multifaceted.

McCabe and Mrs. Miller—The final opium pipe shot with Julie Christie. A film about the wilderness, expansive & untamed, is

Part 3: Directors' Greatest Film Scene Choices and Reasons

reduced to the confines (literally & figuratively) of an opium bed, the rounded outline of the pipe in the foreground becomes the sad rim of a very private universe as it rises in the frame obliterating all.

Medium Cool [1969, Haskell Wexler]—The TV cameraman character, following his lover character, films the *actual* National Guard during the Chicago Convention riot of '68. Unparalleled example of the mix of dramatic reenactment combined w/ real-life events. The tear gas grenade thrown is real and his DOP [director of photography] warns Haskell, "Look out, Haskell, it's real!"

Metropolis [1926, Fritz Lang]—The shift change. [No reason.]

Metropolis—Wide shot of the human machine. Social commentary on a grand scale.

Michael Strogoff (aka *The Soldier and the Lady*) [1937, George Nicholls Jr.]—The torture sequence, blinding with a hot poker of Strogoff. My 1st film experience as a child to believe what was not specifically shown.

Midnight Cowboy [1969, John Schlesinger]—Joe & Ratzo's bus journey from New York to Miami—including Ratzo's death. [Dustin] Hoffman & [Jon] Voight sustain superb acting and honesty in every shot. Schlesinger handles the camera brilliantly.

Midnight Cowboy—The last scene on the bus. I can't help crying every time I see it.

Midnight Cowboy—The death of Ratzo in the bus to Florida. One of film's most powerful demonstrations of the impact, emotionally, of the redeeming power of love.

Midnight Express [1978, Alan Parker]—The opening scene where Billy tapes the drugs to his body and tries to board the airliner. In one scene without dialogue, only with the SFX [special effects] of his nervously pounding heart, Billy establishes his character, snared in bonds *of his own making*. Great visual metaphor of the life he's made for himself.

Directors' Choice

Miller's Crossing [1990, Joel Coen]—The attempted assassination of Albert Finney's character to the tune of "Danny Boy." In a film loaded with great scenes, this one's the best. Again, all images—no dialogue. And though it's violent, it looks so beautiful. Almost poetic.

Mississippi Mermaid [1969, François Truffaut]—Closing shot where snowfall dissolves to grain. The dissolution of a society and of a couple's dreams represented by a magnificent choice of camera technique and lab work.

Mrs. Miniver [1942, William Wyler]—Walter Pidgeon returns home from helping evacuate Dunkirk & is met by Greer Garson. The most exquisite moment of the reuniting of two people I can remember—because of events preceding the moment we are overwhelmed.

Mr. Smith Goes to Washington [1939, Frank Capra]—Jimmy Stewart's filibuster scene. Moving even today. Beautifully staged by Capra & touchingly acted by Stewart.

Mr. Smith Goes to Washington—The filibuster scene in U.S. Senate starring Jimmy Stewart. Stewart is superb, but what makes this scene memorable are the poignant cuts to Harry Carey and Claude Rains.

Modern Times [1936, Charlie Chaplin]—Chaplin trying to operate machinery. Brilliance of execution, concept, and success in epitomizing the spirit of the time.

Mon Oncle [1956, Jacques Tati]—Tea party. Best use of a location for comic effect. The garden becomes a character in this film (also the house).

Mummy, The [1932, Karl Freund]—The mummy comes alive. It chilled me.

Murmur of the Heart (Le Souffle au Coeur) [1971, Louis Malle]—The scene where the mother and son make love. The most sensitive

Part 3: Directors' Greatest Film Scene Choices and Reasons

rendering of the complexity of the human heart, told with a visual simplicity and restraint.

Napoleon [1927, Abel Gance]—Concluding triptych. You are emotionally wrought and then get visually stunned with the massive extras, wide screen, and French flag-tinted film. Carmine Coppola's '80s-era score [for the new release] is an exciting interpretation.

Napoleon—The children crying in the snow. Quality of black and white, action, camera movement.

Nashville [1975, Robert Altman]—The political rally. Altman aesthetically encapsulates the universal flavors of sales presentations, large or small.

Nashville—Opening sequence. Fluid, choreographed well, funny, amazing.

Natural, The [1984, Barry Levinson]—Roy strikes out the "Whammer." This is so beautifully shot it makes you wish the world looked like this. Caleb Deschanel [director of photography] again, three times in a row. No coincidence.

Natural, The—[Robert] Redford's home run in last at-bat to win series. Pure joy to watch—every kid's fantasy.

Network [1976, Sidney Lumet]—Female TV producer fantasizing about the ratings while making love. Nielsen ratings replace sex as the biggest turn-on. Underlines the true aim of TV (et al.): To produce audiences, not programming.

Network—Peter Finch's "I'm mad as hell" scene. Finch is riveting and Paddy Chayevsky's dialogue is among the best ever written for film.

Night and Fog [1955, Alain Resnais]—Corpses in camps. Sobering reality.

Night and Fog—Bulldozers pushing along bodies of holocaust victims while music—classical—plays. Humanity's greatest horror distilled to the most frightening poetry of images imaginable.

Directors' Choice

Night at the Opera, A [1935, Sam Wood]—The "Stateroom Scene"—Marx Bros. & many others pile into small stateroom. Absurdity built on absurdity—simply shot but beautifully played.

Night at the Opera, A—The "stateroom" scene. The style of the Marx brothers comedy was always based around nonsense and this scene reflects the peak of that style.

Night at the Opera, A—Stateroom scene. In which countless people pile into the Marx brothers' stateroom. The reason this is such a great scene is it is quick & funny & choreographed and very original.

Night at the Opera, A—[Respondent called it *Duck Soup*.] The stateroom. Sheer insanity—graphic comedy.

Night at the Opera, A—First cafe scene—with banter between Groucho, friends & Margaret [Dumont]. Can't think of anything ever funnier.

Night on Earth [1992, Jim Jarnusch]—The Italian cabdriver tells the priest about his love life. The funniest scene I have ever witnessed in a film!!!

Nights of Cabiria (aka *Cabiria*) [1957, Federico Fellini]—A wonderful film with many scenes, but when the strong man learns of the death of Giulietta and walks crying on the beach. A wonderful, sensitive scene of a man's realization of a love that he had denied to himself.

North by Northwest [1959, Alfred Hitchcock]—The crop-duster scene—shooting at Cary Grant. Wonderfully staged—given the period (less fancy special effects)—still looks real.

North by Northwest/Psycho—Biplane crop-duster scene/shower scene. Unforgettable Hitchcock moments.

North by Northwest—Mount Rushmore action sequence—great use of locale—great special effects.

Part 3: Directors' Greatest Film Scene Choices and Reasons

North by Northwest—The "redcap" scene. Hitchcock's masterful scene demonstrates futility, powerlessness, & desperation.

North by Northwest—Cary Grant getting off bus in a lone wheat field. The shots tell the scene. Direction. Editing. Camera work.

Nosferatu [1921, F. W. Mumau]—Nosferatu rising from his coffin on ship. Remarkable demonstration of expressionist aesthetics: lighting, camera angle, camera trick.

Nothing But a Man [1964, Michael Roemer]—A white boss confronts Ivan Dixon about organizing black workers into a union. Ivan leaves his job. An American dynamic captured in all of its complexity. The other black workers stay silent as Ivan must choose between denying his true feelings and keeping the job that feeds [his] famil[y].

Nothing Sacred [1937, William Wellman]—Just about everything. Fast paced, brilliantly cast and played.

Notorious [1946, Alfred Hitchcock]—Cary Grant kissing Ingrid Bergman while she is on phone to husband. Hitchcock at his best. Sly when dangerous, humorous when frightened.

Notorious—Ingrid Bergman kissing Cary Grant as he goe[s] from balcony to ringing phone. Such wonderful heat & passion without nudity or overt sex . . . but it sure felt real.

Notorious—Cary Grant coming up the stairs to rescue Ingrid—and leaving w/ her as Claude Rains watches. Certainly one of my fave Hitchcock movies. A very good script, and a different portrayal for Grant—and Bergman at her peak.

No Way Out [1987, Roger Donaldson]—Climactic scene in [Gene] Hackman's office where there are 3 plot twists. Betrayal.

Official Story, The (aka *The Official Version*) [1985, Luis Puenzo]—The description by the wife's returning friend of her torture by the junta. The genius of making a political statement in a purely personal context.

Directors' Choice

Once Upon a Time in America [1984, Sergio Leone]—A scene where De Niro has rented an entire restaurant to seduce his desired. The set design is almost over-romantic but the impression left in the viewer is the power of the ardor or lust of the protagonist.

Once Upon a Time in the West [1969, Sergio Leone]—Opening titles. Another all-visual performance. Sergio Leone sets the tone right here. Jack Elam and the fly are superb.

One Flew Over the Cuckoo's Nest [1975, Milos Forman]—Final scene when Nicholson has a lobotomy and Indian rips up sink and escapes. "Do not go gentle into that good night. / Rage, rage, against the dying of the light." Nicholson was the light.

On the Waterfront [1954, Elia Kazan]—Marlon Brando & Rod Steiger in taxi—"I coulda been a contender." The most influential piece of acting technique in postwar American cinema.

On the Waterfront—"I coulda been somebody." Brando. Performance.

On the Waterfront—[In the] back seat with Brando & Steiger. In one short scene we learn all about Terry Malloy (Brando) and how he got sold out.

On the Waterfront—Back seat shot w/Brando & Steiger ". . . contender." [No reason given.]

On the Waterfront—Back of car; Brando & Steiger. [No reason given.]

On the Waterfront—Scene in taxi—"I coulda been a contender." One of the most poignant scenes in film—archetypal moment; casting, performance, direction.

On the Waterfront—Taxicab scene between Brando & Steiger. The unorthodoxy of a fraternal relationship. Most revelatory!

On the Waterfront—"I coulda been a contender." Beyond all the hype of this scene, Brando proves he is one of our best actors.

On the Waterfront—The scene between Brando and Steiger in the cab vies with that between Brando & [Eva] Marie Saint in saloon.

Part 3: Directors' Greatest Film Scene Choices and Reasons

Although the analogy with his own role in the McCarthy era is invidious, Kazan exactly pictorializes Faulkner's "agony of moral choice."

On the Waterfront—Inside taxi w/Marlon Brando, Rod Steiger. Economy of shot. Acting. Direction.

On the Waterfront—Brando on the roof with his pigeons, talking with the boy. Brando with Steiger in the car as well. Again, aching honesty and simplicity from Kazan, and Brando, Brando saying, "I'd better get down there," to his endless job on the pier—when he knows he *could* have been more. Same with Steiger in the car.

On the Waterfront—End sequence. A moment of good over evil—the little guy wins in spite of shades of gray.

On the Waterfront—Last scene—Battered Brando & ILA "Everybody works!" [No reason given.]

Orphans of the Storm [1921, D. W. Griffith]—Lillian Gish looks for Dorothy Gish. [No reason given.]

Ossessione [1942, Luchino Visconti]—The woman sits down at the end of the day to eat. Pulls the newspaper in front of her. Incredible portrayal of fatigue and emotional exhaustion.

Other People's Money [1991, Norman Jewison]—Stockholders' meeting, [Danny] De Vito and greed vs. [Gregory] Peck and paternalism. Incredible writing. I believe them both. *The* argument for our times.

Our Daily Bread [1934, King Vidor]—The bringing of water to the farm co-op. The rhythm of the piece.

Out of Africa [1985, Sydney Pollack]—Kiss scene. Both the writing and the performance seem to be the best of this scene.

Out of Africa—Almost anything. Because of the camera (directing) giving such a total sense of place (sunsets) and [place]. I felt I'd been to Africa—total accomplishment.

Directors' Choice

Out of the Past [1947, Jacques Tournuer]—Exterior moonlight scene on patio overlooking lake. . . . Man and woman calm (Mitchum/ Greer) & dangerous. A sexual sparring match (jabs only)—[Jane] Greer is lying like a pro—we know it, but don't mind; and same we think for [Robert] Mitchum, until he says: "If there's any dying, I'm dying last."

Ox-Bow Incident, The [1943, William Wellman]—The hanging. All emotions were captured, portrayed & not distorted. Cutting was excellent & film moving & important.

Ox-Bow Incident, The—Henry Fonda reads the letter that Anthony Quinn has written to his wife. Shot with only Fonda's mouth showing behind the face & hat of foreground man. Dared to let words carry the scene.

Paris Is Burning [1990, Jennie Livingston]—End credits. Great song and dance.

Parsifal [1982, Hans Jürgen Syberberg]—When the male Parsifal & the female Parsifal hold hands at the end. Poetic demonstration of the bisexuality of us all.

Pascali's Island [1988, James Dearden]—Pascali (Ben Kingsley) realizes he's misjudged his friends. Jealousy can cloud judgement, in this case destroying lives in a very dramatic & literal sense.

Paths of Glory [1957, Stanley Kubrick]—The battle scene—over the top. Action, excitement, montage. Movement/crane and dolly, zoom, war . . . a sustained action seq[uence] that makes you part of the action.

Paths of Glory—Taking the anthill. Moving camera. Trenches and the insanity of war tempered by the insanity of officers.

Paths of Glory—March to execution. When Timothy Carey is being led to the firing squad the camera dollies with him as he is relentlessly dragged past troops standing at attention. His pleas for mercy go unheeded. This powerful scene captures the brutality of war.

Part 3: Directors' Greatest Film Scene Choices and Reasons

Patton [1969, Franklin Shaffner]—Opening scene. [Script writer] Coppola's decision to open a "war movie" with a monologue is daring and effective. Establishes character and prepares audience for what's to come.

Pawnbroker, The [1965, Sidney Lumet]—When Rod Steiger skewers himself through the hand. The epitome of anger, pain, frustration, and the inhumanity of it all.

Pedestrian, The [1974, Maxmilian Schell]—The "trial" on a TV talk show of the suspected Nazi war criminal. Utter trivialization by TV journalists of the question of truth. The issue has become merely an excuse for putting on a good show. Very German.

Peeping Tom [1959, Michael Powell]—The murder of the girl using the tripod leg while filming her. Wonderfully dark and bizarre and fetishistic.

Persona [1966, Ingmar Bergman]—Split face shot—Bibi Andersson full face. . . . This scene graphically portrays a relationship, an inner conflict, and a moment in the text as perfectly as possible.

Phantom of the Opera [1943, Arthur Lubin]—Chandelier falls. Scared me to death when I was seven, and still does.

Piano, The [1993, Jane Campion]—Piano slowly sinks to sea bottom in an underwater shot. The scene perfectly expresses the built-up emotions depicted.

Piano, The—In the boat where Holly Hunter decides against suicide and pulls free from the rope and back to the surface. All the pain, struggle, and beauty of life as she struggles underwater.

Piano, The—Scene when the piano topples overboard & pulls Ada underwater to drown—she chooses "life." Crane work—underwater "death" so hauntingly filmed; music & image came together to create *magic*.

Piano, The—The climactic scene in which Holly Hunter is snared by the piano's rope, starts to drown, chooses to live, survives . . . and even envisions what her death *would* have been. In some-

Directors' Choice

thing like 45 seconds, the most unpredictable and telling ending in movie history. So much packed into a short climax—and inviting the discussion, did she snare her foot in the rope deliberately or not.

Picnic [1955, Joshua Logan]—Kim Novak coming down the stairs with the "Picnic" theme and "Moonglow" to dance w/ Bill Holden. One of the sexiest moments. Again, a great script. Perfect casting (especially Novak). The entire group all worked. In my opinion, one of the best films ever.

Picnic—Holden & Novak dancing to "Moonglow." Youth dances while regret-sodden elders see their own morality in the youngsters' sexuality. One of the sexiest scenes ever, but painful, too.

Picture of Dorian Gray [1945, Albert Lewin]—Last sequence—the lead character destroying the [painting] which had shown in progress the [character] getting old. Climactic sequence, shocking and revealing. Part black & white—the painting in technicolor showing the change.

Pink Flamingos [1972, John Waters]—Divine eating dog excrement—pure shock value—redefined limits of film & tastelessness.

Pink Panther [1963, Blake Edwards]—Where Inspector C. is talking—got hand caught in world globe.

Pixote [1981, Hector Babenco]—Pixote suckling at the breast of the prostitute. Makes a statement about the cause of sociopathic behavior—the deprivation of love, and the futile search for intimacy. A humanizing note in a savage world.

Place in the Sun, A [1951, George Stevens]—Miss Taylor/Montgomery Clift terrace scene—with the over-the-shoulder shot of Liz. Truly magic. Another great script. By far Stevens' best film—and (in my opinion) the only *great* movie that [Elizabeth Taylor] ever worked in. It's such a great story—and they all worked together so well. Stevens never topped this.

Place in the Sun, A—The kiss. Absolutely beautiful.

Part 3: Directors' Greatest Film Scene Choices and Reasons

Place in the Sun, A—The initial kiss between Elizabeth Taylor & Monty Clift. There is a dissolve in the middle of it that stops the heart. It is the height of romance between two gorgeous young people. The dissolve in the middle of the kiss has a *bonding* effect. In that moment their doomed love is sealed.

Place in the Sun, A—Where the girl (Elizabeth Taylor) visits the boy (Montgomery Clift) in the condemned cell. A great scene adapted from a great book and with its original dramatic power not only intact but enhanced.

Places in the Heart [1984, Robert Benton]—Final shot in film: camera dollies across congregation during communion in church w/ hymn "He Walks with Me." An amazing statement of love in an imperfect & diverse world. We see the alive with the dead, the poor with the well-to-do, old and young, confused and bright, an accidental murderer and victim. What heaven may be like.

Plan 9 from Outer Space [1958, Edward Wood]—Criswell's opening speech. Ed Wood, anti-genius, passionate, incompetent, goes out for art, fumbles in surreal first scene.

Platoon [1986, Oliver Stone]—Overrun of U.S. encampment by V.C. at night. First rate recreation of intense terror, madness, fury, helplessness, confusion, and courage of soldiers fighting hand-to-hand with the enemy.

Player, The [1992, Robert Altman]—A copy style of *Touch of Evil*—beginning sequence. Reveals all in one tracking at the start of the film—revealing the studio and some of its characters—well choreographed.

Player, The—Opening sequence. Camera moves—story.

Player, The—Opening scene. Just a technological masterpiece. One continuous 8½-minute shot. (I've tried it. It can't be done. But Altman did it.)

Player, The—The opening scene, long continuous take. A marvelous technical and acting performance that in one continuous shot

Directors' Choice

set up the mood, the characters, and the environment of the movie.

Player, The—Opening "travel" shot. It immediately established the hectic environment & competitive spirit of the movie studio & introduced many lead characters & ended w/ an intro. to *murder*.

Player, The—Opening sequence. The first 5 minutes are shot without an edit. One fluid camera move while Fred Ward goes off about how films today are cut, cut, cut.

Player, The—The copy of *Citizen Kane*. Just a really great shot. Well planned.

Player, The—Opening scene. Exquisite choreography of a one-take scene.

Player, The—The opening. Staggering—it *never* stopped and it absolutely captured and set up the whole film. *Unbelievable!*

Player, The—Scene at L.A. Club between Robbins and two screenwriters. Tim Robbins, a film executive, can't resist listening to pitch by writers, although he's in personal danger. Perfect blend of suspense and character.

Poltergeist [1982, Tobe Hopper]—Child staring at TV snow, "They're here." The catch phrase caught on around the world.

Pretty Woman [1990, Garry Marshall]—Julia Roberts' return to the store where she was snubbed. Fine acting makes this "get-even" scene work perfectly. She does what all of us have wanted to do at one time or another.

Pride of the Yankees [1942, Sam Wood]—Gary Cooper's farewell address. [No reason given.]

Princess Bride, The [1987, Rob Reiner]—When Peter Falk tells his grandson that the kiss was one of the best kisses of all time. The passing on from old man to young man of a romantic notion.

Producers, The [1968, Mel Brooks]—"Springtime for Hitler" produc-

Part 3: Directors' Greatest Film Scene Choices and Reasons

tion. Captures take no prisoners style of Brooks when he still was possessed by genius.

Psycho [1960, Alfred Hitchcock]—The shower! A "scene" of 70-odd cuts in under a minute.

Psycho—The shower sequence. Murder as sex. Cutting as cutting. Of all Hitchcock's set pieces, the purest.

Psycho—Shower murder. The standard by which all murder scenes should be compared.

Psycho—The murder in the shower. Beautifully choreographed. This awful murder was shot with love and care.

Psycho—Bathroom scene. [No reason given.]

Psycho—Infamous shower scene. Tension and horror set up perfectly with varying angles and you never see a drop of blood on Janet Leigh.

Psycho—Murder scene in shower. Brilliant use of montage; music; best shot of "dead person" in cinema (still photo with water drop).

Psycho—Shower scene. Killing the star in the first half-hour???

Psycho—Shower scene. Brilliant suggestion—montage of violent killing—totally memorable.

Psycho—Shower scene. Use of quick cuts along with music made for great suspense.

Psycho—Shower scene. Horror.

Psycho—Shower murder scene. A horrific, terrifying scene set up with such normal innocence. Amazing editing of image and sound. Horrible images created without really seeing anything.

Psycho—Shower scene. Shocking for its time. . . . Expressed enormity of crime without showing it.

Directors' Choice

Psycho—Shower scene. Strikes a chord of fear that everyone can relate to. It stays with you.

Psycho—Shower scene. For the first time, the audience felt the color red as the blood went down the drain.

Psycho—The bathtub kill. Conception/shooting/editing.

Psycho—The shower scene. The terror, and how it's created by editing.

Psycho—The shower scene. One of the most perfect montages ever cut.

Psycho—Falling down the stairs. The most frightening movie ever made.

Psycho—Tony Perkins holding up corpse of dead mom. Greatest horror scene ever shot.

Psycho—Leigh & Perkins' "snack conversation" in his back parlor. Their dialogue gives all the clues necessary to predict end of story . . . but they're hidden.

Psycho—Murder of P.I. Arbogast. Using anxiety and suspense to detract audience from possibly noticing murderer is a man, not a crazy old woman. Worthwhile trickery.

Public Enemy, The [1931, William Wellman]—End of film scene where [Jimmy] Cagney's mother opens door and his propped-up body falls into camera. A real shocker. I can still hear the audience gasp after some 70 years.

Pumpkin Eater, The [1964, Jack Clayton]—Female lead (J. Woodward) in dept. store alone, breaks into tears, crowd parts, zoom back. When the camera moves back to reveal her crying alone in the crowd we feel her isolation and see how singular grief can be.

Purple Rose of Cairo [1984, Woody Allen]—When actor steps off screen. Surprise.

Purple Rose of Cairo—When character (Jeff Daniels) finally decides to

Part 3: Directors' Greatest Film Scene Choices and Reasons

come off the screen and takes off with Rose (Mia Farrow). Sleight-of-hand perfectly executed. Delightfully blurs the line between one's romantic fantasies, how the movies play upon & fulfill them or seem to, and the pressing need of the real world.

Quiet Man, The [1952, John Ford]—The long fist fight through the countryside. Reality is pushed to the clouds on this one. Perfectly captured in tone and comedy, it is a miracle of film temperament by the master.

Quiet Man, The—J. Wayne & V. McLaglen—"I never hit a man . . ." (says Wayne) and then hits McL. A great love story of a man for his country and his woman.

Quiet Man, The—Near the end of the film—John Wayne drags Maureen O'Hara through the countryside. The photography, direction, and editing were a perfect marriage.

Quiet Man, The—. . . men are working in the field . . . & Mary Kate throw[s] her dowry into the fire. This shows that Mary Kate is finally free of her brother, and now on her own with her husband, Sean Thorton.

Quo Vadis [1951, Mervyn Le Roy]—Climactic finale, when Marcus must watch Ursus fight a wild bull to save his love, Lygia, from death. In this one scene, Director Mervyn LeRoy applies desperate action, vast crowd effects, and interplay between the principals of love, fear, despotism, and literally the conversion of Marcus to Christianity.

Radio Days [1987, Woody Allen]—Opening scene—burglars answer phone & win prize for unwitting residents. Brilliantly quirky, ironic—a perfect "curtain raiser."

Raging Bull [1980, Martin Scorsese]—Fight scene when all goes silent/slo mo. Original, heightened senses, tension.

Raging Bull—[Jake] La Motta is demolished inside the ring. Incredible use of slo mo & black & white to capture blood & sweat sprays—the *sound* enhancing the tragedy—the violence.

Directors' Choice

Raging Bull—Fight with Sugar Ray Robinson (the blood on the ropes). Says everything against fighting—again with *no words*!!!

Raging Bull—Boxing arena. Brilliant editing.

Raging Bull—Boxing scene with Sugar Ray & Jake LaMotta. Astonishing, graphic & poetic depiction of a boxing match that somehow transcends itself to be a haunting visual metaphor of the groveling struggle of a man against the world & himself.

Raging Bull—2nd fight with Sugar Ray. Brutal, violent & ultimately horrifying. When De Niro says, "You never got me down, Ray," you feel as if you truly understand the mind-set of Jake LaMotta.

Raging Bull—Any & all fight [sequences]. The best edited film of all time, shines during these fight sequences.

Raging Bull—Jail scene—LaMotta in jail. Stylized in darkness (very Scorsese).

Raging Bull—De Niro in prison banging his head on wall. It hurts you in the guts to watch him inflict this pain on himself, but the beauty of it is what you *understand*—a tribute to Scorsese and De Niro.

Raiders of the Lost Ark [1981, Stephen Spielberg]—The climactic scene in which the evil Nazis open the ark. The Indiana Jones films have given us many exciting moments, but this tops them all. By combining special effects, opticals, live performances and a great audio component, the director has made this scene the most tense, exciting event of the entire Jones series.

Raiders of the Lost Ark—As they open the Ark—ghosts appear & our heroes are the lone survivors. All senses are stimulated—sight, sound & emotions. You don't have to be religious to feel the impact of a source greater than ourselves. Spielberg excels at this more than any other director.

Raiders of the Lost Ark—Opening sequence. It clearly said, "Watch this, you're in for a treat."

Part 3: Directors' Greatest Film Scene Choices and Reasons

Raiders of the Lost Ark—[Respondent wrote *Indiana Jones*.] Opening seq. with rolling ball in tomb. A truly great seq. that the rest of the film could not live up to.

Rambling Rose [1991, Martha Coolidge]—Scene in which Lukas Haas asks to touch Laura Dern's breasts, etc. Scene could have easily lapsed into bad taste, but under Coolidge's direction, it is both hilarious and touching (no pun intended).

Ran [1985, Akira Kurosawa]—The burning of the castle sequence. So many Kurosawa scenes to pick—this is one of the best.

Rashomon [1950, Akira Kurosawa]—The walk thru the forest. The camera used by a master telling the story & entertaining with beautiful cinematography.

Razor's Edge, The [1946, Edward Goulding]—When the former girlfriend of the male lead sets up drinks for the new alcoholic girlfriend to be tempted. The tension during the scene because we can't quite believe the malice of Gene Tierney and the anxiety of the alcoholic about to take a drink.

Rear Window [1954, Alfred Hitchcock]—L. B. Jeffries watches his girlfriend helplessly as she is found in Thorwald's apartment. The cross-cutting creates as effective suspense as I've ever seen. Makes the passive filmgoer directly identify with Jeffries, the passive voyeur.

Rear Window—The scene in which Jimmy Stewart watches Grace Kelly search Raymond Burr's apt. The tension in that scene is remarkable—as Jimmy Stewart is powerless to help Grace Kelly as she's trapped in the killer's apt. We know she's in danger & Stewart sees it but can't do anything about it. It's great. The audience is caught up totally in the tension.

Rebecca [1940, Alfred Hitchcock]—Dr. Winter's statement "I hated her. . . ." Very dramatic. Beautifully timed and played. Buildup made a great payoff.

Directors' Choice

Red River [1948, Howard Hawks]—The finale, where [John] Wayne fights [Montgomery] Clift, with the drovers looking on, and Joanne Dru shooting at them to break it up. Again, without tricks or gimmicks, director Howard Hawks summed up his film, bringing it to a great conclusion, with action, romance, nuances of man/man love relationships, and boy-gets-girl.

Remains of the Day, The [1993, James Ivory]—The argument when she wants to see his book. Brilliant performances, perfectly edited to make both people understandable. Very painful.

Remains of The Day, The—The scene in which Emma Thompson tries to learn what Mr. Stevens [Anthony Hopkins] is reading. The pivotal scene in the film. Mr. Stevens will never change. He cannot let himself go.

Remains of the Day, The—Emma Thompson tells Anthony Hopkins that she plans to marry & quit post. Cinematic pathos at its best—an hour of film & mutual, unspoken longing set this emotional moment up sublimely.

Repulsion [1965, Roman Polanski]—Hands reach thru the walls. Repulsion.

Requiem for a Heavyweight [1962, Ralph Nelson]—Where manager talks his fighter into wearing a phony wrestler's costume. Manager, fighter, trainer . . . all struggling with what they owe each other versus what they owe/value for themselves. A poignantly tragic scene.

Reversal of Fortune [1990, Barbet Schroeder]—All flashback sequences. Brilliantly structured storytelling & use of voice-under to weave past into present events.

Right Stuff, The [1983, Philip Kaufman]—What I call the "I gotta go" scene. Alan Shephard has been in his Mercury capsule for hours, now he has to urinate. The story (and humor) continue through a series of shots using water and other liquids as the "glue" that holds the scene together. By the time it was over, I had almost wet my pants.

Part 3: Directors' Greatest Film Scene Choices and Reasons

River, The (aka *Louisiana Story*) [1948, Robert Flaherty]—Opening scene of water that becomes the Mississippi River. [No reason given.]

Road Warrior, The (aka *Mad Max 2*) [1981, George Miller]—Mel Gibson's final escape attempt with truck. Incredible action—tension—death as ballet. *Best action scene ever.*

Robin Hood [1922, Allan Dwan]—The original *Robin Hood* film in which Douglas Fairbanks invades the castle of the usurper, Prince John. This scene is recollected from my youth. Douglas Fairbanks was a superb gymnast and was at his best in *Robin Hood*. In this particular scene he plunges his dagger into a massive curtain and, holding on to the dagger, he slides from a balcony down to the main floor—of course, ripping the curtain in half, but who cares?

Rocky [1976, John Avildsen]—When he runs up to [the] statue. Joy, feeling elated.

Rocky—Young guys singing on corner. Reality/entertainment in poor communities.

Roman Holiday [1953, William Wyler]—Scene at the end when she (A. Hepburn) is back as princess & G. Peck has to pretend he doesn't know her personally. Most romantic movie ever made.

Romeo & Juliet [1968, Franco Zeffirelli]—The wedding scene. Extraordinary visual interpretation of the scene. Many wonderful details could be noted, but one incident sums it up. At a screening I attended, there were two teenage girls behind me. They were talking among themselves during the early part of the film, but then quieted down. During the wedding, as the camera craned upward and looked down at the little figures, one said to the other, "They look like little children!" I wished Franco had heard that!

Rope [1948, Alfred Hitchcock]—All sequences. Picture . . . was shot in 9-minute continuous takes.

Directors' Choice

Rose Marie [an early post-WWII German film]—The street singers scenes. Use of very believable characters that fit within the story as a "Greek chorus."

Royal Wedding [1951, Stanley Donen]—[Respondent asked if it was *The Gay Divorcee*.] Fred Astaire dancing on walls and ceiling. Seamless optical work.

Rules of the Game, The (La Règle du Jeu) [1939, Jean Renoir]—The gamekeeper running amok during the costume ball. Comedic slapstick is symbolically used to produce social commentary, as the class relationships of a whole society are depicted as collapsing into chaos.

Rules of the Game, The—Hunting sequence. Powerfully, slyly oblique indictment of frivolous aristocratic lifestyle.

Saboteur [1942, Alfred Hitchcock]—Final scene on Statue of Liberty. Suspense and technical brilliance.

Sand Pebbles, The [1966, Robert Wise]—Steve McQueen shot (and dying). A great climax (in the sense of national power vs. real human power.)

San Francisco [1936, W. S. Van Dyke]—Earthquake sequence. The memorable earthquake climax sequence by montage director John Hoffman. Using Slavko Vorkapich techniques of breaking down a single action into many angles—overlapping and underlapping cuts. Using blurs and hand-held cameras to intensify the reality of the event. Choreographing the intensity of emotion by controlling the amount and kinds of movement on the screen.

San Francisco—Jeannette MacDonald singing "San Francisco" in the nightclub just before the earthquake. Unbelievable performance.

Satyricon [1969, Federico Fellini]—The swine scene. Eroticism visualized.

Scarface [1983, Brian De Palma]—The chain saw scene. Ruthlessly frightening concept & performance.

Part 3: Directors' Greatest Film Scene Choices and Reasons

Scent of a Woman [1992, Martin Brest]—The tango scene. It gives us a glimpse of the desperate and disabled hero's capacity of the love for the good life and underscores the tragedy of his blindness, while offering romance & hope to the other characters.

Scent of a Woman—Al Pacino on the dance floor. Sensuous, sexual, animal, and all fully clothed.

Schindler's List [1993, Stephen Spielberg]—The girl in the colored dress (the only colored object) visible in the crowd. Great tragedy made personal.

Schindler's List—A young girl clad in red appears suddenly in the occupied ghetto. In an otherwise black-and-white film, this is a striking effect.

Schindler's List—Second scene showing girl in red coat. In b/w film these two scenes, especially the second, explain Schindler's motivations.

Schindler's List—The clearing of the ghetto. The handling of mass forces.

Schindler's List—The Nazis depopulating the Crakow ghetto. The inciting moment for one of the most powerful epiphanies (Schindler's) in the entire history of drama.

Schindler's List—Two scenes: The extermination of Crakow ghetto. The medical examination scene in concentration camp yard. You were made to feel the horror of fantasy with S. Spielberg previously. Now, you are made to feel the horror of reality.

Schindler's List—Final scene, where Schindler says farewell, tells them "I should've done more." Schindler speaks for the world in this moment. Beautifully done.

Schindler's List—Where Schindler bemoans the lack of help he gave at the end of movie. Gripping. . . .

Schindler's List—The last scene; the survivors and families visit the grave of Oskar Schindler. As the only color scene in the film, this

Directors' Choice

scene is a wonderful tribute to Schindler and also those who were spared because of him.

Schindler's List—Final scene—rocks on grave. The introduction of the actual holocaust survivors in this scene thrusts the audience into a realization of the truth of the story.

Schindler's List—Schindler asks his bookkeeper (Ben Kingsley) what he can do to help. The height of redemption.

Schindler's List—Shower scene. Takes you into a time & place you would hardly believe & never see.

Schindler's List—Boy hides in toilet. The incredibly moving scene of the kid trying to hide—ending up in the toilet. More powerful than all the skeletons—the dehumanization of individuals. Nothing symbolizes the subtext [more] than this simple scene.

Schindler's List—Prisoners running naked in yard. Newsreel quality of reality. Horrifying juxtaposition of prisoners & captors.

Schindler's List—The restaurant/cabaret scene at opening revealing the carefully orchestrated meeting of two power figures. The character of Schindler is shown... in a purposefully slick, amusing parade of glad-handing & charm.

Schindler's List—Schindler insisting that children be assigned to him because their two fingers could clean shell casings. Desperation of character understood through lie.

Searchers, The [1956, John Ford]—When Martin Pauly [Jeffrey Hunter] & the John Wayne character return from hunting Debbie [Natalie Wood] & Martin get in fight over the girl who has been waiting for him. It might just be that seeing most of John Ford's acting troupe together in this big extended sequence is enough in itself. But the staging, camera work, and acting & drama are pure Americana at its best.

Searchers, The—Closing camera interior as everyone but Ethan enters the house. After 5 years of searching and finding his niece,

Part 3: Directors' Greatest Film Scene Choices and Reasons

Ethan Edwards remains the loner, outside of the family. The lone individual.

Searchers, The—Wayne returns from the Indian camp & says, "Don't ever ask me what I found there!" John Ford created a situation in which the viewer's imagination is twice as violent as anything that could have been filmed. Wayne's expression is priceless!

Serpico [1973, Sidney Lumet]—Auto chase scene in NYC & Queens under elevated [train]. Also scene at the shuttle—Grand Central to Times Square—on/off, etc. [No reason given.]

Seven Beauties [1975, Lina Wertmuller]—Giancarlo Giannini seduces camp commandant (Shirley Stoller). Funny, desperate, biting sarcasm, and probably true.

Seven Samurai [1954, Akira Kurosawa]—Fabulous visual clash of color and movement as various troops attack the fortress. Great editing, sweep, panorama, and editing—again, this could only be done on film.

Seven Samurai—The "quiet" samurai runs off in the night to retrieve a deadly gun from the bandits—alone. Return at first light w/ gun. "Killed two." Then sleeps. Conveys incredible courage, strength, skill, loyalty—without *showing* the actual action—just the before and after—and the response of the farmers. Our minds fill in the rest. Brilliant direction. Genius. (Today it would be a gore-fest.)

Seven Samurai—Sword fight scene. First "intelligent" use of slow motion to indicate power.

Seven Samurai—Long tracking shot through woods toward sun streaks following horseman. [No reason given.]

Seventh Seal, The [1957, Ingmar Bergman]—Death playing chess with the knight. Bergman literally creates a game of life and death during the plague era.

Directors' Choice

Shadowlands [1993, Richard Attenborough]—Death of Debra Winger's character. We see demonstrated the love [the] Anthony Hopkins character has for Debra Winger and her son. She knows he will love and protect the boy as a father would.

Shadows of Forgotten Ancestors [1964, Sergo Paradjanov]—The *whole* movie is a long, swirling connected scene of one man's 16th cent. life in ancient Russia. With a minimum of dialogue and with the most inspired vision I've ever seen, the director takes us from birth to death—[a] message of life lived.

Shane [1953, George Stevens]—Early morning on the ranch—Brandon de Wilde sees Shane practice shooting. If ever an entire audience completely identified with the wonder and feeling of a youngster. It was just marvelous.

Shane—Shane shows the boy his gun and fires it. The pumped-up sound of the first shot heard in this picture is so dramatic, so powerful.

Shane—Final shootout between Alan Ladd & Jack Palance. Classic Western gunfight. Built to beautifully excellent Western mood, characters—white hat vs. black hats.

Shane—Jack Palance showdown (killing) of rebel (Robert E. Lee??). Great action in stark realistic setting of town.

Shane—When the bad guys are beating up on Shane, who's buying a soda pop for the boy, and Van Heflin joins the fray. Probably the best-staged, most realistic screen battle of all time, down to the "WHOOSH" of the ax Van Heflin wields to save Alan Ladd from a crippling beating.

Shane—When Shane rides off at the end & the little boy calls after him. Image of romantic lover disappearing over the horizon.

She Wore a Yellow Ribbon [1949, John Ford]—[Response illegible.]

Shining, The [1980, Stanley Kubrick]—The scene in which Shelly Duvall discovers exactly what her husband has been typing. All the time Shelly has been pleased to see her husband at work

Part 3: Directors' Greatest Film Scene Choices and Reasons

writing his book. When she learns what he's been writing she learns that he has become dangerously insane.

Shoeshine [1946, Vittorio De Sica]—Final shot—2 boys, then panning with horse. Again, the simplicity of the shot, plus the total and devastating impact of what has happened.

Shop on Main Street, The [1965, Jan Kadar and Elmo Klos]—Final slow motion scene at end of movie. The impending & surrounding doom of the holocaust & war is driven home & transcended by this dreamlike moment full of hope & propelled by fear.

Short Cuts [1993, Robert Altman]—Ominous planes "dusting" Los Angeles. Alt[man], as in the sequence above, established a corrupted vision of Los Angeles & the small people who struggled to live there.

Shot in the Dark, A [1964, Blake Edwards]—Opening titles. Perfect timing . . . beautiful choreography . . . all working to the title song, it sets the scene for the movie perfectly.

Silence of the Lambs, The [1990, Jonathan Demme]—First meeting of Hannibal and Clara (?) in the prison. Everything works very well here. And there is magic in Hopkins' portrayal. It is extraordinary that a small man, safely behind bars, can be so frightening. Indirection, suggestion, great scripting, fine handling of the point of view to enhance the woman's reaction to his power. Intellectual, psychological, sexual, even professional tension. An incredible antagonist—and somehow, against all odds, he manages to get us to accept her as a worthy opponent. Wonderful camera & lighting. Everything that follows can be accepted after this scene.

Silence of the Lambs, The—First meeting with Hopkins. An acting tour de force. We are both repelled and drawn to Hopkins' character. He works the audience as a conductor works an orchestra.

Silence of the Lambs, The—Anthony Hopkins & Jodie Foster interrogation in the cage. Intellectual terror with only implied violence.

Directors' Choice

Silence of the Lambs, The—Where Hopkins reads Foster as poor white trash trying to escape her background. She stands like a deer in headlights. Mesmerizing interplay between two excellent actors. Insightful and revealing beyond words spoken.

Silence of the Lambs, The—Jodie Foster enters home of true serial killer—slowly realizes she has found him. Eerie, nail-biting, quirky suspense. Audience is "ahead" of Foster's realization—brilliantly spun out.

Singin' in the Rain [1952, Gene Kelly and Stanley Donen]—Splashing. Well, you know.

Singin' in the Rain—Kelly dancing the title song. The joyous feeling displayed in creative choreography epitomizes the best of film musicals.

Singin' in the Rain—Gene Kelly's dance. Speaks for itself.

Singin' in the Rain—"Singing in the Rain." The epitome of the Hollywood musical.

Singin' in the Rain—Gene Kelly dancing from puddle to puddle. This scene has charm, wit and innovation. Even to this day it remains the zenith of musical numbers and choreography.

Singin' in the Rain—Gene Kelly dances into rain. [No reason given.]

Singin' in the Rain—"Singing in the Rain"—with "Moses Supposes" as a close second. Have there been better musical sequences? These particularly utilize the film form.

Singin' in the Rain—Gene Kelly dancing the title number. This is one of the most charming and memorable musical numbers in cinema history. Perhaps its simplicity combined with a great piece of music and a great dancer is what makes this scene stand above all others in musicals.

Singin' in the Rain—Gene Kelly dances title song. The sheer joy of it.

Singin' in the Rain—Gene Kelly's dance with garbage can lids. Great choreography that expressed the film title.

Part 3: Directors' Greatest Film Scene Choices and Reasons

Singin' in the Rain—Kelly dancing down that street. All the elements—performer, camera, set design in perfect harmony.

Singin' in the Rain—The "Singing in the Rain" musical number. Seamless combination of performance, choreography, camera, editing and music. When the camera finally sweeps up and around it takes the audience with it.

Singin' in the Rain—Kelly performing title song. Has lifted my spirits for 44 years.

Singin' in the Rain—[Respondent called it *An American in Paris.*] Gene Kelly singing: "Singin' in the Rain." Choreography. Special effects. Camera work. Direction.

Singin' in the Rain—Gene Kelly dancing in the rain. The magic is in the pure & simple (?) performance that Gene Kelly makes look magical. His talent transcends the difficulty factor & he makes it look easy/timeless. Makes you feel good every time you see it.

Singin' in the Rain—"Singin' in the Rain" sequence. Epitome of musical sequences.

Singin' in the Rain—Gene Kelly's dance to the title song. Sheer joy—seamless cutting and happily conceived & performed.

Singin' in the Rain—"Good Morning" number. Direction and editing outstanding.

Singin' in the Rain—The "Make 'em Laugh" number. The whole conception and performance by Mr. Kelly and Mr. [Donald] O'Connor.

Sleeper [1973, Woody Allen]—Woody Allen & hosts pass by a 22nd-century McDonalds. Greatest sight gag ever.

S.O.B. [1981, Blake Edwards]—Felix's friends steal his body from the mortuary. It has all the Blake Edwards trademarks . . . a preposterous idea that grows out of the characters and plot, good timing, pacing, and writing. It is hilarious in content.

Some Like It Hot [1959, Billy Wilder]—Joe E. Brown, "Nobody's

Directors' Choice

Perfect"—end of film. The best comedy line I can remember—perfectly delivered—enhancing—already wonderful film.

Some Like It Hot—Scene where Jack Lemmon & Tony Curtis first appear in drag—shocking plot twist—beautiful costumes & makeup.

Someone to Watch Over Me [1987, Ridley Scott]—The scene in the restaurant when Mimi Rogers has fallen in love w/ [Tom] Berringer. The lighting, music, the look—all the best. This is certainly one of my favorites. Scott made no mistakes—a '40s picture in every way. Perfect (again) casting took an ordinary script into a great film—and New York never looked better. R. Scott's best.

Sophie's Choice [1982, Alan Pakula]—Sophie must choose which of [her] children will die. The pain she feels is powerfully conveyed. Beautiful lighting!

Sophie's Choice—[Respondent called this *The French Lieutenant's Woman*.] Where Meryl Streep's character is to choose which child shall live. Absolutely compelling—unbearable in its reality—a *blend* of brilliant direction and acting.

Sorcerer [1977, William Friedkin]—Roy Scheider must cross the rope bridge with nitro-laden truck. I still can't believe they shot this. Incredible production and suspense.

Sound of Music, The [1965, Robert Wise]—Closing—as the Von Trapp family cross over the mountains from Nazi-occupied Austria into Switzerland. The Von Trapps have eluded capture by the Germans and are free to start their life anew.

Stagecoach [1939, John Ford]—Anything. Every sequence adds to the development of a rich, mythic—yet sparingly simple—story.

Starman [1984, John Carpenter]—Starman revives dead deer in parking lot. Inspirational—shows character and possibilities through Earth woman's eyes.

Star Wars [1977, George Lucas]—Attack on the Death Star. A film

Part 3: Directors' Greatest Film Scene Choices and Reasons

that taught a generation of kids how to see, this [sequence] began modern special effects.

Star Wars—Dogfight over the Death Star. [No reason given.]

Star Wars—Opening scene—rebels versus the Empire in a spaceship gun battle. First of the modern sci-fi westerns; established a whole new genre and acceptance of sci-fi/fantasy films.

Star Wars—Opening credits [and] throughout! Great special effects!

Star Wars—Earliest scene aboard the Millennium Falcon. Scene climaxes when the power fails on the bridge and Han Solo slams his hand above the control console to restore the ship for blastoff. Scene is remarkable for its texture—the first time we ever saw a spaceship that looked like a tired old DC-3. It is also a condensed statement of the theme—brave, handsome, foolhardy young kids in hot planes, cavalierly setting off to do battle against the most evil forces you can imagine. At stake for the wise-cracking heroes is escape from ennui or bad debt. For the universe, however, there's more in the balance—it could be the end of all that is good. Incidentally, this scene, with all of its stylistic clues, tells us we are in the hands of a master storyteller. He knows the roots of all great stories and [is] a master of their vital conventions. He will not disappoint us. We surrender to him and are lifted away on board the Millennium Falcon.

Star Wars—The bar scene. A first. Creatures that just "were" . . .

Star Wars—Where Luke is guided to trust his force and fly his plane by intuition. Highly charged climactic moment where the protagonist learns his more important lesson in the most crucial moment of the film.

Star Wars—1st time when they enter "light speed."The sensation of movement has never been felt more by an audience sitting in a theater. In one quick scene we are hurtled & transformed thru time & space. Genius pure & simple.

Directors' Choice

State of the Union [1948, Frank Capra]—[Mistakenly called *The Best Man* by the respondent.] Adolph Menjou trying to pour himself a drink while Katherine Hepburn prattles on. Two wonderful actors demonstrating their timing and a director with enough sense to let them do their thing without a million "cuts."

Stavisky [1973, Alain Resnais]—Blood drops onto white ermine fur. Startling visual which takes metaphor and myth and creates a shot which foreshadows the story as well as comment on character.

Sting, The [1973, George Roy Hill]—Close, [Paul] Newman & [Robert] Redford leave. Money turns out to be less than "everything."

Strangers on a Train [1951, Alfred Hitchcock]—The tennis match and the cigarette lighter. Unmatched suspense. Hitchcock at his best.

Strangers on a Train—Shots of murdered girl—seen through her fallen glasses—interesting angle—especially effective in black & white.

Strangers on a Train—Merry-go-round sequence. Uncanny elements of childhood ride becoming terrifying.

Streetcar Named Desire, A [1951, Elia Kazan]—Moon cake scene as spoken by [Marlon] Brando. Drama at its best. Tour de force run full of emotion, transition.

Sullivan's Travels [1941, Preston Sturges]—Joel McCrea visits a black church and has his spirits revived by seeing a Disney cartoon. One of the best uses of "film within a film"—amazing journey from realism to laughter to tears.

Sullivan's Travels—In church watching cartoon. Dramatic resolution of hero's conflict.

Sunrise [1927, F. W. Mumau]—Trolley ride into city. Expressive use of background space to reflect foreground emotions.

Sunset Boulevard [1950, Billy Wilder]—Final staircase scene—"I'm ready for my closeup, Mr. de Mille." The perfect end of an incredibly well-made film.

Part 3: Directors' Greatest Film Scene Choices and Reasons

Sunset Boulevard—"I'm ready for my closeup, Mr. de Mille...."Closing shot of Norma Desmond believing she is back on her set—doing a film.

Sunset Boulevard—Corpse in the pool. Says so much about Hollywood and his lips don't move!!!

Sunset Boulevard—End: Norma speaking: "No one leaves a star, that's what makes them a star!" Drama, ego, insanity at its peak! Great direction—great acting. Hollywood at its best!!

Swing Time [1936, George Stevens]—Final dance sequence—"Never Gonna Dance." It is a perfect synthesis of text, choreography, cinematography. The film is furthered w/o text. The action of the dance is a scene.

Swing Time—Fred Astaire sings & dances his sense of loss on losing [Ginger] Rogers. Economy of technique & acting contrast with "straight-to-the-heart" music.

Tale of Two Cities, A [1935, Jack Conway]—Camera tilts as guillotine blade falls to the heavens. A reasonably good film up until the last moment—when choice of "delivering the fall of the blade"—gave me a reason to always remember the film.

Taste of Honey, A [1968, Tony Richardson]—Rita Tushingham walks out of her apt.—holds a lit sparkler—freeze frame. The simple moment—with the unexpected ending—crystallized a beautiful & touching film.

Taxi Driver [1976, Martin Scorsese]—Travis Bickle's "You talking' to me?!" scene before the mirror. An electric moment giving insight into madness.

Taxi Driver—Travis confronts himself in the mirror. [No reason given.]

Taxi Driver—A bizarre and cranked up [Robert] De Niro talking to himself as he preps how he will use his gun (to mirror). The suspension of disbelief is practically obliterated and the moviegoer is in the room with De Niro. He could be talking to you with the lines, "ARE YOU TALKING TO ME?"

Directors' Choice

Taxi Driver—De Niro is practicing in front of the mirror with guns (in his apartment). We know that Travis Bickle is over the edge.

Taxi Driver—The end sequence. You can taste death. The realism was power.

Tenant, The [1976, Roman Polanski]—Tarkovsky is back in chair—just when you thought he was in control. Polanski's staging, editing & timing sweep the viewer along—a very manipulative scene—coupled w/Phillipe Sardi's haunting score.

Ten Commandments, The [1956, Cecil B. de Mille]—Opening of the Red Sea. DeMille pulls out all the stops to create one of the most dramatic sequences ever. Composition, music, special effects, and high theatrics make this memorable.

Ten Commandments, The—Moses parting the Red Sea. Brought special effects to epic proportions.

Ten Commandments, The—Moses (Charlton Heston) starting to lead the Israelites out of Egypt. The magnitude of the scene and the feeling it engenders of an entire population freeing itself from tyranny makes this the best scene of its kind in all of cinema.

Thelma and Louise [1991, Ridley Scott]—The two women torment the truck driver & blow up his truck. Satisfied a lot of female revenge fantasies.

Things to Come [1936, William Menzies]—When the spacemen arrive. [No reason given.]

Thin Man, The [1934, W. S. Van Dyke]—William Powell shooting the Christmas ornaments off the tree. Powell and [Myrna] Loy at their best in one of those scenes when you give it to the actors.

Thin Man, The—Any *Thin Man* picture. Any scene between Wm. Powell & Myrna Loy. Elegance & sophisticated comedy at its best.

Third Man, The [1949, Carol Reed]—The chase scene in the sewers.

Part 3: Directors' Greatest Film Scene Choices and Reasons

The invincible, corrupt, cynical Harry Lime gets chased through the sewers and is finally shot by his friend who still believes in justice.

Third Man, The—Ferris wheel scene; [Orson] Welles & [Joseph] Cotten. Spectacular location, chilling rationale of evil.

Third Man, The—The balloon man scene. Reed's lighting and use of "Chinese angles" make this sequence particularly memorable for me.

Third Man, The—Chase through Vienna streets. The use of music and shadows . . . very eerie.

39 Steps, The [1935, Alfred Hitchcock]—Mr. Memory unmasked. Encapsulation of greatest spy movie ever made.

39 Steps, The—The scene where the housekeeper discovers the corpse, lets out a scream which becomes the whistle of the train out of the tunnel. Again, brilliant editing not only visual—but of sound—the shock of the woman's open mouth, out of which we hear the piercing scream of the whistle.

39 Steps, The—When Robert Donat & the girl handcuffed together escape in the rain from the motor car, get hotel room & spend the night. Suspense, action, comedy, & pure charm. Wonderful acting.

This Happy Breed [1944, David Lean]—The scene where a number of generations wait to attend a funeral. Noel Coward dialogue that sparkles.

Thomas Crown Affair, The [1968, Norman Jewison]—Library scene. 360 degree camera movement with Steve McQueen and Faye Dunaway, along with music is breathtaking.

Throne of Blood [1957, Akira Kurosawa]—Climactic shower of arrows. Dynamic tension and imagery.

Throne of Blood—Opening scene w/ driving rain, [Toshiro] Mifune on horseback. Great mood setter for entire film. Reveals interior

Directors' Choice

of the main character while foreshadowing the character's inevitable downfall.

To Kill a Mockingbird [1962, Robert Mulligan]—After he loses the case and is walking out of the courtroom, the Reverend says, "Stand up, Scout. Your father's passing." It makes my eyes tear to even describe this powerful scene. It is almost a "shot" in its scale, but it is built toward and paid off as a full scene. What a quiet, powerful statement of the man's integrity, nobility, & honor! What a recognition of who he is and what he has done. What a contrast to the surface story of having lost his case. Perhaps most moving to me is the wise return at this moment to our child/narrator's viewpoint, and her awareness of how it was the Reverend who pointed out this truth. At the edge of it all hovers the frightening fact that she might have missed the chance to honor her father—except for the promptings of that wise man.

To Kill a Mockingbird—Last sequence—from walk through the woods till end. From a child's point of view the innocence and horror of an historical era are movingly captured.

Tombstone [1993, George Cosmatos]—Saloon, Curly Bill has just demonstrated his art of twirling his pistols. Doc Holliday mimics him by twirling a coffee cup as he would a pistol. This is the pure putdown to Curly Bill.

Tombstone—The gun-and-cup twirling competition between Ringo and Doc Holliday in the bar. . . . Val Kilmer's playful, but possibly lethal mimicry of Michael Biehn's considerably expert gunplay, using only a cup, is exciting and funny and dangerous.

Tom Jones [1963, Tony Richardson]—The eating scene. Sex was never mentioned, but was always there. It rivals whoever first used the roaring fireplace to make the same statement.

Tom Jones—Albert Finney eating dinner with friend. Sexual tension, fun.

Part 3: Directors' Greatest Film Scene Choices and Reasons

Tom Jones—Eating scene. Everything is said & done. Literally very sexual, yet they're just eating fully clothed.

Tootsie [1982, Sydney Pollack]—The reveal scene when Hoffman (as Michael Dorsey) is doing the live soap [and he] tears the wig off and lets the whole world know who he is! Again, the structure of this *brilliant* script—that takes us to this moment. Certainly one of the *best* movies *ever*. Perfect in every way.

Top Hat [1935, Mark Sandrich]—Any Fred Astaire–Ginger Rogers dance routine from their many B & W movies of the '30s. All are splendid examples of the special quality of music-based scenes to merit repeated viewings. Movies, books, plays are seen but a few times but music bears *repeated* experiencing. Add the dancing of Astaire and Rogers and the scene can be watched forever. The kind of movie you'd take to a desert island.

Touch of Evil [1958, Orson Welles]—Opening credits thru explosion One of the best designed single shots in [the] history of film. One complete shot runs about 7–8 minutes.

Touch of Evil—The long crane shot revealing the first scene sequence. It revealed the location and characters all in one move. Approx. 9 minutes.

Touch of Evil—The film's single take opening—a battle for the viewer between Welles' cinematic mastery & storytelling.... If you need to have an explanation for this scene, the whole survey you are undertaking is in jeopardy.... This one can get by on one word: ART.

Touch of Evil—Grandy has Vargas' wife taken to a hotel and drugged. Quinlan kills Grandy. The cinematography, quick cuts and eerie lighting from a swinging light bulb perfectly complement this chilling assault—Quinlan's first truly evil deed.

Touch of Evil—[Respondent called it *Repulsion*.] Opening scene—long continuous shot from trunk of car to explosion at U.S.-Mexico

Directors' Choice

border. Completely captures atmosphere of border town and of the rest of the movie. Incredible technical and artistic achievement.

Traffic [1970, Jacques Tati]—Long track, imitating [Jean-Luc] Godard's *Breathless*, among [??] the huge traffic jam/accident. Great physical comedian & director using the camera to create a comic hell.

Tramp, The [1915, Charlie Chaplin]—Charlie Chaplin's final exit (that became his signature)—the jaunty walk and iris down! (Toss-up with the *preparation and eating of the shoe* from *The Gold Rush*.) The tramp was beaten and rejected, but then there comes a look of hope and skip in his step—you know he'll overcome and survive!

Treasure of the Sierra Madre, The [1948, John Huston]—Walter Huston's dance of glee as [Humphrey] Bogart & [Tim] Holt watch. This scene capsulizes the gold prospector's search and defines the characters and their greed!

Treasure of the Sierra Madre, The—Walter Huston jumping for joy when gold is discovered. The audience, waiting and hoping for a strike, now jumps with him. Total involvement.

Treasure of the Sierra Madre, The—Old miner Walter Huston tells Dobsey [Humphrey Bogart] that the treasure of gold has been "blown back" to the mountains where they mined it. A scene similar to that in *The Killing* but here *dialogue* is used to convey the disaster that has befallen the miners. Blowing gold dust not as effective as blowing bills—and Huston's laughter is redemptive.

Treasure of the Sierra Madre, The—The gold bags are ripped open & the dust goes flying to the wind. It was a satisfying ending similar to the scene in *The Killing* where the paper money goes flying.

Treasure of the Sierra Madre, The—Walter Huston's crazy dance over the empty gold bags. A mad Bolero marking the end of a trail of

Part 3: Directors' Greatest Film Scene Choices and Reasons

greed, betrayal, killing, which could have been inspired only by the Devil. A defining moment.

Treasure of the Sierra Madre, The—The 3-way dialogue between the trio—Bogart, Huston, Holt—where Huston literally tells the entire movie we're to see! John Huston economically settled the audience in for a walloping good ride, through the genius of his father, Walter, recounting "gold tales," and the reactions of the other two.

Treasure of the Sierra Madre, The—Bogart's confrontation with the bandits and death. The whole film builds to this climax. Great suspense, terror. Bogart's final character collapse is beautiful.

Treasure of the Sierra Madre, The—The "up there!" sequence. The utter and savage power of Mr. [Walter] Huston's performance, caught completely.

Treasure of the Sierra Madre, The—Opening scene with Bogart [and] Huston. Anti-hero characters.

Treasure of the Sierra Madre, The—Campfire with Bogart and Holt where "Dobbs" decides to kill his friend and steal all the gold. ... We see into the heart of darkness in Bogart, whose greed and paranoia drive him to attempt murder ... all for the gold he will lose anyway.

Treasure of the Sierra Madre, The—All scenes. [No reason given.]

Trial, The [1962, Orson Welles]—Wide shot of bureau scene. I felt the insanity of bureaucracy.

Triumph of the Will [1936, Leni Riefenstahl]—Plane flying, landing, crowds. Camera work. Editing.

Triumph of the Will—The sequence of youth hailing from various provinces saluting their domiciles. "And you, comrade?" "From the Zaar!" Beautifully shot & edited to make it appear all have joined the Nazi party.

Directors' Choice

Truly, Madly, Deeply [1990, Anthony Minghella]—The moment when the ghost returns to his bereaved wife, playing the piano in their apartment. In which the (irrelevant) distortions of truth and memory are dramatized with indelible and eloquent simplicity.

2001: A Space Odyssey [1968, Stanley Kubrick]—The primitive natives' bone-weapon becoming the space ship docking. Just unforgettable!

2001: A Space Odyssey—Cut from bone to satellite. [No reason given.]

2001: A Space Odyssey—The origin of man *and the transition* to the spaceship. Millions of years in one dissolve. And the *definition of a tool*. Brilliant.

2001: A Space Odyssey—Opening scene of film. In a sort series of scenes Kubrick establishes the world of primitive man and goes from the discovery of a tool to the space shuttle in one cut.

2001: A Space Odyssey—The dawn of man (apes discover bones as weapons). Cinematically brilliant. Super symbolism. Pointed observation about man's birth thru violence.

2001: A Space Odyssey—The "man-apes" tableau. Moment when we see bone (tool) thrust high above dx [sic] to monolith. Notwithstanding the aural and visual splendor of this predawn of man set piece, the scene transcends itself and hurtles the viewer from a unknown reality to another unknown reality—and provides the bridge for both.

2001: A Space Odyssey—Dissolve from ape-man bone to orbiting bomb. 2 million years in one perfect edit—entire sci fi genre boiled down to 2 seconds.

2001: A Space Odyssey—Flying bone turns into floating spaceship. The greatest transition in the history of film. Kubrick is the only director who could make a single cut span millions of years—and have it make sense.

Part 3: Directors' Greatest Film Scene Choices and Reasons

2001: A Space Odyssey—Hominid "discovering" bone as tool. Sense of moment; development; music; "bravura" effect achieved & sustained.

2001: A Space Odyssey—Discovery of the tool (an animal bone). Combination of the music (Richard Strauss, "Thus Spake Zarathustra"); low angle on ape man; slow motion on cross-cutting with animals falling to the ground.

2001: A Space Odyssey—Travel to Jupiter scene (lights, colors, etc.). Groundbreaking use of lights, colors, special effects.

2001: A Space Odyssey—Hal's murder of hibernating crew. No words; classic example of montage rhythm; clean, efficient technological violence.

2001: A Space Odyssey—"Blue Danube" planet dance. The start of modern sci-fi movies—great wit.

2001: A Space Odyssey—Open—come up over the planets. Great special effects—before computer enhancement was being used regularly.

2001: A Space Odyssey—The astronaut vs. the computer as he tries to talk Hal 9000 into allowing reentry into the spacecraft. . . . First moment where we understand the cold, logical evil of technology [that] will one day simply decide to terminate humanity.

2001: A Space Odyssey—Trip from Earth to the Moon. Stunning evocation of future space travel: its ordinariness, its quirkiness, its impersonality, and (with the music, "The Blue Danube") its extraordinary beauty.

2001: A Space Odyssey—"The Stargate" (man meets the monolith). An extraordinary montage—a visual trip—that puts a philosophical exclamation point on a thought-provoking film.

2001: A Space Odyssey—Space/time warp. Pure wonderment & mind expansion.

Directors' Choice

2001: A Space Odyssey—Astronaut Dave Bowman lobotomizes Hal by methodically disconnecting the memory modules. The scene is a turning point in the film. Up to that point the technology is shown to be superior to human intellect, but absolute power corrupts absolutely and humanity proves stronger.

Two Women [1960, Vittorio De Sica]—Sophia Loren in the roadside rape of her daughter sequence. Most moving dramatic performance and camera work.

Umberto D [1952, Vittorio De Sica]—Old man puts hand out to beg, cannot do it, pretends to be feeling for rain. Heart wrenching! and unbelievable. Also, a *surprise*.

Umberto D—Umberto tries to trick his little dog Flag by abandoning him in the park. A wrenching metaphor for how society treats the aged and impoverished in a world that professes to value love and attachment.

Un Chien Andelou [1928, Luis Buñuel]—Cutting the eye with a razor. The scene is incredibly beautiful despite the implied violence. (A pig's eye was actually used.)

Unforgiven [1992, Clint Eastwood]—The shootout in the saloon. Intense action in a compressed space.

Unforgiven—The gunfight in the tavern. As inevitable as the denouement in any Greek drama, this sequence delivers the texture of life in the old West with such kinesthesia that one can almost smell the foul air in that room; an intense presentation of what it means to do the walk if you're going to do the talk.

Unforgiven—Ride thru the rain. You felt as cold and as miserable as the actors were supposed to feel—I should say the characters, not actors.

Unforgiven—Shooting in the outhouse. What a comment on violence in the old West.

Untouchables, The [1987, Brian De Palma]—Baby carriage sequence

Part 3: Directors' Greatest Film Scene Choices and Reasons

in Grand Central—Brian De Palma at his best—very Hitchcockian.

Untouchables, The—Shootout in train station. A tribute to Eisenstein's *Battleship Potemkin*. Will they ever rescue the baby carriage?

Vertigo [1958, Alfred Hitchcock]—Hotel room—transformation of Kim Novak into Madelaine. A great synthesis of form, content, narrative, and emotion.

Vertigo—Jimmy Stewart sees Kim Novak fall from the tower. In this scene the plot & emotions all come together as you realize the reason & conclusion for his fears—& at the same time the horror of her death.

Victor/Victoria [1982, Blake Edwards]—"Le Jazz Hot" number. A beautifully staged musical number that moves the story forward with reaction shots ending in the shock of revealing a man being a woman.

Viva Zapata! [1952, Elia Kazan]—Zapata's body (Brando) is placed in the plaza by townspeople: "He is not dead—he is in the hills." Illustrates a great one cannot be killed, for there will always be superstitions and believers.

Wages of Fear [1953, Henri-Georges Clouzot]—Explosion of 1st truck. Underplaying event, using close observation of reality (i.e., flash of light, shock wave blowing tobacco).

Wages of Fear—Trucks moving through mountains carrying explosives to an oil fire. Hazardous, edge-of-your-seat terror. Builds constantly until one driver stops to urinate. The audience does the same figuratively, not literally.

Way Down East [1920, D. W. Griffith]—Ice floe scene. [No reason given.]

Way Down East—The snowcapped scene w/ Richard Barthelmess. [No reason given.]

Way Down East—Lillian Gish on the ice floe. The suspense.

Directors' Choice

West Side Story [1961, Robert Wise and Jerome Robbins]—Big dance fight scene. [No reason given.]

West Side Story—"Tonight/Rumble" quintet. Great synthesis of drama & music on stage. Robert Wise (director of film) used multiple locations & visual moods to make it cinematically magical.

What Ever Happened to Baby Jane? [1962, Robert Aldrich]—Last scene on the beach. Acting, camera work.

What's Up, Doc? [1972, Peter Bogdanovich]—Hotel room catching on fire. Really hilarious just-keeps-getting-worse scene where *everyone* gets involved, like it or not. (The whole film is a true classic of comedy.) Shot well. Good coverage, tight editing, good performances, SFX [special effects], etc.

When Harry Met Sally [1989, Rob Reiner]—Meg Ryan fakes orgasm.

When Harry Met Sally—Diner scene where Sally acts out the big O. The elderly lady customer who said "I want what she had" immediately afterward.

When Harry Met Sally—Sally's simulated orgasm in a crowded restaurant. One of the first contemporary relationship films to deal frankly with sex; a whole new level of acceptance of modern morals.

When Harry Met Sally—Orgasm scene. Meg Ryan at her best!

White Heat [1949, Raoul Walsh]—Jimmy Cagney, just before the oil tank explodes, "Top of the world, Ma!" Cagney's most famous scene—an all-time camp classic. Representative of the fantasy early Hollywood was capable of creating.

Who Framed Roger Rabbit? [1988, Robert Zemeckis]—Opening scene. Wonderful funny animation.

Wild Bunch, The [1969, Sam Peckinpah]—Climactic scene where the bunch decide to "get Angel" back, walking to their death. The greatest heroic, cathartic scene in movie history.

Part 3: Directors' Greatest Film Scene Choices and Reasons

Wild Bunch, The—The critical face-off, where the bunch shoot and kill the Mexican warlord. . . . Given the overwhelming odds the Americans face, a la the Spartans at the bridge, it is a thrilling moment—they're dead men but still alive!

Wild Bunch, The—The last shootout for Pike and the bunch. Forget all you know or thought you knew, this violence is poetic.

Wild Strawberries [1957, Ingmar Bergman]—Last scene. Hero is rejected by his true love, returns to idealized views of mother & father. The scene powerfully captures the elusive nuance of character the film has struggled to delineate.

Wings [1927, William Wellman]—Buddy Rogers shoots down Dick Arlen. The mistake he never forgot.

Witness [1985, Peter Weir]—Raising barn. A spirit & a time come alive.

Witness—Rachel heals John Book's gunshot wound. Everything is told with very little dialogue. Eloquent images—she holds his hand, the moment when Book, coming out of delirium, looks at her.

Witness—The scene between Harrison Ford and Kelly McGillis in the barn. Its romantic quality.

Wizard of Oz, The [1939, Victor Fleming]—Transition from B&W Kansas to color of Oz. While done as much for economic reasons . . . very effective.

Wizard of Oz, The—Remove the screen to reveal the wizard is not really an all-powerful wizard. Teaches us to look beyond appearances.

Wizard of Oz, The—Yellow brick road. What a way to start an adventure.

Wizard of Oz, The—Dorothy & Co. meet the wizard. Scaring the shit out of kids for over 50 years!

Wolfen [1981, Michael Wadleigh]—The speeded up, low travel shot across deserted empty lots in N.Y.C. It terrified me. I had never seen anything like it. The point of view of a predator, but who or what kind baffled me . . . so fast, so low, so out of control.

Woman of the Dunes [1964, Hiroshi Teshigahara]—The man tries to escape from the sand pit and the sand keeps giving way. It was the single shot that expressed the central idea of the film.

Women on the Verge of a Nervous Breakdown [1988, Pedro Almodovar]— Valium mixed into gazpacho. Humorous yet deadpan campy melodrama.

Wuthering Heights [1939, William Wyler]—Cathy's death scene. All of film's creators combined to produce a perfect blend of regret and rage, anguish and anger.

Yankee Doodle Dandy [1942, Michael Curtiz]—Jimmy Cagney performing title song. Transcendent moment.

Yentl [1983, Barbra Streisand]—Wedding night. Inventive, funny.

Young Frankenstein [1974, Mel Brooks]—"Puttin' on the Ritz." I will never hear this song again without seeing this scene in my mind.

Z [1968, Constantin Costa-Gavras]—The end sequence. After so much arrogance and deceit the bad guys lose . . . for the moment.

Zelig [1983, Woody Allen]—Any [scene in which] Zelig appears— baseball. Woody Allen's comic genius at its technical and creative best.

Zero de Conduite [1933, Juan Vigo]—The children pillow-fighting. Humor and visual beauty.

Miscellaneous:

Bonnie & Clyde/Godfather, The—The killing of B & C/The killing of Sonny Corleone. These were the "kill" scenes which, because of editing and shooting, were most effective.

Part 3: Directors' Greatest Film Scene Choices and Reasons

Boom Town/San Francisco/Test Pilot—Virtually any of their [Clark Gable and Spencer Tracy's] scenes together, in all the films they appeared in. The directors wisely let the "chemistry" of the two actors impel any scenes they were in—à la Tracy and Hepburn, etc.—and without any "directorial touches."

Bullitt/French Connection—The car chase. These exciting moments were the first of their kind.

Cinerama motion pictures [various directors]—One of the first Cineramas was of the Grand Canyon, and the most memorable scene in it was flying over the edge of the canyon. This was the first experience of most audiences with the superwide motion picture screen and the physical effect it could produce on the viewer. Many outstanding superwide screen films have been made, particularly with the development of Omnimax, but that early Cinerama experience showed the way.

Any of the many Busby Berkeley visual fantasies. Never done better.

[Charlie] Chaplin skating in closed dept. store to impress girlfriend, not realizing safety rail is removed. Combination of comedy & fear & audience having different info. than characters.

PART 4
Art Defined and Its Origins

What Is Art?

Can we take what we have learned about great scenes in film and apply it to art and aesthetics in general? We think so. What is art? What makes great art? Current fashion is to either give up defining art altogether or to define it so broadly that almost anything is allowed as art (see Menand, 1998). Just how difficult and polemical the debate over "what is art" has become is well illustrated by Jasmina Reza's one-act play *Art*, where the purchase of an expensive white-on-white abstract painting by one of the characters nearly destroys the friendship of three men. At least one thing does seem clear in attempting to define art: Any definition of art must be equally appropriate for an Australian aboriginal rock painting as it is for a Japanese kabuki drama, a Jackson Pollack painting, or an Orson Welles film.

Our film data suggest that at its most fundamental, art must accomplish two things—it must exhibit craft on the part of the artist and elicit emotion in the viewer. At its most basic, *art is craft plus emotion*. The level of craft exhibited in works of art from around the world varies widely from the casual dabbing of pigment onto a canvas or construction of a few poorly formed sentences to the masterful application of paint on canvas based on training and rare ability or the skill and talent required to write a great novel. Emotions, sensations, and feelings evoked in the viewer by art works also vary—both in type of emotion evoked (beauty, romance, pathos, fear, awe, etc.) and in their amplitude, from the slightest perceptible twinge in a viewer to being completely overwhelmed emotionally. The greater the level of craft involved in an artwork's production, the higher we would place it on a scale of artistic achievement, as with Robert Altman's complex and highly crafted opening shot in *The Player*, or the design and brushwork in a Vermeer painting. Likewise, the greater the aesthetic emotion evoked in the viewer, the greater the artistic achievement, as with the emotions evoked in the last scene from *Casablanca* or Michelangelo's paintings on the ceiling of the Sistine Chapel. Craft represents the application of human agency, human activity, human skill, to elements available to the artist. Nature unshaped by human agency also evokes powerful emotions in human beings, as with seascapes and sunsets, but it is not "art."

The distinction between *present* and *represent* (re-present) may be helpful here. Nature presents, to be perceived and appreciated by human beings, sometimes with great aesthetic emotion, sensation, and feeling. But nature's presentation is what it is, nothing more. It does not stand for anything else. It does not represent anything but itself: A sunset is a sunset. Art, on the other hand, is not what it is. It is more. A work of art *re-presents*; it stands for something else as it is perceived and appreciated. All things—both nature and art—are screened by the human mind during perception, but art is one step removed from nature, itself having been first screened and *re-presented* by the artist prior to being perceived by the viewer. If a putative work of art has not been *re-presented*, it is not art, but a constituent of nature. Moreover, there are degrees of *re-presentation*, some being minimal, as with a simple collage of driftwood embodying minimal craft and human agency. Film, in contrast, based as it is on shadows on celluloid, is the height of *re-presentation* (McCracken, 1998).

Thus, we have two major dimensions in art, one being craft/

human agency exhibited by the artist, the other aesthetic emotions, sensations, and feelings evoked in the viewer. All existing objects, manmade and otherwise, can be placed in the two-dimensional space these concepts form, as illustrated in Figure 1. On the vertical axis items can vary from untouched natural objects such as an undistinguished stone or a stunning waterfall to objects produced by human agency that involve high levels of craft such as ball bearings or a great film. The horizontal axis illustrates an object's potential to evoke aesthetic emotion, sensation, and feeling. Some objects have a great aesthetic potential—for example, sunsets and great films—others have little or no such potential, as with ball bearings and stones. Objects in the upper right quadrant are manmade and tend to have utilitarian uses and go largely unappreciated aesthetically. Aesthetically unappreciated natural objects such as sticks and stones are found in the lower right quadrant. Natural objects with high potential for aesthetic appreciation such as sunsets and seascapes are found in the lower left quadrant. Art, manmade objects with potential for aesthetic appreciation, are found only in the upper left quadrant. The films *Citizen Kane* and *Casablanca* would be placed far up in the upper left-hand corner of the upper left quadrant, as would paintings by Jan Vermeer and sculptures by Michelangelo. A white-on-white painting or simple collage of driftwood, with minimal exhibition of craft and modest aesthetic potential, would be placed in the lower right corner of the upper left quadrant.

Art has at least two other characteristics that should be mentioned: They comprise third and fourth dimensions. All art exists in a social context. Its creation and viewing always take place in a social context, with shared meaning between the artist and the audience. Both the creation and the appreciation of art presuppose a degree of involvement by artist and viewer in the society's economy, religion, customs, and belief systems. The artist and viewer's involvement need not be profound, but some sharing of social context must ordinarily occur.

Art must also have personal relevance for the creator and, especially, for the viewer. If a work of art lacks personal meaning for the viewer, there is no way for the viewer to adequately engage the

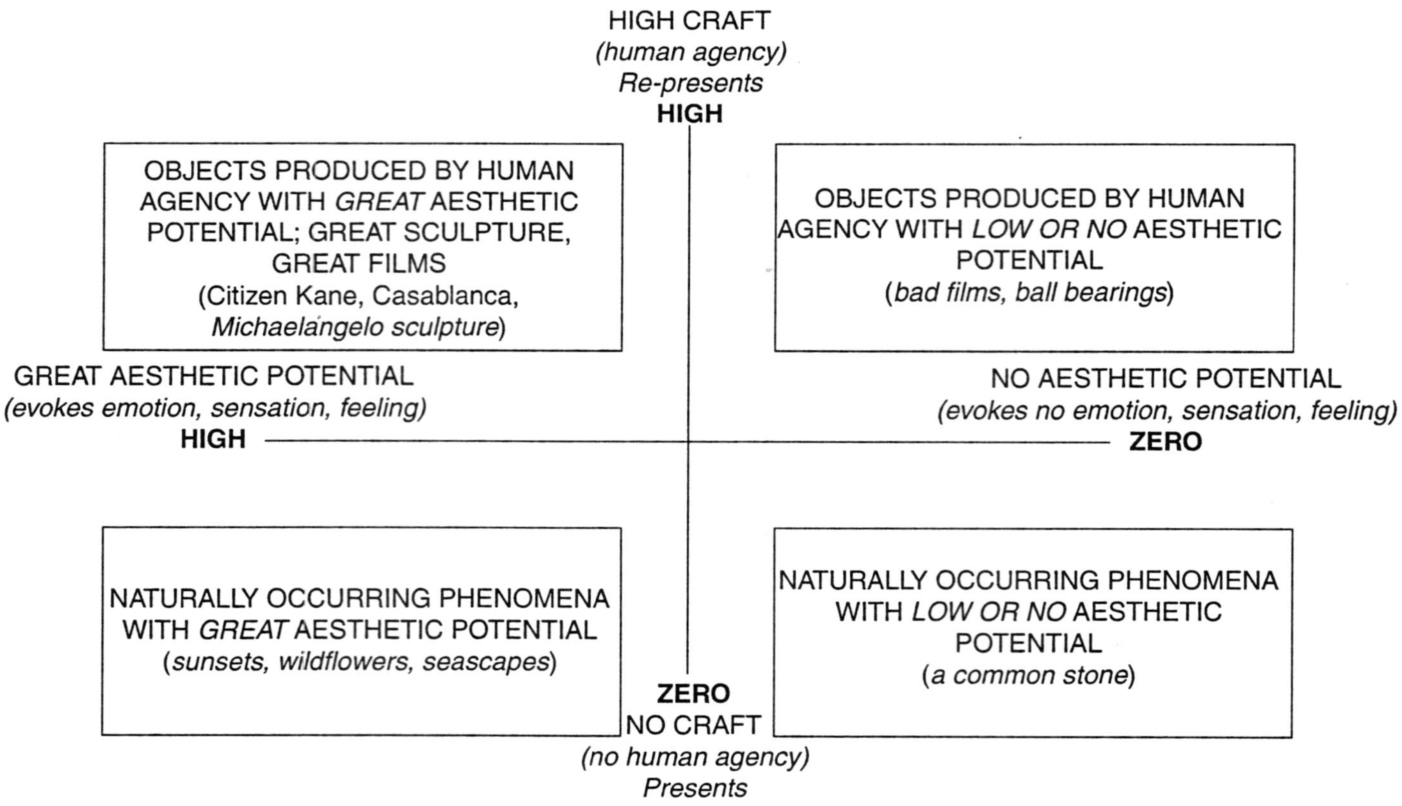

	HIGH CRAFT *(human agency)* Re-presents **HIGH**	
OBJECTS PRODUCED BY HUMAN AGENCY WITH *GREAT AESTHETIC POTENTIAL*; GREAT SCULPTURE, GREAT FILMS *(Citizen Kane, Casablanca, Michaelàngelo sculpture)*		OBJECTS PRODUCED BY HUMAN AGENCY WITH *LOW OR NO AESTHETIC POTENTIAL* *(bad films, ball bearings)*

GREAT AESTHETIC POTENTIAL —— **HIGH** ———————— **ZERO** —— NO AESTHETIC POTENTIAL
(evokes emotion, sensation, feeling)   **ZERO**   **NO CRAFT**   *(evokes no emotion, sensation, feeling)*

	(no human agency) Presents	
NATURALLY OCCURRING PHENOMENA WITH *GREAT AESTHETIC POTENTIAL* *(sunsets, wildflowers, seascapes)*		NATURALLY OCCURRING PHENOMENA WITH *LOW OR NO AESTHETIC POTENTIAL* *(a common stone)*

Figure 1. TWO DIMENSIONS OF ART

artwork aesthetically. The importance of personal relevance is well illustrated by the following example from anthropology. An elderly Native American man once said to the anthropologist Mary Austen, who was interviewing him on his music, "You see Piuty man singin' sometime, and cryin' when he sing. It ain't what he singin' make him cry. It what he thinkin' about when he sing make him cry" (Greenway, 1964: 23). The personal relevance dimension can range from zero, or even negative, to high.

A fifth consideration, perhaps another dimension that characterizes art, states that art can never be adequately appreciated passively. Art appreciation involves the participation of the viewer. The viewer must at some point become mentally involved and emotionally receptive, exhibiting what might be called *aesthetic intention*. In effect, the viewer must open his or her heart at least a little to experience what the work of art offers. The film patron goes to a movie theater explicitly to enjoy a film, to engage the work aesthetically. Visitors to art galleries are ordinarily there to enjoy the displayed art works. If an art viewer is intent upon not enjoying a work of art, he or she will likely succeed. Physical participation in art appreciation may also be required, as in many religious ceremonies and interactive theater.

In summary, our research encourages us to define art as craft plus emotion. The difference between great films and great sunsets is the presence of craft and human agency, and the difference between ball bearings and great films is aesthetic emotion. If a work does not elicit aesthetic emotion in viewers, it is not art. Likewise, if craft is not present, it is not art. Social embeddedness, personal relevance, and aesthetic intention on the part of the viewer are critical in defining the aesthetic experience.

Where Does Artistic Merit Exist?

Where does the merit in great films such as *Apocalypse Now* or *Singin' in the Rain* exist? Where does the merit in a Rembrandt painting or a Bernini sculpture reside? For that matter, where does the lack of merit in an obviously inferior work of art reside?

Directors' Choice

Many artists believe that the artistic merit in the work they have created, whatever its medium—film, drama, painting, sculpture, music, poetry—resides in the work of art itself. Quality, or the lack of it, is, for many artists, inherent in the crafted object, existing independent of viewers, time, and space. The merit in a great film such as *Citizen Kane* in this view is said to exist irrespective of whether it is showing on a screen in Westwood, California, thirty years ago or today, or sitting in a can on the surface of some deserted planet 1,000 light years from here, never again to be screened. For many artists, merit is a Platonic-like quality that resides in the object, and it is up to the viewer to "see" or find the merit. If the audience doesn't "get it," it is the audience's fault, because the merit was there.

Psychologists, in contrast, often tend to see the viewer or consumer of art as the locus of artistic merit. If the consumer is sufficiently predisposed psychologically, emotionally, culturally, then the art will touch them. The value of a work of art is inside the viewer. That is why, some psychologists would say, some consumers will see a specific work of art as wonderful and worthwhile while others will see it as having no merit. For many psychologists, art is a kind of Rorschach test, like inkblots onto which the viewer projects whatever is in his or her mind. The artwork only furnishes the opportunity to project what is already inside the viewer.

A psychological anthropologist, in contrast, is more likely to take a middle-ground position between the psychologist and the artist—what might be called an ecological approach—and say the artistic merit of a work of art resides in the total context in which it is viewed, an interaction between the art object, the setting in which it is viewed, and the viewer. The impact of a series of "great" edits in a film scene such as the shower scene in *Psycho* is dependent upon fears that the viewer brings to the film—fear of knives, fear of being cut, feelings of vulnerability while standing naked and defenseless in the steamy confines of a shower. Take away the fears that most viewers bring to the scene's showing, and those quick edits and screeching noises on the sound track lose their emotional impact. Yet it takes Hitchcock's mastery of camera and editing to elicit and give expression to fears that are only latent in the viewer. Without the viewer's fears, the shower scene loses its emotional impact. Without Hitchcock's skills in crafting the shower scene, the viewer's fears are never expressed. The power and greatness of the shower scene in *Psycho* lies in both what the viewer brings to the theater and what is showing on the screen. The gasping and screaming of others in the audience adds to the viewer's emotional pandemonium. A fellow we know fainted the first time he saw the scene. The merit of the scene lies in the total context, in the interaction between an artwork, the setting in which the scene is viewed, and the viewer. Artistic merit resides in the ecology of art.

There is a saying that great novels require great readers of novels. Great films likewise require great viewers. Ultimately, a film is only as good as its audience, and an audience is only as good as the film. Art needs viewers; viewers need art!

Film: A Pinnacle of Art

Writing in the mid-nineteenth century, the German composer Richard Wagner, whose operas were often based on German legends, gave expression to an idea that had been common in German cultural criticism circles for a century. For Wagner, the theater, which to him meant opera, was the principal form of public art—the supreme art, the crown of civilization (Wagner, 1992: 16).

We agree with Wagner and suggest that technological advances led to opera being superseded as the supreme art. Opera involves a synthesis of all historically preceding art forms—theater, acting, drama, poetry, storytelling, music, architecture, sculpture, painting, and costume design. Like opera, movie-making involves an amalgamation with all these earlier art forms, but with the addition of three nineteenth-century inventions: photography, the motion picture camera, and film editing. In a way, all previous art forms anticipated film; in film, a great artistic convergence occurred in this century, reaching a pinnacle, perhaps in the late 1930s, from which it has not retreated.

Film, either on the theater screen or less suitably the television tube, is arguably the most emotionally potent of all the arts and has largely replaced those other two great forms of narrative art and the elicitors of emotion in the agora of minds: the stage play (including opera) and the novel. (The emotions film-viewing evokes may have to a significant degree also replaced, at least in many persons, the emotional outlets once associated with religion.) As Gore Vidal, who has plied the trades of both novelist and screenwriter, has said, "There is no such thing as a famous novelist now, any more than there is such thing as a famous poet.... Today, where literature was, movies are.... Art is now sight and sound; and the books are shut" (Vidal, 1992: 3–5). Movies are, Vidal says, "all emotion" (1998). Today, movies, more than any art form in history, hold a greater percentage of viewers transfixed, gripped in an embrace as waves of emotions and feelings roll through the mind and define consciousness. As the pinnacle art form, film is perfectly suited to human beings, nature's most emotional and feeling-steeped creatures.

The Human Mind and the Origins of Art

Consilience and Art

In revealing the vital role that emotions play in film appreciation, our study of great film scenes provides the basis for some educated speculation on the evolutionary origins of art in society. To understand the origins of art and the aesthetic experience, we must turn to biology and evolutionary theory. Human beings are biological organisms having much in common with the many other creatures of the Earth. But we also possess a number of relatively unique characteristics that animals with whom we share the Earth do not possess—at least in well-developed form—that are vital to understanding the origins of art and our experience of it.

Thanks in large measure to the efforts of Edward O. Wilson, the well-known Harvard biologist, a major effort is now under way in the sciences and just beginning in the arts to unite all human knowledge into a single corpus of understanding. Wilson is a leader in this effort, which he calls "consilience," a nineteenth-century term meaning the joining or jumping-together of knowledge by "linking of facts and fact-based theory across disciplines to create a common

Part 4: Art Defined and Its Origins

groundwork of explanation" (Wilson, 1998: 8). Consilience involves connecting the natural or "hard" sciences (physics, chemistry, biology) with each other and with the so-called soft sciences, (anthropology, sociology, psychology, economics, even political science) in a single body of knowledge that shares facts and many basic principles or laws. Such a linking is becoming a reality for the natural sciences and is just getting started for the social sciences. A dream for many is to be able to include the arts, among humankind's most exalted activities, in such a web of knowledge. A linking-together of knowledge regarding art and science would provide much-needed insight into human nature and the societies we humans create. Consilience also offers the hope of telling us more about the nature of art, its origins, and the important role it has long played in human affairs. Such understanding may be helpful in pointing to the future of both science and art and to the presently unimaginable ways we may come to understand and appreciate the universe.

Dualistic Thinking

When it comes to understanding human nature and human beings' place in the world, thinking in Western society, at least dating back to many Greek philosophers including Aristotle, has been characterized by dualistic thought. Until the time of Charles Darwin and the publication of his famous book, *The Origin of Species*, in 1859, it was generally assumed that human beings, having been created by God, were separate from nature, fundamentally different from the other life forms found on Earth. For more than 2,000 years, this view of human beings' separation from nature helped prevent people from better understanding their true place in the world. Since Darwin's time the belief in humankind's separation from the natural order has gradually given way to a view that we are a part of nature and arrived on this Earth in the same way as did all the other organisms, through biological evolution.

The second form of dualistic thinking that held back understanding, and which has only begun to give way in recent decades, is called the mind-body dichotomy. This view, traceable in explicit form to the French philosopher René Descartes (1596–1650), holds that a human being is a union of two separate and distinct substances, a body and a soul. The soul is usually equated with the mind and consciousness, producing such mental phenomena as thinking and emotions, and is regarded as separate from the material body. Body-mind dualism is no longer taken seriously by most scientists, who assume that the mind and body are one and the same entity. As Edward O. Wilson has said, "Virtually all contemporary scientists and philosophers expert on the subject agree that the mind, which comprises consciousness and rational process, is the brain at work" (1998: 98).

If we are to understand art in the broadest sense, in the sense of consilience—the unification of the physical and social sciences with art—we must look to science, specifically to biology and the evolutionary origins of the human body, brain, and mind. We must also understand the evolution of human society and the role that art has played in society's development. We must understand how art is appreciated in terms of brain function. Only then will we understand why we so love it. In what follows, a speculative effort will be made to briefly and roughly sketch the origins of art from a consilience perspective.

Bonobos Watch Movies

So far as we know, human beings are the only species to both make and appreciate art. But one other species does seem to possess at least a rudimentary ability to appreciate movies. Our closest relatives in the animal kingdom are the great apes, and among the apes, the chimpanzee is believed to be our closest relative. Of the three varieties of chimps, the Bonobo is thought to be the smartest and most humanlike. Sue Savage-Rumbaugh, an anthropologist at Georgia State University, studies Bonobos at a 55-acre laboratory near Atlanta, Georgia. At their home on the reserve, the Bonobos watch a lot of television. What kinds of programs do they like? They like home videos featuring human beings they know from around the lab. They also like suspenseful stories with interesting endings. And what are their favorite movies? They like films about human beings trying to relate to apelike creatures. They like *Tarzan*, *Iceman*, *Quest for Fire*, and Clint Eastwood's movies with the orangutan (Dreifus, 1998). Clearly, some of the precursors of human film-viewing aesthetics are present in the Bonobos. The apelike creatures we evolved from may have been somewhat similar to the Bonobos.

In the Beginning

The universe is presently thought to be about 14 billion years old. We don't know what happened before that, but the topic is a subject of scientific research and debate. More than four and one-half billion years ago, our solar system (the sun and its planets) began to condense out of a large dust and gas cloud. The cloud had formed out of ancient stars that had long ago exploded and scattered their ashes in space. The compacting force from a nearby supernova may have provided the impetus for the cloud's condensation. Life—that is to say, molecules based on nucleic acids (DNA and RNA) capable of self-replication—is thought to have begun on Earth about 3.6 billion years ago. The first seeds of life may have originated here on Earth, "home grown," so to speak, or possibly life was "seeded" here by a meteorite from somewhere else, perhaps another planet (Mars?) or another star system.

Once life began on Earth, its future was guided thereafter by the principle of natural selection, first noted by Charles Darwin in the mid-nineteenth century. Natural selection is a mechanism whereby life forms favorably suited to their environment are preserved in the next generation while unfavorable forms are eliminated. It is "competition among replicators," as Steven Pinker, an MIT psychologist, succinctly points out (Pinker, 1997: 174). Natural selection is always active among all life forms on Earth, including human beings, accounting for the presence of all living forms on the planet. Natural selection explains the design in the living world without the presence of a designer. It is responsible for the design of our bodies, our brains, and, ultimately, our minds, including our intellectual capabilities and our most exalted emotions. To understand why human beings everywhere love and appreciate art, one must turn to natural selection.

Following the origin of life on Earth, things were pretty boring for about the next 3 billion years or so, as the many different forms remained relatively simple in their design and behavior. Then about 540 million years ago, for reasons that are not fully understood, a great explosion of diversity occurred. Within a few million years there was a proliferation of many new life forms featuring a plethora of body designs and survival strategies. Over the ensuing tens of millions of years many of these radically new forms failed to survive. But some did, and through natural selection they went on to give rise to the amazing diversity of life found on Earth today. The first land plants appeared 410 million years ago. One body design whose origins can be traced to that great period of biological creativity, which is called the Cambrian Explosion, are the chordates, the family of life forms with spinal cords. Fish, amphibians, reptiles (including dinosaurs), birds, and mammals are chordates, and each appeared in succession over the past 500 million years as natural selection slowly shaped each species' body design and behavior. The extinction of the dinosaurs 65 million years ago opened up new environments for the mammals; their numbers and variety exploded on the scene, leading to the great diversity we now see from shrews to whales. One group of mammals that prospered greatly from the dinosaurs' demise was the primates, the biological order that includes Old World and New World monkeys, great apes, and human beings. Origins of the order of primates can be traced by fossil teeth from as early as 80 million years ago. Small primates were living in trees 65 to 40 million years ago.

The Human Family Lineage

The secret of how we human beings acquired our capacity to create and appreciate art is found in the past 5 million or so years of our evolution. In this section we briefly sketch how paleoanthropologists draw the past few million years of our family lineage. The study of human evolutionary origins is complex, and the scenario presented here may eventually prove to be inaccurate in some detail, but it is probably pretty valid in general. Paleoanthropologists often don't agree on the species names of fossils of our ancestors, but there is fairly strong agreement on the stages of human evolution and the

Part 4: Art Defined and Its Origins

sequence in which various traits appeared. The sketch we present here is much simplified.

Human beings belong to the biological superfamily *Hominoidea*, which includes the great apes (chimps, gorillas, orangutans, and gibbons). The evolution of the great ape superfamily can be traced back many millions of years. Fossil *Hominoidea* dating 35–30 million years ago have been found in Egypt, from a time when the area was a lush tropical forest and marshland. Other *Hominoidea* fossils from a creature known as *Dryopithecus*, who existed over a wide area from Africa to India, date from about 30 to 12 million years ago. The ape-like *Dryopithecus* is thought to be the ancestor to the great apes and human beings. One by one the ancestors of the great apes are believed to have split off from the line traced to *Dryopithecus*, leading eventually to the great apes living today. About 5 million years ago the ancestors of the modern chimpanzee and human beings split. One line became chimps, the other became humans.

The line that eventually led to humans underwent rather rapid change (evolutionarily speaking) over the next 5 million years, adding first one remarkable trait, then another. As each of these traits was added, they helped our ancestors survive in their local environments. In the meantime, the branch that became chimps underwent their own evolution but in failing to acquire the traits the human line was adding, remained apes. By about 4.4 million years ago, our ancestors had attained bipedal walking posture, a trait no ape or monkey possesses. The acquisition of upright posture necessitated some radical redesign of the pelvis and limb bones as well as the nervous system. Walking upright, as any toddler knows, requires a pretty good balancing act that must be managed by the brain (see Table 15 and Figure 2).

For a 2-million-year period, from about 4.4 to about 2.5 million years ago, our ancestors and a variety of species that were close cousins, known collectively as australopithecines, lived in East and South Africa. Several varieties, or species, of australopithecines are believed to have existed during their 2-million-year tenure in Africa, with more than one species sometimes coexisting at the same time. At least two species, *Australopithecus afarensis* and *Australopithecus*

Table 15. HUMAN FAMILY LINEAGE

Name/Species	Distribution	Appearance–Extinction (years ago)	Height	Brain size	Importance	Culture
Dryopithecus	Africa, India	30 million–12 million	—	—	Ancestor to great apes & humans	Ape-like, possible knuckle walker
Chimp-hominid (human like) ancestor	West Africa	8 million–5 million	3.25–5.5 ft	450 cc	Species from which humans and chimps separated	Chimp-like, long arms, knuckle walker, used very crude tools—sticks, stone hammers
Australopithecus (anamensis, afarensis, & africanus)	East and South Africa	4 million–2.5 million	3.25–4.0 ft	400–500 cc	Fully erect posture, many brain & other changes necessitated by erect posture	Tool use same as modern chimps
Homo habilis	East and South Africa	2.3 million–1.6 million	3.25–5.0 ft	500–800 cc	First to use stone tools (crudely produced); first evidence of language beginnings	Hunted & scavenged on the savanna. Oldowan culture
Homo erectus	Began in East Africa & spread out over Asia & Europe	1.9 million–perhaps 30,000	4.25–6.0 ft	750–1250 cc	Improved techniques for making stone tools. Improved use of language. Perhaps used fire. Less aggressive, more friendly. Increased capacity to reason, plan for future & determine cause & effect. Capable of using water craft for transportation.	Skilled hunters & gatherers. Perhaps bonding of males & females, beginnings of family. Achulean culture.

178

Neanderthal	Europe	200,000–27,000	5.0–5.8 ft	Average = 1,450 cc	Evolved from *Homo erectus* in Europe. Possessed language and first evidence of beginnings of religion with deliberate burial of dead, perhaps accompanied by flowers. Though brains were large, lacked modern human mental & emotional capacity. Likely became extinct by 27,000 years ago. May have bred with more modern humans.	Efficient hunters & gatherers, well-crafted stone tools. As far as can be determined, lacked art & modern capacity for appreciation of beauty. Mousterian culture.
Early *Homo sapiens*	Africa, Western Asia	120,000–60,000	5.25–6.1 ft	1,200–1,700 cc	Modern robust bodies; brain size about same as modern humans. Unchanging technology suggests a lack of creativity, perhaps less than full self-awareness.	Skilled hunters & gatherers, retouched flakes & flake blades & points. Little evidence of art or religion or appreciation of beauty.
Modern humans *Homo sapiens sapiens*	Worldwide	50,000–present	4.5–6.75 ft	1,000–2,000 cc (average = 1,350 cc)	Fully self-aware & capable of rational thought. A wide range of emotions essential for normal mental functioning. Emotions of beauty, ectasy, awe, & the sublime frequently experienced in contexts of art & religion.	Culture ranging from Stone Age to atomic energy. Art & religion essential parts of lifestyle.

Source: Eccles (1991) and Pinker (1997)

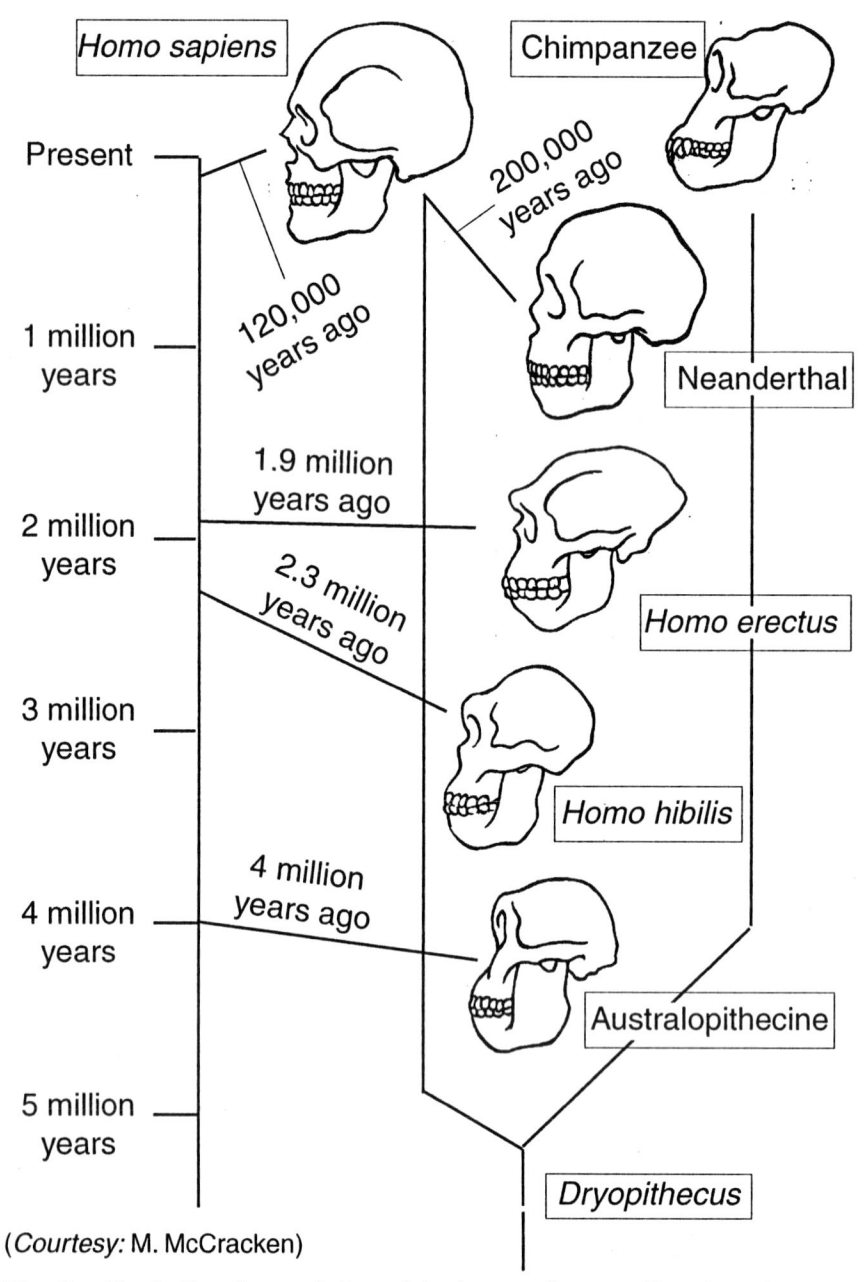

Timeline illustrating the evolution of the human lineage. Note how the part of the skull enclosing the brain increases in size with time, as the brain case moves upward and forward to a position above the face.

Figure 2. Human Lineage

Part 4: Art Defined and Its Origins

africanus, are thought to be ancestral to modern human beings (Tattersall, 1998: 185). The australopithecines were about four feet tall, and their brains ranged from 400 to 500 cubic centimeters (cc), not much different from the modern chimpanzee's 450 cc. (Average brain capacity of a modern human being is 1,350 cc, with a range from 1,000 to 2,000 cc.) The australopithecines probably possessed only a small inventory of tools, probably using sticks and stones as implements, much as chimpanzees now do. No evidence has been found of australopithecines manufacturing more sophisticated tools or implements. They didn't have the brains for it. In fact, much of the way of life of the australopithecines probably did not differ greatly from that of the modern chimpanzees. Moreover, there is no evidence of a language among these individuals, with their communication probably not going much beyond the wide range of gestures and the more than 30 named and identified vocalizations made by wild chimpanzees (Tattersall, 1998: 60). Undoubtedly the australopithecines possessed nothing that could remotely be considered art or religion. These two most human of traits would have to wait.

About 2.3 million years ago, something important began to happen in one group of australopithecines. They became a little taller, perhaps as tall as five feet in height, and their brain capacity expanded dramatically. From the 400–500 cc range of australopithecines, this group, which we know as *Homo habilis*, featured brains that ranged from 500 to 800 cc in size, with an average of about 700 cc. This was a watershed increase, and it led to the presence of two new abilities that had never been seen on Earth prior to that time. The first was *Homo habilis*'s ability to manufacture stone tools—primitively shaped flakes, choppers, and scrapers called collectively by archaeologists the Oldowan assemblage or culture. By later standards these stone tools were very crudely formed, to be sure, but they were deliberately shaped nevertheless. Manufacture of such tools is thought to have been associated with an increase in *Homo habilis*'s hand-eye coordination and perhaps with an increase in capacity to conceive of a product before making it (Eccles, 1991: 70).

The second ability is revealed on the fossilized interior bony surfaces of the skull of *Homo habilis*. What is described as a "fullness" in two areas of *Homo habilis*'s brain (the inferior frontal lobe and the inferior parietal lobe) is something not previously seen in other apes or australopithecines. Areas where such fullness is found in *Homo habilis*'s brain are closely associated with the use of language in modern human beings. From this we may infer that *Homo habilis* seems to have had the rudimentary beginnings of human language (Eccles, 1991: 23–24). Scientists are presently attempting to unravel what it was in the environment of the australopithecines that led to natural selection endowing *Homo habilis* with the ability to make stone tools and presumably to use rudimentary language.

After appearing on the scene about 2.3 million years ago, *Homo habilis* apparently remained largely unchanged for a long period of time. They seemed not to have improved their tool-making ability or to have increased their capacity for language. The reign of *Homo habilis* represents a long period of biological and cultural stasis. Nature, that is to say, natural selection, does not change a species more than it has to. Species only change enough to get the job done, to survive and reproduce. Any further change would be wasteful of energy, and that is one thing nature does not ordinarily waste.

By 1.6 million years ago, a new species thought to have descended from *Homo habilis* and to be ancestor to modern human beings appeared on the scene in East Africa. Known as *Homo erectus*, with a brain capacity of 850 cc, this species represents another major advancement in human evolution and mental capacity. Several hundred thousand years later, at least one variety of this species ended up with a brain capacity of more than 1,200 cc, at the low end of the modern range. About the same height as their predecessors, Homo erectus are notable for several reasons. First, they developed new and better ways of making stone tools. These tools, known as the Acheulian assemblage or culture, are far more finely crafted that *Homo habilis*'s Oldowan tools, with flakes removed from the entire surface of the stone tool and a high degree of purposeful shaping and symmetry, not just the crude removal of two-inch-long flakes that could be used for cutting, from a stone core, as with Oldowan tools.

The more skillful manufacture of stone tools by *Homo erectus* probably reflects greater hand-eye coordination and increased ability to think and plan for the future, and it was undoubtedly accompanied by changes in the way they lived. (By 400,000 years ago, descendants of *Homo erectus* in Germany were making and presumably using skillfully crafted spears reflecting essentially modern hand-eye coordination; see Dennell, 1997: 767.) It is possible that *Homo erectus* manufactured crude dwellings and clothing. Perhaps males gave up some of their fighting in competition for females and devoted more of their energy to involvement in some form of proto-family in which males tended to bond to some degree with females and participate in the rearing of the young—something chimpanzees, for example, do not do. With their larger brains, the young of *Homo erectus* were born in a more immature state and thus childhood was prolonged. As technological knowledge increased and there was more group cooperation, more technical and social knowledge had to be passed on to the young if they were to survive. Males could play an important role in the transmission of their knowledge to the young. An increased capacity for language likely helped in passing on this knowledge. Greater brain power undoubtedly led to major increases in the ability to plan and carry out actions, and improvements in cause-and-effect reasoning may have occurred.

In addition to better tool-making abilities and a probable increase in capacity for language, *Homo erectus* was the migratory race of proto-humans. They possessed an unusual wanderlust not seen in their predecessors. Over a period of several hundred thousand years, *Homo erectus* migrated out of East Africa, where they originated, through the Middle East into Asia and China and south into Java and other Indonesian islands. In Indonesia 800,000 years ago they apparently crossed several miles of open water in "water craft" to reach the island of Flores, which is located about 300 miles east of Java. *Homo erectus* also migrated into Europe, where extensive remains have been found in Spain dating to 650,000 years ago. *Homo erectus* may have survived in Southeast Asia as a separate species until about 30,000 years ago.

Homo erectus possessed another trait that was crucial in human evolution. Unlike their predecessors the australopithecines and *Homo habilis*, whose brains showed no pronounced or speedy tendency to become ever larger over a period of several hundred thousand years in many different environments, *Homo erectus*'s brains seem to have continued to increase in size over the many generations in most of the environments where they resided.

Among the *Homo erectus* who migrated to China, their brains eventually reached 1,250 cc in size; brain capacity ended up somewhat smaller for those who occupied Southeast Asia. Most researchers believe *Homo erectus* in Europe evolved into the well-known Neanderthals, who on average possessed brains a littler larger than our own. And interestingly, although there are no indications of religion and art among the *Homo erectus* in Asia, among the Neanderthals, who inhabited Europe and the Middle East starting about 200,000 years ago, we find a few instances of deliberate burials of the dead and perhaps even floral tributes placed with the deceased dating to 80,000 years ago (Eccles, 1991: 115). Most researchers believe the Neanderthals eventually became extinct, with at least a few surviving until about 27,000 years ago.

Beginning more than 1 million years ago, while their brains were still in the 800 cubic centimeter size range, the *Homo erectus* that remained in Africa slowly began to take on more humanlike features (Abbate et al., 1998: 458; Bower, 1998: 356). Over the next 900,000 years or so, these direct ancestors of ours, whose remains have been found in northeast Africa in the region of the Red Sea and the Horn of Africa, gradually evolved bodies and heads that were indistinguishable from those of modern human beings. By about 100,000 or more years ago their brains were the same size as ours.

The modern human brain weighs about 2.75 pounds and is composed of 100 billion nerve cells (Wilson, 1998: 81) that work in concert to maintain a human body, execute needed behaviors, and create a human mind. As of 1995, genetic data show the human brain structure is prescribed by at least 3,195 separate genes, 50 percent more than any other organ or tissue in the body (Wilson, 1998: 97). Scientists are still counting, with the final number of genes influencing brain structure likely to be much higher. Out of an estimated total of between 50,000 and 100,000 genes in the total human genetic code, at the very least between 3 and 6 percent of human genes determine the brain's structure. The large number of genes involved in the growth of the human brain provides an immense source of raw material in the form of genetic mutations upon which natural selection can operate to design the brain functions needed for our ancestors' survival in their physical and increasingly complex social environment. Potential mutations in the many genes and the variability in brain function they prescribe provide much grist for natural selection's evolutionary mill. Variation in those nearly 3,200 known genes helps account for the great differences we see in how modern people think and feel, including how differently they respond to individual films. However, large numbers and the lack of contemporary isolation of human populations have put an end to the 4-million-year era of hominid brain-size increase and structural modification. New potentially favorable mutations get swamped in the large numbers of people now living.

Tripling the size of the brain from *Australopithecus* to *Homo sapiens* involved many complex design problems for nature. One was a problem of head size and birth. A human being must be born in a highly immature state while the brain is only a fraction of its eventual adult size, or else the mother's pelvis could never accommodate the infant's delivery. The bone-encircled outlet of the human female pelvis is about as large as it can get without radical redesign of woman's anatomy for standing upright and walking. It is estimated that human brain size at birth is but 26 percent of adult size, in comparison to 60 percent for apes, an estimated 46 percent for *Homo habilis*, and 35 to 29 percent for *Homo erectus* (Eccles, 1991: 107). Moreover, the birth of young in such a highly immature and helpless state in a species that lived by foraging necessitated a social structure that provided help and support for mothers with infants. Large-brained immature infants require a long infancy and childhood to provide time for their brains to grow and for them to learn the intricacies of survival—knowledge handed down through close social living.

A second problem posed by the increasing brain size of our ancestors involved energy requirements. It takes a considerable amount of precious bodily energy to grow a large brain, and even more energy to operate it. It is estimated that a newborn human being's brain consumes about 60 percent of the energy the baby takes in; the figure for an adult is somewhere around 20 percent, still extraordinarily high for a 2 1/2-pound organ comprising less than 2 percent of the body weight of a 150-pound person. Some researchers believe evolution was forced to make tradeoffs to feed the brain's ravenous energy needs. Prior to birth the human baby's placenta invades the uterine lining more deeply than other primates' placentas, and it is more aggressive in pulling nutrients from the mother's bloodstream. The human being's larger brain appears to be balanced with a smaller gastrointestinal track in comparison with other primates, which perhaps freed up energy from growing and maintaining intestinal tissue for brain growth (Gibbons, 1998: 345–347).

But growing a larger brain still didn't solve all the needs for increased computing power in our ancestors. Structural alterations in the brain were also required. The increasing importance of language in our ancestors from *Homo habilis* on, as well as the rising complexity of their mental and social life, placed heavy demands on the need for more brain computing power that could not be met through size increase alone. If nature had relied on size increase alone, our heads would have simply been too large for survival. We would have looked like the large-headed aliens seen in cartoons, an easy meal for a hungry leopard. Instead of going for size increases alone, nature also went for reorganization. The brain is composed of two halves, the right and left hemispheres. In lower animals the two halves pretty much share the same functions. One way to increase brain power is to allocate different functions to the halves. Instead of having symmetry between the two hemispheres, our hominid ancestors began to develop what is called asymmetry between the right and left sides. There are indications of the beginnings of asymmetry in the brain areas associated with speech in the common ancestor of humans and chimps. Such beginnings of asymmetry have been passed down to present-day chimpanzees and perhaps to other apes. Brain asymmetry suggesting right-handedness has been found in *Homo habilis* fossils a little less than 2 million years old, and archaeologists have determined that the earliest stone tools were mostly made by right-handed individuals (Tattersall, 1998: 76).

The human brain, in contrast, is highly asymmetrical, with one side able to perform tasks that are difficult or impossible for the other side to execute. The right side tends to specialize in nonverbal ideation and social abilities, while the left side is highly specialized for language. The right side notes visual similarities and perceives forms; the left notes conceptual similarities and details. The left side analyzes words and their meanings, the right side synthesizes gestalt (Eccles, 1991: 211). By developing asymmetry in functions and structures, evolution was able to get more "bang for the buck," so to speak, from the same volume of neural tissue.

Although our ancestors had attained the same brain volume as ours by 100,000 years ago, they were still apparently not our equals mentally. Steven Pinker has pointed out that though anatomically modern-appearing fossils of human beings date to more than 100,000 years ago in Africa and, shortly thereafter, in the Middle East, judging from their archaeological remains, their lifestyle did not differ appreciably from either their *Homo erectus* predecessors or from the Neanderthals. Because these ancestors' overall brain capacity was much the same as ours, we have to assume that their brains were organized and functioned somewhat differently from ours, Pinker believes (1997: 202). The study of paleopsychology will provide answers to the questions; one way they differed may have been in emotions.

Emotions and Their Function

Now, the fun part. Earlier we mentioned Western society's ancient tendency toward dualistic thinking when it came to understanding human beings and their place in nature and the relationship of body to mind. Another pervasive example of dualistic thinking also exists and, like the former examples, has long held back our understanding of human nature. When discussing the nature of the human mind there is a long tradition of drawing a hard line between emotions and rational thought. Most people see a fundamental difference between the two: Rational thought is cool and logical, emotion-free and desirable; it is quintessentially human. Emotions, in comparison, are viewed as a lower type of mental activity, more primitive and muddled, characteristic of animals, likely to contaminate rational thought and lead the clear-thinking individual astray.

Studies of brain functions now show that such a dualism of rational thought and emotion is wrong and, in fact, could not be further from the truth. Researchers now believe that rational thought and emotions, far from being separate activities, are best seen as two aspects of the same mental process—namely, mental activity that is adaptive and helps keep the individual alive and reproducing. Our culture's long tendency to discount the value of emotions has led to the neglect of their scientific study; only recently have emotions begun to receive the scientific attention they deserve.

In 1872 Charles Darwin published a book entitled *The Expression of Emotions in Man and Animals*. From the study of the facial expressions of sulky monkeys, dogs, the insane, and even his own wailing infant he concluded that different species have common ways of expressing emotions, which reinforced his belief in the shared ancestry of animals and humans (Mlot, 1998: 1005). But Darwin's work on emotions was largely overlooked and stimulated little research over the next one hundred years. After much neglect, researchers have begun to pick up where Darwin left off. Scientists are now beginning to recognize that, as Edward O. Wilson says, "passion is inseverably linked to reason. Emotion is not just a perturbation of reason but a vital part of it" (Wilson, 1998: 106). According to Wilson, the rational mind does not float above the irrational, free to engage in pure thought. Instead, rational thought and emotions are *entwined*. Furthermore, emotions are essential for maintaining rational thought. "Without the stimulus and guidance of emotion, rational thought slows and degenerates," Wilson says (1998: 113). This can be seen in the fact that the "higher," more recently acquired centers of the brain in the neocortex communicate with each other, primarily or even exclusively through the evolutionarily older and more "primitive" parts of the brain that control the emotions (Tattersall, 1998: 71–72).

Scientists now see the human brain as an information-processing system designed by several hundred million years of biological evolution to keep the individual alive and reproducing so that the positive traits that individuals possess, including genetically based mental traits, may be passed on to the next generation. Survival in any environment is complex and multifaceted, especially the increasingly complex social environment that our ancestors faced from australopithecines on. In our ancestors' complex world, an individual had to skillfully sort through a welter of information about what was going on around him and make life-and-death choices about what to do: to go over there or stay here; to approach or hold his or her ground; to eat this or try a little of that. In a less genetically and behaviorally complex species, nature solves such problems by hardwiring individuals to respond to selected information in the same way every time. We human beings, for example, are hardwired to close our eyes when an object threatens to hit the open eye, and we instantly withdraw upon contact with a hot surface. But as the complexity of essential information increases, hardwiring becomes less and less effective. There are too many options that must be considered if chances of survival and reproduction are to be maximized.

As essential information in an evolving species' environment became increasingly complex and the behavioral choices ever more varied, nature had to find some method by which to prioritize potential behaviors—some means by which the creatures could set goals in a complex world and get moving toward those goals. Psychologists believe that *emotions* are the mechanisms by which brains set their highest goals. As Steven Pinker says, "An animal cannot pursue all its goals at once" (1997: 373) but must prioritize them, rank order them so that behaviors critical to survival and reproduction get top priority and less-important goals fall farther down the list. Once the brain sets a goal, an emotion to get the individual moving toward that goal is stimulated. When an emotion has been triggered, a "cascade of subgoals and sub-subgoals that we call thinking and acting" ensues, says Pinker (1997: 373). Like Wilson, Pinker believes that no fine line exists between thinking and emotions, feelings and sensations. They are woven together. Thinking and emotions are a part of the same process, not separate as the dualists' view held.

Emotions are adaptive; they are crucial for survival. "Mental processes . . . are not organized around thought or reason but around emotional ideals. . . . emotions . . . set our agenda. And they do so without our being aware of them. Far from being disorganizing, they are the focal point of the mental system's activity," says psychologist Robert Ornstein (1991: 94–96).

Because emotions are adaptive, it does not mean they are always perfectly appropriate. Sometimes they are not. But over the long haul, evolutionarily speaking, they work well enough for most people most of the time to optimize survival and reproduction (Ornstein, 1991: 94). "Emotions rarely disorganize thought to the person's detriment," says Ornstein (1991: 88). They direct the mind toward particular conclusions; they are short-circuit deliberations.

Among simple organisms with a slim behavioral repertoire, a few emotions for goal-setting will do the job. The repertoire of high-priority goals remained relatively simple: eat, survive (don't get eaten), and reproduce about summed things up. Fear, hunger, thirst, and sexual desire are enough. But as life gets more complex, more emotions are added by natural selection. Fear and terror, followed closely by the drives of thirst and hunger, are among the most basic emotions, the first to appear in animals. These emotions represent high-priority goals often requiring time-sensitive behavior in which delay threatens physical survival. Love, that is to say sexual attraction, is another powerful emotion that appeared early in the history of life. Without sexual attraction there is no reproduction, and so beneficial traits do not get passed on to the next generation. Love is also an emotion associated with other social bonds that are highly conducive to survival. Is it any wonder, then, that great scenes in the movies so often invoke the emotions of fear, terror, and love?

With the appearance of the mammals and their more complex social systems involving group living and competition and cooperation among group members, strategies for survival and reproduction became increasingly more complicated. With greater complexity came the need to make choices among a greater variety of behaviors. This meant brains had to (1) set *more* goals, and (2) work with a greater *variety* of goals. Thus, natural selection (evolution)

Part 4: Art Defined and Its Origins

provided for a wider array of emotions. Complexity took a big jump with the first appearance of the primates and again with the common ancestors of the apes and human beings. Like their cousins the chimpanzees, our australopithecine ancestors must have experienced a wide array of emotions, all vital for survival in their world. The emotional array likely increased with *Homo habilis* and *Homo erectus*. By the time the first *Homo sapiens* appeared on the scene in East Africa more than 100,000 years ago, the species' emotional repertoire would have been impressive.

But their emotional repertoire still wasn't what we would call human. We suggest that even with otherwise apparently physically modern bodies and head size, people living 100 millennia ago were not emotionally—and therefore rationally—the equal of modern people. There is scant evidence that these *Homo sapiens* ancestors of ours had either art or religion, cultural traits that in their full form apparently did not exist much before about 50,000 years ago. If these traits did exist, it seems likely that they existed in rudimentary form. Our modern-bodied ancestors of 100,000 years ago seem to have been sufficiently lacking in imagination and creativity that they continued making the same kinds of tools as their predecessors had, and they seem to have done so for at least another 60,000 years. Archaeologists have determined that objects we would definitely call art, including beautiful figurines several inches high carved from stone and wonderfully crafted spear-thrower handles, appeared quite suddenly in Europe about 35,000 years ago. These items had no obvious utilitarian functions, as objects found that predate that time had. No more than 5,000 years after the appearance of these carvings in the archaeological record, magnificent paintings began to appear on the walls of caves in Europe.

The suddenness of the appearance of magnificent art among our ancestors about 35,000 years ago seemed to occur with little evidence of transition forms leading up to these exquisite works; there is apparently an absence of any prolonged period of learning time where the skills were gradually mastered. The sudden appearance of art in Europe, along with its apparent absence in the Neanderthals and *Homo erectus* in Asia, suggests a biological change, one or more chance mutations in the preceding generations of *Homo sapiens* in Africa. Biologists know that the change from one species to another in an evolving line of organisms tends to not take place gradually with incremental modifications over a very long period of time, but happens rather quickly, sometimes almost overnight, evolutionally speaking.

Religion and art are two of the most emotion-intense activities in which human beings participate. Both art and religion worldwide tend to be identified with emotions associated with the sublime: beauty, awe, ecstasy, and rapture. These emotions heighten consciousness as no others, perhaps accentuating consciousness of self, as opposed to consciousness of things other than the self. Because these emotions are so closely associated with art and religion, we can speculate that these emotions or mental traits are closely allied with the origins of art and religion, and were not present in our ancestors prior to about 60,000 years ago, some 25,000 years prior to the appearance in Europe of the first known art and religion.

In what is clearly speculation, it seems reasonable that some time around 60,000 years ago, give or take a few thousand years, probably just prior to the last wave of migration of *Homo sapiens* out of northeast Africa into the Middle East—from where, over the next 30,000 or so years, they spread out over most of the globe—a mutation or series of mutations in genes governing brain functions occurred in one or more isolated populations of *Homo sapiens* living in East Africa. Human beings settled Australia at a maximum of about 60,000 to 50,000 years ago (Piazza, 1998:637), and no well-dated archaeological site has been found there that is older than 35,000 years, so the genetic changes would have had to occur in the African mother population prior to migration out of Africa to Australia. Modern human beings, known as Cro-Magnons, arrived in Europe about 40,000 years ago and, like the Australians, had also migrated there from an African homeland. These mutations made those individuals more capable of experiencing a new set of emotions, what we call beauty and the sublime, ecstasy, and awe. We say "more capable" because these traits may have existed in rudimentary form earlier, but were not strong enough to fully influence behavior and

Part 4: Art Defined and Its Origins

institute the full development of art and religion. These mutations formed the basis of the transition from *Homo sapiens* (our ancestors of 100,000 years ago) to *Homo sapiens sapiens* (we human beings). Based on current research, we suggest that the mutations took place in a single individual or series of individuals living in a small isolated population of *Homo sapiens* somewhere around the Horn of Africa, and because that individual (or those individuals) was (were) likely male, the trait was quickly transmitted to descendants in the group and on to future generations. These mutations had the effect of raising the overall cognitive powers of those who possessed them (they could think more rationally) and, more importantly for our purposes, led to an increased capacity for a more enriched emotional life for the individual.

With this new emotional capacity our ancestors immediately began to experience the world in different and richer ways. In addition to greater overall computing power, besides old emotions such as lust, anger, fear, contentment, sadness, and hunger, *Homo sapiens sapiens* became increasingly aware of emotions and feelings never truly seen on Earth before. Out of this grew the capacity to experience beauty, awe, and the sublime. The greater complexity of the mental interior of these individuals was unlike that seen in preceding generations, dating back billions of years. Very suddenly, consciousness was hugely enlarged, brimming with new emotions, feelings, and sensations that literally cried out for expression. The newly enriched mental interior needed an outlet.

This event, these mutations and their mental consequences, represents a fundamental transition in the evolution of the universe physically, biologically, and culturally. Matter, in the form of human beings, became more self-aware, and for the first time that we know of, matter truly began to contemplate its nature and to experience beauty in all its dimensions in the world. During the first 10 billion or so years of the universe, or at least this part of the universe, matter had no awareness of itself. During the next 3.8 billion years or so of evolution of life on Earth, life was dominated by what goes on *outside* the organism—that is to say, the external environment. Almost overnight things changed fundamentally. One species came to be increasingly dominated by what was going on *in its own mental interior*. From this interior this species (our own) would reform, reshape, and recreate the exterior world as no species had previously. *Homo sapiens sapiens*'s fate was not dominated by the natural exterior world, as was the case with all predecessor species, but by the conjurings, eruptions, and machinations of its own mental interior.

Origins of Art and Religion

> There was a kind of behavioral revolution [in Africa] 50,000 years ago. Nobody made art before 50,000 years ago; everybody did afterward.
> —Richard Klein, archaeologist, Stanford University
> (Appenzeller, 1998: 1454)

As the big-brained, essentially artless and religionless *Homo sapiens* living in Africa sixty or so thousand years ago were positioned to migrate out of northeast Africa and begin colonizing and conquering the world, they lacked at least one major trait to successfully accomplish the job—powerful emotions relating to beauty, awe, ecstasy, the sublime. The culture of these early humans probably consisted of a hodgepodge of knowledge, beliefs, customs, and manufactured items, some ephemeral, others useful and essential. Included were crudely constructed stories and tales, lore about animals and plants, local geographic knowledge, knowledge about people and their behavior, probably simple concepts about death and speculation on what follows death. But all this information, this cultural inventory, was somewhat disconnected and amorphous, not fully synthesized into a systematic body of emotion-laden thought. One or, more likely, a series of mutations occurred in these ancestors of ours that expanded their emotional repertoire and laid the full foundation for art and religion. Art objects—sculptures, paintings, and perhaps costumes—became a focus of these new emotional capacities. Stories once told as secular tales or myths, knowledge communicated about people, animals, plants, geography, and thoughts on death and its meaning began to become annealed into a single system of thought that became the focal point for these new emotions.

Part 4: Art Defined and Its Origins

The formerly disparate products of early humans' thinking agglutinated into a relatively coherent system held together by a new complex of emotions and feelings. In evolutionary terms, these thought systems and their associated behavior—what anthropologists call *culture*—evolved relatively recently, perhaps within the last fifty, even forty, millennia, among people who had the capacity for the requisite emotions. Art began as a means of expressing emotion. Religion grew out of art and evolved as an outlet for emotions, emotions that had a biological substrate. Thus, biology initiated culture, in this case art and religion, much as purely physical processes had earlier initiated biology.

Out of this new species of ape's rich mental interior grew the need to express what was being experienced. We all have experienced the feeling of having an emotion that just has to be let out. Every artist, regardless of his or her chosen medium, knows the feeling of absolutely having to give artistic vent to an emotion or feeling, to get it out of one's mind and into the world. This is precisely the experience of our ancestors. And in it lies the spark of creativity and inspiration that is at the heart of all higher subsequent human achievements. Because of one or a small number of mutations, our predecessors suddenly had a real human mind, and that mind demanded expression. In this need lies the origin of art.

Out of art and the need to re-present the world grew religion and the ensuing synthesis of beliefs and knowledge into the societies' system of sacred thought. The first real religious emotions and feelings grew out of the newly increased capacity to experience beauty, awe, ecstasy, and enchantment, which in turn led to the creation of gods and the full development of religious-based beliefs. The increased emotional complexity led to greater capacity to employ and sustain higher levels of rational thought. With art and religion flowing from the same emotional wellspring, art and religion rapidly evolved in tandem, each feeding into the other's growth and evolution. Art then, and to this day, remains based upon the expression and embodiment of the feelings of beauty, awe, ecstasy, and enchantment. And those feelings, not intellectual rationalizations, are also the true basis of real religion everywhere. As noted earlier, until the time of Jan Vermeer in the seventeenth century, nearly all art worldwide was religious in derivation and context.

The art and religion that grew out of the newly enriched mental interior of our *Homo sapiens sapiens* forebears provided historic assistance to survival. Art and religion, along with language, which, in a simpler configuration, had developed earlier, turned out to be much more useful in survival and an asset in the expansion of human beings over the face of the Earth than did large teeth for a tiger or the fast legs of the antelope. Religion and art improved group solidarity by getting group members to think alike, experience the same emotions at the same time, and believe in the same things, thereby better regulating group behavior. Art and religion kept group members on the same page in an ever-increasingly complex social environment. Language, which had been evolving for more than two million years, got a boost from the enlarged emotional repertoire and increased rational capacity upon which art and religion were predicated, making possible better communication; more effective exchange of information almost always improves survival chances in any situation.

With a richer mental interior leading to art and religion and the consequent improvement of survival chances, a positive feedback loop was established. Art and religion increased the chances of survival for those who had the genetically based emotional traits; improved chances of survival led to increased numbers in groups featuring the genetic mutation(s). More group members in turn made for a richer mental interior, which led to more language, art, and religion. This feedback loop assured that any further mutations leading to increased brain capacity for a richer emotional repertoire, capacity for rational thought, and richer mental interior would be favored by natural selection. Thus in bootstrap fashion this feedback loop rapidly (in evolutionary terms, perhaps a few thousand years) led to the appearance by about 35,000 years ago of art judged to be the highest quality in any age. With the requisite biologically based emotions fully in place, a whole system of religious and artistic thought was probably fully established in Europe by 35,000 years ago, as well as the other areas where the last wave of those out of

Part 4: Art Defined and Its Origins

Africa migrated. Some of the first art produced in Europe—carvings and cave paintings—remains some of the most beautiful ever produced.

The recently discovered cave at Chauvet in south central France contains 300-plus magnificent images of animals on its walls dating back more than 30,000 years. Of the Cro-Magnons who painted them, Ian Tattersall, curator in the Department of Anthropology at the American Museum of Natural History in New York City, has said, "Art was emphatically not an occasional or incidental occupation among these people; it was central to their experience of their environment and to the way they explained the world" (Tattersall, 1998: 11).

It is important to note that no society of *Homo sapiens sapiens*, regardless of technological simplicity, is known to have existed without art and religion. Such a society would not be viable in competition with other societies that possess these cultural traits and their associated emotions.

Homo sapiens became *Homo sapiens sapiens* with the acquisition of the full human repertoire of emotions and capacity for reason. Art, its origins and appreciation, is grounded in biology and follows the emotions, not vice versa. The emotions do not go where the art is! This proposition is evident in our study of great film scenes. As the directors in our study recognized, great film scenes tend to be emotion laden, where craft has been fine-tuned to evoke emotions, emotions that are biologically based. If great art were not grounded in the biology of emotions, it would be possible to talk about great art in emotion-free terms. This, we assert, cannot ordinarily be done. Craft can be spoken of in emotion-free terms, but not art.

The Biology of Emotions

If art goes where emotions lie, and not vice versa, we must look for great and enduring art in the sectors of human life where high levels of emotion are found. High levels of emotion tend to be determined by what Edward O. Wilson calls *epigenetic rules*, the predisposition to experience the world in a particular way and learn certain behaviors in preference to other behaviors (Wilson, 1998: 150). Powerful emotions, as might be expected, tend to cluster in areas strongly related to survival and reproduction, fear and tension (safety), love and romance, bonding to others and to community, bonding to a geographical area, and to factors relating to one's mental efforts to delineate a satisfying place in society and the universe.

It is very exciting that researchers now believe they are close to discovering the physical basis of emotions. Investigators believe the underlying bases, or substrate, of emotions in human beings, as well as other creatures, are called *neuropeptides*, or ligands. Neuropeptides are biological substances that are produced inside the cells in one part of the body and circulate through blood or other body fluids to a second site, where they become attached to the surface of a cell, often a nerve cell in the brain or some other part of the nervous system. The neuropeptides attach to the cell's surface at sites known as a receptors, where specific neuropeptides bind to specific sites on the cell in lock-and-key fashion. Information is conveyed when binding occurs. Neuropeptides are informational substances. Once a neuropeptide is locked onto the receptor at the cell's surface, a message is transmitted to the cell's interior for the cell to begin a highly specific task, such as accessing the cell's nucleus (the storehouse of information containing the individual's total genetic code), for the information necessary to begin producing a new protein that the cell or some other cell in the body can use. When a neuropeptide locks on to a nerve cell, either in the brain or somewhere else in the body, the attachment of the neuropeptide affects the cell's firing potential, the timing and conditions, and the manner in which that cell is allowed to fire and thus transmit information to other cells.

In the brain, the attachment of the neuropeptide to a nerve cell and the cell's subsequent firing becomes the emotion that the individual experiences. Candace B. Pert is a leading figure in this research. In 1972 she discovered the opiate receptor in the human brain, the site where the body's own morphinelike substance, called endorphin, docks to produce pleasurable effects similar to those produced by opiates such as opium and morphine. Had she been a male making the same discovery, Pert would have stood a good chance of winning the Nobel

Prize. Because she is a woman, and because of the politics of science (particularly in decades past), she did not.

Pert writes, "From my perspective, emotions are what link the body and mind into bodymind" (1997: 350). "The brain is a big hormone bag! Pockets of peptide juices are released from both glands and brain cells, after which they bind with specific receptors that enable them to act at sites far from where the juices originated" (1997: 181). "Mind," she says, "doesn't dominate body, it *becomes* body—body and mind are one" (1997: 187). "Emotions are constantly regulating what we experience as 'reality.' The decision about what sensory information travels to your brain and what gets filtered out depends on what signals the receptors are receiving from the peptides" (1997: 147).

Pert defines emotions in the broadest terms. They include familiar human experiences of anger, fear, and sadness along with joy, contentment, and courage. She also includes basic sensations such as pleasure and pain and drives such as hunger and thirst, as well as an assortment of "intangible, subjective experiences that are probably unique to humans, such as spiritual inspiration, awe, bliss, and other states of consciousness that we all have experienced" (Pert, 1997: 131–132).

Pert believes that neuropeptides are the substrates of emotion. They are the "molecular underpinnings of what we experience as feelings, sensations, thoughts, drives, perhaps even spirit or soul" (1997: 130). "The same simple physiology of emotions," she says, "has been preserved and used again and again over evolutionary eons and across species" (1997: 131). Pert believes there may be a specific peptide for each emotion (1997: 145).

The parts of the brain where the peptides and their receptors are the richest are the parts that have been implicated in expression of emotions. Emotions, Pert suggests, can be understood as basic molecular, biological processes (1997: 178). She writes:

> The mind as we experience it is immaterial, yet it has a physical substrate, which is both the body and the brain. It may also be said to have a nonmaterial, nonphysical substrate that has to do with the flow of that information. The mind, then, is that which holds

the network together, often acting below our consciousness, linking and coordinating the major systems and their organs and cells in an intelligently orchestrated symphony of life. Thus, we might refer to the whole system as a psychosomatic information network, linking *psyche*, which comprises all that is of an ostensibly nonmaterial nature, such as mind, emotion, and soul, to *soma*, which is the material world of molecules, cells, and organs. (Pert, 1997: 185).

The human brain probably does not contain any completely new structures not shared with our primate and mammal relatives (Tattersall, 1998: 72). Moreover, thus far, every neuropeptide found in humans has been found in other animals. For example, the neuropeptide that locks on to the opium receptor on human brain cells, known as endorphin, which brings pleasure and positive feelings, has been found in all animals and in insects. So far researchers have found nearly 100 different neuropeptides among the 100 billion or so nerve cells in the human brain and in the rest of the body. Some researchers now believe that the real power of the human brain and the rest of the nervous system, its real computing power, lies not so much in the nerves themselves—with their trillions of connections with each other—which are of course essential, but in the orchestration, the dance of the neuropeptides as they circulate throughout the body stimulating the firing potential of first one bundle of nerves, then another (Pert, 1997: 139, 148). The multitude of interactions, of course, are exceedingly complex. This great dance is the language of the brain/body information system that comprises the whole person, the music that keeps the individual alive and reproducing. It was the modifications of this information system that led to the development of art and religion, by making possible a new suite of powerful emotions.

In her book *Molecules of Emotion*, Pert sums up:

Emotional states or moods are produced by the various neuropeptide ligands, and what we experience as an emotion or a feeling is also a mechanism for activating a particular neuronal circuit—*simultaneously throughout the brain and the body*—which generates a behavior involving the whole creature, with all the necessary physiological changes that behavior would require. This fits nicely with

UCSF psychologist Paul Ekman's elegant formulation that such emotion is experienced throughout the organism and not in just the head or the body, and has a corresponding facial expression. It's part of the constellation of bodily changes that occurs with each shift of subjective feeling. (Pert, 1977: 144)

Candace Pert echoes Steven Pinker's view of emotions; both seem to anticipate a new scientific discipline to be called *paleolithic psychology* or perhaps *paleolithic neurobiology*.

One extremely important purpose of emotions from an evolutionary perspective is to help us decide what to remember and what to forget: The cavewoman who could remember which cave had the gentle guy who gave her food is more likely to be our foremother than the cavewoman who confused it with the cave that held the killer bear. (Pert, 1997: 144)

What Is Beauty and Why Are We Attracted to It?

Beauty: What Is It?

If the full experience of beauty is unique to human beings, what exactly is *beauty*? Plato (427?–347? B.C.), writing in the fifth century B.C., regarded beauty (along with truth, love, goodness, justice, and so on) as an active force in the universe. For him, it was an aspect of the ideal and spiritual powers that propel reality (Angeles, 1991: 24). The degree to which an object had this property determined how beautiful it was.

Most people today would not go as far as Plato in attributing beauty solely to a "real" quality possessed by objects, being more inclined to attribute some major portion of this exalted experience to the propensities of the viewer, an interaction, as with our concept of art quality, between object and viewer. We are reminded of an anecdote we once heard involving the well-known anthropologist Margaret Mead that illustrates this object/viewer interaction. It seems Dr. Mead and a native were out hiking one morning in the mountains on the native's South Pacific homeland. While trudging up a hill they came to a spot that presented a magnificent vista of a mist-filled valley and more mountains in the distance. "Oh! Isn't that beautiful," Dr. Mead exclaimed. "Yes," said the native, "I'm going to remember where that nest of bees is located. I'll get some honey there" he said, pointing to a nearby beehive. Dr. Mead and her native companion both saw beauty in the situation, but they weren't talking about the same scene.

There is a sense whereby beauty might be more possessed by an object than our anecdote from Dr. Mead suggests. Mathematicians and physicists often speak of *mathematical beauty* in their motivations and use it as a heuristic tool in their search for mathematical proof and physical laws. Harking back to Occam's razor—the principle of the preference of simplicity and economy in an explanation—an elegant and tidy proof or equation for a physical law is much preferred to one that is unruly and said to be "ugly." In mathematics and physics an ugly, or even homely, equation is probably one that is either incomplete or wrong, unlikely to be included in the high pantheon of mathematical truths that describe the true structure of the world.

Paul Dirac, one of the most able and well-known physicists of this century, was famous for being motivated by considerations of mathematical beauty. It may well be that many things human beings perceive as beautiful, from scenic vistas to works of art as different as poems, dances, and film, possess structures that reflect or are similar to structures that are in some way fundamental to the nature of the world we human beings occupy, the physical world, our social world, or the world of our mental interior. The elegance of a physicist's equation, one could argue, is more than just a pretty construction of the human mind. Paul Dirac's beautiful equations are not just beautiful to the physicist, they work in the "real world," where the rubber meets the road. The fact that you can turn on your television set and see a picture argues strongly there is some as yet poorly understood relationship between mathematical beauty—and perhaps other forms of beauty—and the deep structure of the universe. As they say, "Scratch a mathematician and you'll find a Platonist." Perhaps there are instances in film or other art forms where craft has been so deftly applied—as in the construction of an elegant mathematical equation—that the deep structure of the universe has been tapped into, perhaps as in a paleolithic ivory carving or a Dutch master's still life, a *Pietà* of Michelangelo, or a scene from *Citizen Kane* or series of cuts from *Doctor Zhivago* or *City Lights*.

The overwhelming majority of instances of the beauty we experience seem to have a more mundane explanation. Beauty is an interaction between an object (natural or human made) and the perceiver, specifically the perceiver's neurobiology. Culture and our experience—that is to say, learning—dictate in large measure what we experience as beautiful, but the experience itself is steered by our biology. The capacity for experiencing beauty is inbuilt in our brains and nervous systems. Genetic evolution has programmed us with the predisposition to view selected things in the environment as beautiful, while other categories are excluded.

For example, we appear to be equipped innately to perceive beauty in others, especially in women. It has been recognized since the nineteenth century that photographic composites, or blends, of a number of faces are likely to be judged more attractive than most of the individual faces that went into the blend. Recently researchers in Britain and Japan made composites of the faces of both British and Japanese women. They then made composites of the faces of only those women from the two groups with the highest attractiveness ratings. Then they made a third composite, a caricature really, exaggerating the distinctive attributes between the second (more attractive) and first (average) composites. Both men and women in those nations judged the first composite attractive, the second more attractive, and the third composite even more so. The procedure was repeated making composites of Caucasian men's faces, with similar results, except that the caricatures were not preferred. The authors suggest that highly attractive faces are systematically different in shape from the average, and perhaps attractive facial features may signal sexual maturity and fertility, emotional responsiveness or a "cuteness" such as found in the young that elicits protectiveness (Perrett, May, and Yoshikawa, 1994: 241). Women, and to a lesser extent men, with relatively high cheekbones, thin jaws, relatively large eyes, and a shorter distance between mouth and chin and nose and chin tended to be seen as more attractive. Apparently, we are to some degree hard-wired to perceive these features in others as attractive. As Nancy L. Etcoff, a neuropsychologist at Harvard Medical School in Boston is quoted as saying, "the assumption that beauty is an arbitrary cultural convention may simply not be true" (Bower, 1994: 182).

Beauty and the great efforts to which people go to appear attractive may be related to what biologists call a *supernormal stimulus*, which Wilson defines as "the preference during communication for signals that exaggerate the norms even if they rarely occur in nature" (1998: 231). The silver-washed fritillary is a silver-dappled orange butterfly found in cleared woodlands from Western Europe to Japan. Males of this species instinctively recognize females by their unique color and flight movements and chase them. But males are even more attracted to models that flap their wings and feature "the biggest, brightest, and most rapidly moving wings" (Wilson, 1998: 231). Although no such super-females in the human species exist, the males prefer an idealized form. Wilson suggests something analogous to the male silver-washed fritillary may be going on in human males when women paint their faces to make the eyes appear larger, the lips redder and larger, and the skin smoother. Perhaps, he suggests, we are only accentuating features we are innately attracted to. In most fertile women, the waist-to-hip ratio is between .67 and .80, in contrast to a ratio of between .80 and .95 in men, children, and postmenopausal women. Research in most cultures has shown that a .70 or lower ratio is considered most attractive. This is the same proportion as the ideal of a woman with a 36-24-36 hourglass shape. Interestingly, as Steven Pinker points out, the Venus figurines carved by Upper Paleolithic hunters 20,000 or more years ago have the same proportions (Pinker, 1997: 485). When it comes to human female beauty, and presumably in male beauty also, there is a preferred geometry. Perhaps there is a preferred geometry expressed in most high-quality art.

Similarly, researchers have found people consistently show preferences when it comes to selecting the most desirable habitats or environments from a variety of choices. In this research, the human brain is regarded "as an evolved organ especially designed to analyze and respond appropriately to opportunities and constraints that existed in [our] ancestral environments" (Heerwagen and Orians, 1993: 139). Selection of a habitat, a place to explore, occupy, and attempt to survive in, appears to involve emotional responses to key features of the environment, with "positive" and "negative" feelings that lead to rejection, exploration, or settlement. High-quality habitats with ample opportunities for survival should evoke strong positive emotional responses, whereas poor habitats, where survival chances are slim, should evoke weaker or negative responses (Orians and Heerwagen, 1992: 555). Research shows that savanna-like environments are consistently preferred and are chosen by research subjects over other environments. Deserts are least preferred. In a savanna, presumably the environment where human beings evolved, a flat grassland with scattered trees offers views, ample opportunity for undetected exploration, and subsistence off a variety of foods found at ground level, in trees, and off animals living there. The fact that no other natural environment can compare in life-sustaining opportunities is believed to account for generalized positive bias in modern people for the savanna. Tree shapes characteristic of the savanna—low trunks (easy to climb) and broad canopies (more shelter)—were also most preferred (Heerwagen and Orians, 1993: 160). Dense forests where undetected danger may lurk and unpredictability abounds make us ill at ease. Plants constitute a vital part of a habitat, and the presence of flowers usually signals quality food resources. Flowers can be eaten and sometimes produce edible fruit; furthermore, they are a sign of a productive environment. Little wonder we respond to flowers so positively and find them beautiful.

The emotional responses evoked by paintings and photographs have been similarly studied. Those featuring a road winding around a hill and disappearing into the distance tend to evoke in us a sense of mystery, inviting exploration, telling us there is more to be learned: Where does the road lead? Paintings and photographs have been used to study what is believed to be our innate need to seek refuge and find shelter as night approaches. One study of the content of paintings of sunrises and sunsets showed that paintings of sunsets frequently contain high refuge symbolism—houses, churches, buildings in the foreground all providing a sense of shelter and safety from the night—in contrast to paintings of sunrises, where the majority had no refuge symbolism. Nighttime has long been a time for settling in and nesting for our species and its predecessors. Wandering about at night not properly sheltered increases the chances that, for that individual, morning will never come. Sunrise, when what lies ahead can be seen, has long been a time to get going and make something of the day (Heerwagen and Orians, 1993: 147–150).

Researchers such as Wilson and Pinker believe that the perception of the beautiful tends to center on situations or stimuli that in the evolutionary past have been associated with or conducive to health and safety—that is to say, survival—and opportunities for reproduction. Such conditions tend to activate the neurobiology substrates that underlie the experience of the beautiful. Because beauty is associated with survival and reproduction, it is an attractant. We desire to move closer to it, enfold it, incorporate it into ourselves, and preserve it. (The effort to preserve beauty explains why we take so many photographs that usually turn out badly—because of the desire to hold on to and preserve a beautiful, healthful situation or scene.) Beauty produces pleasure, and pleasure equates with survival. The ugly and grotesque, the malformed, the disharmonic, the malproportioned, constitute threats to survival evolutionarily speaking and lead to an absence of opportunities for reproduction. We shun such situations and ordinarily avoid them because they produce unpleasant feelings and mental pain. A little of the ugly or disharmonic can be incorporated into the structure of a work of art—or life—for richness or a desired effect but, like disharmonic notes in a melody, a little ordinarily goes a long way.

The emotions and feelings associated with the experience of beauty, and its close cousins awe, the sublime, ecstasy, and enchantment, lie at the heart of aestheticism and art. These emotions also lie, as noted above, at the heart of religion, and the two likely owe their origins to the same emotional wellsprings. There is no evidence that these emotions are found in any well-developed form in other animals as a major component of their mental life. They are more or less unique to humans. The appreciation of beauty and awe are supreme human traits. And art, anchored as it is in beauty and its allied emotions, is a supreme human accomplishment.

The human brain is filled with circuitry that provides us with the capacity and predisposition to view certain stimuli in selected emotional terms. Herein lies the basis of the experience of the beautiful and other emotions. Great artists, knowingly or not, utilized these predispositions to orchestrate a viewer's response to their works. The more an artist is able to connect a work of art with these ancient response patterns, the more enthusiastic his or her audience over the generations is likely to be. In a very real sense, great art is closely connected to and derives from our species' history.

On the Innate Attraction to Beauty

Edward O. Wilson has proposed that human beings have an innate emotional affiliation for other living organisms. He calls this emotion and its accompanying set of behaviors *biophilia*, and he believes it is a part of "ultimate human nature" (Wilson, 1993: 31). We propose that as with biophilia, human beings also have an innate affiliation for that which is beautiful and, just as moths fly toward the light and birds migrate in their season, we are innately predisposed to experience emotions and feelings associated with beauty and to seek out and acquire the beautiful, as if to make beauty a part of ourselves. Like biophilia, "beautyphilia" is a part of ultimate human nature.

These thoughts on the origins of art and the human mind are admittedly speculative but in their larger configuration are grounded in anthropological and biological fact. Regardless of their ultimate validity, we hope they illustrate how deeply and how long human beings have been enmeshed with their art and how very important it is to us and how very unwise it is for some to criticize, marginalize, and completely privatize its production. We hope these thoughts will prove to be of use to others in investigating such matters.

Directors' Choice

Watching Emotions of Others

Human beings are innately predisposed to respond to the expressed emotions of other human beings and, to a lesser extent, animals. When someone in our presence expresses an emotion of any kind—joy, fear, anger, sadness—it is typically very difficult for us to remain neutral and uninvolved. The expression of emotion is a form of communication with deep evolutionary roots and ordinarily involves information that pertains in one way or another to survival and reproduction. Neighbors of our ancestors who didn't respond to the emotions of others probably didn't have as many opportunities to become our ancestors. And it doesn't matter a whole lot whether the emotions expressed by others are the real thing or faked, so long as they seem real. This is the basis of acting and the theater.

The existence of pictures—that is to say, drawings, reproductions, or photographs—is a relatively new feature of the human environment. The first known "real" drawings appeared only about 35,000 years ago on cave walls in Europe.[1] The first method for taking photographs is only just over 150 years old. In a very significant sense, as far as the human mind is concerned, what is portrayed in a photograph or moving picture can be just as real as the real thing. A film of waves crashing on a beautiful seashore can produce many of the same emotions as viewing a real seashore. Watching people express emotions on film can be as emotional for the viewer as watching them in real life. Because we are evolutionarily mentally programmed to respond to the emotions of others, we respond to people expressing emotions in pictures and on film much as we would to them in the flesh. This is the true basis of the power of film to evoke

---

[1] Crude scratchings on a rock of what appears to be the back of a woman's head and arms were recently found in Israel, dating from 250,000 years ago (Bower, April 11, 1998: 238). The scratchings, however, are extremely crude and considerable imagination must be used to see the form as a woman. It is really more of a Rorschach test from the Paleolithic. A plaque made of polished mammoth tooth with crevices filled with red ochre has been found in Hungary that is 50,000 to 100,000 years old. A piece of flint with concentric arches incised on it is 54,000 years old (Appenzeller, 1998: 1453). The latter two artifacts could be the work of some of the first true human artists as we would define them.

emotions in us. The same is true of theater, paintings, and sculptures and their power to evoke our emotions. In poetry and literature, reading about people expressing emotions or even discussing emotions in the abstract can arouse an emotional response in us.

In fact, we have become so accustomed to watching the images of others emoting on film (or television) and responding to their emotions that many people often find themselves preferring, as playwright/actor Sam Shepard says, "the image to the human being" (Shepard, 1998).

Emotion helps explain our fascination with celebrities—in this case, movie, TV, and entertainment personalities. Celebrities are people with whom we emote on the silver screen or television tube. In our evolutionary past we emoted primarily, in most cases almost exclusively, with those in our small band or village. Mentally, celebrities are members of our village. We are genetically programmed to take an interest in those in our village—it was beneficial for survival. We bond with people with whom we emote; it doesn't matter if the emotion is only via the television tube or movie screen. We bond with celebrities, even though there is no reciprocation. And we identify with films because they contain a magical blend of emotion—awe, the sublime, ecstasy, and enchantment—and effective presentation through craft.

AFTERWORD

Commercial Applications

Our research suggests that each individual has a unique Aesthetic Emotion/Feelings Sensation Potential Profile (Aesthetic Potential Profile, or APP), a pattern or array of emotions, feelings, and sensations that is most likely to be elicited in a range of aesthetic contexts. Profiles can be specific for specific art forms—for instance, a different profile for movies versus paintings may exist in the same individual. We believe that individual profiles exist and can be described empirically; they are probably relatively stable over time and probabalistic in their elicitation. In practice we assess and make judgments concerning the APPs of others all the time. We say, "I know Joe will love this movie," or "I don't think Sue would like that film; it's not her type." We all understand that some people are softies for films that evoke romantic emotions and feelings, while others prefer to be terrorized, still others are most "turned on" by action and special effects, and some get their kicks from more cerebral films.

Communities and subgroups within a community also possess Aesthetic Potential Profiles. Many women, for instance, prefer films with romantic themes; boys like high action films; people with high education levels are more likely to patronize low-budget art films, to cite three well-known examples. Group profiles can be empirically described in the same way they are for individuals. Group differences occur with age, education, and income level *as well as many other social and psychological variables that can be defined through further research*. Nations and cultures also exhibit macro APPs in the same way as do individuals and groups. What deeply pleases one macro group may leave another unmoved, even offended.

Individual films may also be described in terms of their unique Aesthetic Potential Profiles and their potential to evoke emotions in an individual, group, or nation. A film's aesthetic potential can be matched with the aesthetic profile of candidate audiences at any stage of the filmmaking process from script through marketing. Individual artists, insofar as they have their own detectable style, will also elicit their own Aesthetic Potential Profiles in selected audiences. The APP of a Hitchcock film differs from that of a Chaplin film as a Norman Rockwell painting differs from that of a Jackson Pollack painting. The profile of a Woody Allen film likely evokes an identifiable APP in a range of audiences that will vary from the patterns evoked by a John Ford or Henry Jaglom film. The same is true for actors: Clint Eastwood's Aesthetic Potential Profile differs from Al Pacino's, Michelle Pfeiffer's, or Meryl Streep's. As with individual, group, and national profiles, the APP evoked by an artist's work is empirically describable and probabalistic in its occurrence.

We believe great potential exists for using APP theory to both understand film aesthetics and to make and market movies.

Gore Vidal, one of our most gifted writers and thinkers, once said that as he moved, he hoped graciously, toward the door marked "Exit," it occurred to him that the only thing he ever really liked to do was go to the movies. As we move toward the exit, we think we know what he means.

Bibliography

Abbate, Ernesto, et al., "A One-Million-Year-Old *Homo* Cranium from the Danakil (Afar) Depression of Eritrea." *Nature*, Vol. 393, June 4, 1998, pp. 458–460.

Amberg, George. *The New York Times Film Reviews: A One-Volume Selection 1913–1970*. Arno Press, published in cooperation with Quadrangle Books, Inc., 1971.

Angeles, Peter A. *Dictionary of Philosophy*, New York: Harper Perennial, 1991. First published 1981 by Harper Collins.

Appenzeller, Tim. "Art: Evolution or Revolution." *Science*, Vol. 282, November 20, 1998, pp. 1451–1454.

A. W. "Astor Offers 'On the Waterfront.'" *New York Times*. July 29, 1954. Reprinted in: *The New York Times at the Movies*, Arleen Keylin and Christine Bent, eds. New York: Arno Press, 1979, p. 156.

Bogdanovich, Peter. *Who the Devil Made It: Conversations with Legendary Film Directors*. New York: Ballantine Books, 1997.

Bower, B. "Facial Beauty May Lie More Than Skin Deep." *Science News*, Vol. 145, March 19, 1994, p. 182.

———. "Cutting-Edge Pursuits in Stone Age." *Science News*, Vol. 153, April 11, 1998, p. 238.

———. "Ancient Skull Fills Big Fossil Gap." *Science News*, Vol. 153, June 6, 1998, p. 356.

Canby, Vincent. "The French Connection." *New York Times*. October 8, 1971. Reprinted in *The New York Times at the Movies*, Arleen Keylin and Christine Bent, eds. New York: Arno Press, 1979, p. 81.

———. "'Kane' at 50 Dazzles Yet with Its High Spirits." *New York Times*. April 28, 1991.

Cannon, Terry. "Dumping Guilt on Innocent Victims." *People's World*, September 8, 1979, p. 10.

"Cashiers du Cinema." 1964 interview with Orson Welles that appeared in *The Great American Films*, Los Angeles County Art Museum, November 15, 1973.

Corliss, Richard. "A Masterpiece Restored to the Screen." *Time*, February 6, 1989.

Crowther, Bosley. "Casablanca, with Humphrey Bogart and Ingrid Bergman." *New York Times*, November 27, 1942. Reprinted in *The New York Times at the Movies*, Arleen Keylin and Christine Bent, eds. New York: Arno Press, 1979, p. 47.

Dennell, Robin. "The World's Oldest Spears." *Nature*, Vol. 385, February 27, 1997, pp. 767–768.

Director's Guild of America Directory of Members. Director's Guild of America, Inc. Los Angeles, CA, 1993, 1992.

Dreifus, Claudia. "She Talks to Apes and, According to Her, They Talk Back." *New York Times*, April 14, 1998.

Eccles, John C. *Evolution of the Brain: Creation of the Self*. New York: Routledge, 1991.

Firth, Raymond. "Art and Anthropology." Pp. 15–39 in *Anthropology, Art, and Aesthetics*, Jeremy Coote and Anthony Sheldon, eds. Originally published in 1992, reprinted 1995. Oxford: Clarendon Press.

French, Philip. "The World's Favorite Citizen." *Observer* (London), July 7, 1991.

Friedkin, William. "Anatomy of a Chase." *Action*, March-April 1972, pp. 8–10, 18,19.

Giannetti, Louis. *Understanding Movies*. Englewood Cliffs, NJ: Prentice-Hall, Inc., 1990.

Gibbons, Ann. "Solving the Brain's Energy Crisis." *Science*, Vol. 280, May 29, 1998, pp. 345–347.

Glaser, Barney and Anselm L. Strauss. *The Discovery of Grounded Theory: Strategies for Qualitative Research*. Hawthorne, NY: Aldine de Gruyter, 1967.

Gold, Richard. "AFIs Restored 'Lawrence' Touted by H'w'd Heavies." *Variety*, December 15, 1988.

Greenway, John. *Literature Among the Primitives*. Hatboro, PA: Folklore Associates, 1964.

Harmetz, Aljean. "You Must Remember This." *New York Times*, April 5, 1992.

Heerwagen, Judith H. and Gordon H. Orians. "Humans, Habitats, and Aesthetics." Pp. 138–172 in *The Biophelia Hypothesis*, Stephen R. Kellart and Edward O. Wilson, eds. Washington, D.C.: Inland Press/Shearwater Books, 1993.

Hubbert, Steve. Personal communication, 1998.

Bibliography

Hunter, Allan. (ed.). *Movie Classics*. New York: Chambers, 1992.

Katz, Ephriam. *The Film Encyclopedia*. New York: Harper & Row, 1979.

Kock, Howard. "Casablanca? They'll Play It Forever, Sam." *Screen Actor*, Spring 1986, p. 31.

Konigsberg, Ira. *The Compleat Film Directory*. New York: Meridian Book, New American Library. 1987.

Mayer, David. *Eisenstein's Potemkin: A Shot-by-Shot Presentation*. New York: Grossman Publishers, 1972.

McBride, Joseph. "Wise Move Raises 'Kane' for Viewers." *Variety*, May 1, 1991.

McCracken, Michael J. Personal communication. 1998.

Menand, Louis. "What Is 'Art'?" *The New Yorker*, February 9, 1998, pp. 39–41.

Miller, Frank. *Casablanca: As Time Goes By: 50th Anniversary Commemorative*. Atlanta: Turner Publishing Inc. 1992.

Mlot, Christine. "Probing the Biology of Emotion." *Science*, Vol. 280, May 15, 1998, pp. 1005–1007.

"The 100 Best Movies." *Newsweek* Extra. Summer 1998.

Orians, Gordon H. and Judith H. Heerwagen. "Evolved Responses to Landscape." Pp. 555–598 in *The Adapted Mind: Evolutionary Psychology and the Generation of Culture*, Jerome H. Barkow, Leda Cosmides, and John Tooby, eds. New York: Oxford University Press, 1992.

Ornstein, Robert. *The Evolution of Consciousness*. New York: Prentice Hall Press, 1991.

Perrett, D. I., K. A. May, and S. Yoshikawa. "Facial Shape and Judgements of Female Attractiveness." *Nature*, Vol. 368, March 17, 1994, pp. 239–242.

Pert, Candace B. *Molecules of Emotion*. New York: Scribner. 1997.

Piazza, Alberto. "Towards a Genetic History of China." *Nature*, Vol. 395, October 15, 1998, pp. 636–639.

Pinker, Steven. *How the Mind Works*. New York: W. W. Norton & Co., 1997.

Pollack, Sidney. Interview, Bravo Television Network. June 26, 1998.

Rebello, Stephen. *Alfred Hitchcock and the Making of* Psycho. New York: Harper Perennial, 1991.

Schulberg, Bud. "You Was My Bruthah, Charlie." *GQ*, October 1994, pp. 240–245.

Shepard, Sam. "Sam Shepard: Stalking Himself." PBS documentary aired July 8, 1998.

Stringer, Christopher, and Clive Gamble. *In Search of the Neanderthals: Solving the Puzzle of Human Origins*. New York: Thames and Hudson, 1995.

Tattersall, Ian. *Becoming Human: Evolution and Human Uniqueness*. New York: Harcourt Brace & Co., 1998.

Vidal, Gore. *Screening History*. Cambridge, MA: Harvard University Press, 1992.

———. Interview with Charlie Rose, PBS television, April 12, 1998.

Wagner, Richard. *On Music and Drama*. Albert Goldman and Evert Sprinchorn, eds., translated by H. Ashton Ellis. Lincoln: University of Nebraska Press, 1992.

Wilson, Edward O. *Consilience: The Unity of Knowledge*. New York: Alfred A. Knopf, 1998.

———. "Biophilia and the Conservation Ethic." Pp. 31–69 in *The Biophilia Hypothesis*, Stephen R. Kellert and Edward O. Wilson, eds., Washington, D.C.: Inland Press/ Shearwater Books, 1993.

Wollen, Peter. *Singin' in the Rain*. London: BFI Publishing, British Film Institute, 1992.

APPENDIX A

The Questionnaire and Letter

Copies of the cover letter and accompanying questionnaire mailed to the directors in this research.

February 3, 1994

FILM AESTHETICS
3930 South Swenson Street • Suite 810 • Las Vegas, NV 89119
(702) 735-4988

Mr. ▓▓▓▓▓▓▓▓▓▓

Dear Mr. ▓▓▓▓▓:

Film Aesthetics is a research effort by a small group of film and social science professionals to better understand the art of film making. One aspect of this research is to compile a list of "great" scenes from films. Since the director's role — more than any other — is central to film making, we believe that directors offer a unique and especially valuable perspective on quality and greatness in films. We are therefore asking a random sample of directors who are members of the Directors Guild of America to nominate great scenes from the movies for further analysis.

On the following page, please nominate up to 10 movie scenes that you consider the "greatest," "most memorable," or "most distinguished." It is not necessary to rank the scenes on your list. Please identify the scene by giving the title of the film, a brief description of the scene, and major reasons for your selection. We use the word scene to mean the following:

"A section of a motion picture which is unified as to time and place . . . made up from a series of shots of varying angles . . . " (Ephraim Katz, *The Film Encyclopedia*. New York: Harper and Row, 1979)

"A unified action within the film's plot that normally takes place in a single location and in a single period of time." (Ira Konigsberg, *The Complete Film Dictionary*. New York: Penguin Books U.S.A., 1987)

"An imprecise unit of film, composed of a number of interrelated shots, unified usually by a central concern — a location, an incident, or a minor dramatic climax." (Louis Giannetti, *Understanding Movies*, fifth edition, Englewood Cliffs, NY: Prentice Hall, 1990)

We know your time is valuable and appreciate your help.

Sincerely yours,

Robert D. McCracken, Ph.D.
Principal Investigator

February 3, 1994

Dear Mr. ▓▓▓▓▓:

We understand your time is valuable. We are willing to send you a $20 bill by return mail if you will thoughtfully complete this questionnaire and return it.

Yours truly,

Robert D. McCracken, Ph.D.

FILM AESTHETICS

I. Greatest Scenes

#	Title of Film	Scene	Reasons
1.			
2.			
3.			
4.			
5.			
6.			
7.			
8.			
9.			
10.			

II. Greatest Single Shot

Please also select one or two of your candidates for the greatest single shot (a single camera setup) in the history of film and reasons for your choice.

#	Title of Film	Shot	Reasons
1.			
2.			

Additional Comments:

I give permission for the authors of this research to quote me in scholarly work on this research.
☐ Yes   ☐ No

I would like to be informed of the results of this survey.
☐ Yes   ☐ No

(Please print)
Name _____
Address: _____
_____

FILM AESTHETICS

APPENDIX B
Great Directors

Director/ Films/Great scene nominations	Total number of films with great scenes listed	Total number of great scenes nominations
W. Allen	9	15
Annie Hall (1977) 3		
Broadway Danny Rose (1984) 1		
Husbands and Wives (1992) 1		
Love and Death (1975) 1		
Manhattan (1979) 4		
Purple Rose of Cairo (1985) 1		
Radio Days (1987) 1		
Sleeper (1973) 1		
Zelig (1983) 1		
R. Altman	4	16
McCabe & Mrs. Miller (1971) 3		
Nashville (1975) 2		
The Player (1992) 10		
Short Cuts (1993) 1		
R. Attenborough	3	3
A Bridge Too Far (1977) 1		
Gandhi (1982) 1		
Shadowlands (1994) 1		

Directors' Choice

Director/ Films/Great scene nominations	Total number of films with great scenes listed	Total number of great scenes nominations
I. Bergman *Persona* (1966) 1 *The Seventh Seal* (1957) 1 *Wild Strawberries* (1957) 1	3	3
B. Bertolucci *The Conformist* (1970) 1 *The Last Emperor* (1987) 1 *The Last Tango in Paris* (1972) 2	3	4
F. Capra *Arsenic & Old Lace* (1944) 1 *It Happened One Night* (1934) 1 *It's A Wonderful Life* (1946) 4 *Mr. Smith Goes to Washington* (1939) 2 *State of the Union* (1948) 1	5	9
C. Chaplin *City Lights* (1931) 6 *The Gold Rush* (1925) 13 *The Great Dictator* (1940) 6 *The Kid* (1921) 2 *Modern Times* (1936) 1 *The Tramp* (1915) 1	6	29
F. F. Coppola *Apocalypse Now* (1979) 23 *The Conversation* (1974) 1 *The Cotton Club* (1984) 1 *The Godfather* (1972) 14 *The Godfather, Part II* (1974) 3	5	42
M. Curtiz *Adventures of Robin Hood* (1938) 2 *Casablanca* (1942) 30 *Yankee Doodle Dandy* (1942) 1	3	33

Appendix B: Great Directors

Director/ Films/Great scene nominations	Total number of films with great scenes listed	Total number of great scenes nominations
V. De Sica	4	6
Bicycle Thief (1948) 2		
Shoeshine (1946) 1		
Two Women (1960) 1		
Umberto D (1952) 2		
Disney Studios	3	7
Bambi (1942) 3		
Fantasia (1940) 3		
Lady and the Tramp (1955) 1		
B. Edwards	4	4
The Pink Panther (1964) 1		
A Shot in the Dark (1964) 1		
S.O.B. (1981) 1		
Victor/Victoria (1982) 1		
S. Eisenstein	3	19
Alexander Nevsky (1938) 3		
The Battleship Potemkin (1925) 14		
Ivan the Terrible (1945) 2		
F. Fellini	7	12
Amarcord (1973) 1		
And the Ship Sails On (1983) 1		
8½ (1963) 5		
Fellini's Roma (1972) 1		
La Dolce Vita (1959) 2		
Nights of Cabiria (1956) 1		
Satyricon (1969) 1		
J. Ford	9	18
The Grapes of Wrath (1940) 3		
How Green Was My Valley (1941) 1		
The Hurricane (1937) 1		
The Informer (1935) 3		
The Man Who Shot Liberty Valance (1962) 1		

Directors' Choice

Director/ Films/Great scene nominations	Total number of films with great scenes listed	Total number of great scenes nominations

J. Ford (continued)
    The Quiet Man (1952) 4
    The Searchers (1956) 3
    She Wore a Yellow Ribbon (1949) 1
    Stagecoach (1939) 1		

H. Hawks
    The Big Sleep (1946) 1
    Red River (1948) 1
	3	3

A. Hitchcock
    The Birds (1963) 1
    Foreign Correspondent (1940) 1
    The Lady Vanishes (1938) 1
    North by Northwest (1959) 5
    Notorious (1946) 3
    Psycho (1960) 22
    Rear Window (1954) 2
    Rebecca (1940) 1
    Rope (1948) 1
    Saboteur (1942) 1
    Strangers on a Train (1951) 3
    The 39 Steps (1935) 3
    Vertigo (1958) 2
	13	46

J. Huston
    The African Queen (1951) 2
    Key Largo (1948) 2
    Maltese Falcon (1941) 3
    The Man Who Would Be King (1975) 2
    The Treasure of the Sierra Madre (1948) 11
	5	20

E. Kazan
    On the Waterfront (1954) 13
    A Streetcar Named Desire (1951) 1
    Viva Zapata (1952) 1
	3	15

Appendix B: Great Directors

Director/ Films/Great scene nominations	Total number of films with great scenes listed	Total number of great scenes nominations
S. Kubrick	6	33

    A Clockwork Orange (1971) 2
    Dr. Strangelove or: How I Learned to Stop Worrying and Love the Bomb (1964) 7
    The Killing (1956) 1
    Paths of Glory (1957) 3
    The Shining (1980) 1
    2001: A Space Odyssey (1968) 19

A. Kurosawa	5	8

    Kagemusha (1980) 1
    Ran (1985) 1
    Rashomon (1950) 1
    The Seven Samurai (1954) 3
    Throne of Blood (1957) 2

D. Lean	7	28

    The Bridge on the River Kwai (1957) 6
    Brief Encounter (1945) 1
    Doctor Zhivago (1965) 3
    Great Expectations (1946) 1
    In Which We Serve (1942) 1
    Lawrence of Arabia (1962) 15
    This Happy Breed (1944) 1

S. Lumet	3	4

    Network (1976) 2
    The Pawnbroker (1965) 1
    Serpico (1973) 1

L. McCarey	3	3

    An Affair to Remember (1956) 1
    The Awful Truth (1937) 1
    Duck Soup (1933) 1

Directors' Choice

Director/ Films/Great scene nominations	Total number of films with great scenes listed	Total number of great scenes nominations

R. Polanski
    Chinatown (1974) 1
    Repulsion (1965) 2
    The Tenant (1976) 1
	3	4

R. Reiner
    A Few Good Men (1992) 2
    The Princess Bride (1987) 1
    When Harry Met Sally (1989) 4
	3	7

J. Renoir
    French Can-Can (1954) 1
    The Grand Illusion (1937) 6
    The Rules of the Game (1939) 2
	3	9

A. Resnais
    Hiroshima Mon Amour (1959) 4
    Night and Fog (1956) 2
    Stavisky (1973) 1
	3	7

M. Scorsese
    Cape Fear (1991) 2
    The Color of Money (1986) 2
    Good Fellas (1990) 4
    Raging Bull (1980) 9
    Taxi Driver (1976) 5
	5	22

R. Scott
    Alien (1979) 3
    Someone to Watch Over Me (1987) 1
    Thelma and Louise (1991) 1
	3	5

S. Spielberg
    Close Encounters of the Third Kind (1977) 6
    Empire of the Sun (1987) 1
    E.T., The Extra-Terrestrial (1982) 7
    Indiana Jones and the Last Crusade (1989) 1
	9	43

Appendix B: Great Directors

Director/ Films/Great scene nominations	Total number of films with great scenes listed	Total number of great scenes nominations

S. Spielberg (continued)
  Indiana Jones and the Temple of Doom (1984) 1
  Jaws (1975) 6
  Jurassic Park (1993) 1
  Raiders of the Lost Ark (1981) 4
  Schindler's List (1993) 16		

G. Stevens
  Giant (1956) 1
  Gunga Din (1939) 2
  A Place in the Sun (1951) 4
  Shane (1953) 6
  Swing Time (1936) 2
	5	15

F. Truffaut
  Day for Night (1973) 2
  The 400 Blows (1959) 3
  Jules and Jim (1961) 1
  Mississippi Mermaid (1968) 1
	4	7

O. Welles
  Citizen Kane (1941) 31
  The Lady from Shanghai (1948) 3
  The Magnificent Ambersons (1942) 3
  Touch of Evil (1958) 4
  The Trial (1962) 1
	5	42

W. Wellman
  Nothing Sacred (1937) 1
  The Ox-Bow Incident (1943) 2
  The Public Enemy (1931) 1
  Wings (1927) 1
	4	5

B. Wilder
  The Apartment (1960) 1
  Double Indemnity (1944) 2
  Some Like It Hot (1959) 2
  Sunset Boulevard (1950) 4
	4	9

Directors' Choice

Director/ Films/Great scene nominations	Total number of films with great scenes listed	Total number of great scenes nominations
R. Wise	5	6
The Haunting (1963) 1		
I Want to Live! (1958) 1		
The Sand Pebbles (1966) 1		
The Sound of Music (1965) 1		
West Side Story (1961) 2		
W. Wyler	9	19
Ben-Hur (1959) 7		
The Best Years of Our Lives (1946) 4		
Dodsworth (1936) 1		
Jezebel (1938) 2		
The Letter (1940) 1		
The Little Foxes (1941) 1		
Mrs. Miniver (1942) 1		
Roman Holiday (1953) 1		
Wuthering Heights (1939) 1		

APPENDIX C

Terms Participants Used to Connote Emotions, Feelings, and Sensations

The following list contains nearly 450 words gleaned from the responses to our survey that connote emotions, feelings, and sensations. The reader may not agree that all terms in this list connote emotions, feelings, and sensations sufficiently strongly to warrant inclusion here, but even if 50 or 100 terms were deleted, the list would still be lengthy. Either way, the list constitutes a virtual lexicon of emotion- and sensation-related terms and demonstrates the reliance directors made on the use of such terminology in describing why a film scene is great. It illustrates the kaleidoscope of emotions we all experience when viewing movies.

Directors' Choice

aching
admiration
adrenaline going
aesthetic
aesthetically
aesthetics
affected me
always remember
amazing
ambiance
anger
anguish
animal
anticipation
anxiety
archetypical
ardor
astonishing
atmosphere
attention
audacious behavior
audiences react
awe
awe-inspiring
awesome

baffled [me]
ballet
ballistic
bang [introduction with]
beaten [the Tramp]
beautiful
beauty
believable
bewilderment
bewitching
bizarre
blasting [sound of]
boggles the mind
breathing irregular
breathtaking

brutal
brutality
build [tension]
building [fear]
builds and builds
build up [tension]

calm
can't be forgotten
catharsis
cathartic
charisma
charm
charming
cheered
chilled
chilling
chills
choreographic [intensity of emotion]
claustrophobic
cold
compassion
compelling
conflicting [images]
confusion
continues in minds
convinced
convincing
courage
crackling
craziness
crying

danger
dangerous
dangers
daring
dark
dazzle
deeply
delicacy

delight
depravity
desirable
desire
despair
desperate
desperation
devastating
dignified
disgust
doom
doomed [love]
draining
drama
dramatic
dramatically
dramatized
drawn [to Hopkins]
dread
dreamlike

edge-of-your-seat
eerie
eerily
ego
elated
electric
electrifying
elegance
elegant
eloquent
embarrassment
emotion
emotional
emotionally
emotions
engaging
entertaining
epiphanies
epiphany
erotic
eroticism

230

Appendix C: Terms Participants Used

esprit of soldiers
excitement
exciting
exhaustion
exhilarating
experience
experiencing
exploded
expressive
exquisite
eyes tear

fantasies
fantasy
farewell [emotional]
fascinating
fascination
fatigue
fear
fearless
fears
feel
feel good
feeling
feelings
felt
ferocity
fetishistic
forbidden
foreboding
freedom
fresh
frightening
frustration
fulfilling
fun
funny
futility

gams [beautiful]
gasp
gentle

giddy
glamor
glee
glorious
goose bumps
gore [graphic]
gorgeous
grace [and subtlety]
gratifying
greed
grief
grim
gripping
gruesome
gut-wrenching

happily
happy
hardly believe
haunting
hauntingly
hazardous
heart contract [makes]
heartbreak
heartbreaking
heartlessness
heart-wrenching
heat
heightened senses
helpfulness
heroic
honest
honesty
hope
hopeless
hopelessness
hoping
horrible
horrific
horrified
horrifying
horror

horrors
human
humanity [of characters]
hunger
hurtled and transformed
hurtles the viewer
hurts
hysteria

identified [with]
imagination [my]
imaginations [let our]
imagine
impact
impression
indelible
inhumanity
innocence
insanity
inspiration
inspirational
intense
intensely
intensifying
intensity
interesting
intimacy
intimate
intoxication
intriguing
involved
isolation

joy
joyful
joyous

kinesthesia

languorous

Directors' Choice

laughter	nostalgia	regret
lifting	nudity	rejected
loathsome		release
loneliness	opens my heart	relish
longing	otherness	repellant
looked	outrageous	repelled
lost	overwhelmed	repulsion
love	overwhelming	resentment
loving		revealing
lust	pain	revenge
lust/heat	painful	rigid [character]
	painfully	riveting
mad [men going]	panic	romance
mad Bolero	passion	romantic
madness	passionate	
magic	passions	sad
magical	pathos	sadness
manipulative	patriotic	satisfied
melodrama	physical effect	satisfying
memorable	physiologically	savage
memory	piercing	scare
menace	pitiable	scared
mesmerizing	poetic	scares
methedrine-like	poetry	scarier
mind	poignance	scaring
mind expansion	poignancy	scary
mind fills in the rest	poignant	scream
mind-numbing	power	screams
misanthropic	powerful	seductive
miserable	powerfully	sensation
misguidedness	powerless	sense
mood	powerlessness	senses
moods	pretty	sensitive
moved	pride	sensuous
moving	primal	sentimental
mystery	primal desire	sentimentality
	proud	separated forever
nail-biting	psychological	sex
nervously beating		sexiest
heart	rage	sexual
never forget	rawest	sexual sparring
nightmare	realization	sexy

Appendix C: Terms Participants Used

shamelessly
shock
shocked
shocker
shocking
slyest
smell
sobering
spectacle
spectacular
spirit broken
splendor
spooky
staggering
startled
startling
stays with you
sticks in mind
stifled
stirred
stirring
strength
striking
strong
stunned
stunning
stupidity
subconscious appeal
sublime
sublimely
subtlety
suggestion
surprise
surprises

surprising
surreal
surrender
suspend belief - disbelief
suspense
suspenseful
sweep [the viewer along]
sweet [love scene]
sympathetic
sympathy

taste
tastelessness
tear
tear-filled
tears
tender
tenderness
tense
tension
terrified
terrifying
terror
theatrics
threat
thrilling
tone
touching
touchingly
tragedy
tragic
transcendent

transports the audience
trapped
treat
turn-on

ugly
unbearable
unbelievable
uncontrolled
understand
understated
unexpected
unforgettable
unfulfillment
unpredictable
unsettling
urgency [sense of]

violence
violent
virtue
vulnerable

warm
wet my pants
wit
wittily
women in peril
wonder
wonderment
wrenching
wrought

zinger

Index

A

A Bout de Souffle. See: *Breathless*
Abrahams, Jim, 60
"Adagio," 96
Adlon, Percy, 67
Adventures of Robin Hood, The, 60, 222
Affair to Remember, An, 60, 225
African Queen, The, 34, 60, 224
Aguirre, the Wrath of God, 60
Airplane!, 60
Albinoni, 96
Aldrich, Robert, 160
Alexander Nevsky, 60–61, 223
Alien, 61–62, 226
All About Eve, 62
Allen, Woody, 4, 22, 24, 25, 35, 37, 63, 74, 107, 116, 117–118, 132, 133, 145, 162, 212, 221
All Quiet on the Western Front, 36, 62, 90
All That Jazz, 62
All That Money Can Buy, 62
Almodovar, Pedro, 162
Almond, Paul, 109
Altman, Robert, 24, 28, 42, 118, 121, 129, 143, 166, 221
Amadeus, 63
Amarcord, 63, 225
American in Paris, An, 63
And the Ship Sails On, 37, 63, 223

Andersson, Bibi, 127
Andrews, Dana, 70
Annie Hall, 63, 221
Antonioni, Michelangelo, 71
Apartment, The, 63, 227
Apocalypse Now, 3, 18, 20, 22, 30, 35, 52–53, 64–66, 169, 222
"April Come She Will," 103
Arau, Alfonso, 116
Aristotle, 173
Arlen, Dick, 161
Arsenic and Old Lace, 66, 222
Art, 165
Ashby, Hal, 69, 72
Asquith, Anthony, 74
Astaire, Fred, 74, 138, 149, 153
"As Time Goes By," 79
Astor, Mary, 117
Attenborough, Richard, 24, 73, 96, 142, 221
Au Revoir les Enfants, 66
Auntie Mame, 66
Austen, Mary, 169
Australopithecus spp., 177–181, 185, 189
Autant-Lara, Claude, 86
Avildsen, John, 137
Awful Truth, The, 66, 225
Axel, Gabriel, 67
Ayres, Lew, 36, 62

B

Babenco, Hector, 128
Babette's Feast, 67

Bacall, Lauren, 111
Bacon, Lloyd, 93
Bad Day at Black Rock, 67
Bad Lands, 67
Baghdad Cafe, 67
Baker, Joe Don, 80
Ballard, Carroll, 71
Bambi, 67, 223
Bancroft, Anne, 102
Bang the Drum Slowly, 67
Barrault, John-Louis, 80
Barron, Steven, 89
Barthelmess, Richard, 159
Battleship Potemkin, The, 3, 18, 19, 20, 22, 48–50, 68–69, 101, 159, 223
Beatty, Warren, 118
Beauty and the Beast, 69
"Begin the Beguine," 74
Being There, 69
Belmondo, Jean-Paul, 73
Ben-Hur, 20, 69, 101, 228
Benton, Robert, 129
Beresford, Bruce, 72
Bergen, Candace, 76
Bergman, Ingmar, 24, 127, 141, 161, 222
Bergman, Ingrid, 21, 56–58, 76–80, 123
Berkeley, Busby, 93, 163
Bernini, Gian, 169
Bernstein, Leonard, 44
Berringer, Tom, 146
Bertolucci, Bernardo, 24, 85, 113, 114, 222
Besson, Luc, 113
Best Years of Our Lives, The, 69–70, 228

Directors' Choice

Bicycle Thief, 70, 223
Biehn, Michael, 152
Big, 70
Big Sleep, The, 70, 224
Billy Jack, 70
Birds, The, 70, 224
Birth of a Nation, 71
Black Orpheus, 71
Black Stallion, The, 71
Black Stallion Returns, 71
Block, Robert, 53
Blockheads, 71
Blow-Up, 71
"Blue Danube," 21, 157
Blue Velvet, 72
Blystone, John, 71
Body Heat, 72
Bogart, Humphrey, 21, 29, 35, 56–58, 60, 70, 76–80, 111, 117, 154–155
Bogdanovich, Peter, 160
Bold and the Brave, The, 72
Bonnie & Clyde, 72, 162
Boom Town, 163
Boorman, John, 86
Borgnine, Ernest, 67
Bound for Glory, 72
Bozzuffi, Marcel, 47
Brando, Marlon, 18, 28, 35, 41, 43–44, 52, 98, 124–125, 148, 159
Brazil, 72
Breaker Morant, 72
Breathless, 73, 153
Brest, Martin, 139
Bridge on the River Kwai, The, 21, 36, 73, 225
Bridges at Toko-Ri, The, 73
Bridge Too Far, A, 73–74, 221
Brief Encounter, 74, 225
Broadway Danny Rose, 74, 221
Broadway Melody of 1940, The, 74
Brooks, Mel, 130, 162
Brooks, Richard, 108
Brown, Joe E., 145
Browning Version, The, 74
Bruckman, Clyde, 91, 97
Bujold, Genevieve, 109, 112
Bull Durham, 74
Bullitt, 74, 163
Buñuel, Luis, 158
Burr, Raymond, 135

Butch Cassidy and the Sundance Kid, 21, 74–75
"By a Waterfall," 93
Bye, Bye, Birdie, 75

C

Cabaret, 75
Cabeza de Vaca, 75–76
Cabiria. See: Nights of Cabiria
Caddyshack, 76
Caesar and Cleopatra, 76
Cagney, Jimmy, 33, 132, 160, 162
Caine Mutiny, The, 76
Caine, Michael, 118
Campion, Jane, 127
Camus, Marcel, 71
Canby, Vincent, 47
Cape Fear, 76, 226
Capra, Frank, 24, 66, 109, 120, 148, 222
Carey, Harry, 120
Carey, Timothy, 126
Carnal Knowledge, 76
Carné, Marcel, 80
Caron, Leslie, 63
Carpenter, John, 146
Carson, Jack, 117
Casablanca, 2, 3, 18, 20, 21, 22, 32, 37, 56–58, 76–80, 166, 167, 168, 222
Chandler, Jeff, 70
Chaplin, Charlie, 4, 20, 21, 23, 24, 29, 34, 83, 99–100, 104, 111, 120, 154, 163, 212, 222
Chariots of Fire, 80
Charley Varrick, 80
Chase, Chevy, 76
Chayevsky, Paddy, 121
Cher, 42
Cherrill, Virginia, 83
Children of Paradise, 80
Chinatown, 80, 226
Christie, Julie, 88, 118
Cimino, Michael, 86
Cinema Paradiso, 80
Citizen Kane, 2, 3, 18, 19, 20, 21, 28, 45–47, 80–83, 113, 130, 167, 168, 170, 227
City Lights, 20, 29, 83, 222
Clayton, Jack, 104, 132
Clément, René, 93

Clementi, Pierre, 85
Cleopatra, 83–84
Cliffhanger, 84
Clift, Montgomery, 21, 33, 128–129, 136
Clockwork Orange, A, 84, 225
Close Encounters of the Third Kind, 20, 84, 226
Clouzot, Henri-Georges, 87, 159
Coen, Joel, 120
Color of Money, The, 85, 226
Conformist, The, 85, 222
Connery, Sean, 118
Conrad, Joseph, 46, 52
Conversation, The, 71, 85, 222
Conway, Jack, 149
Coogan, Jackie, 111
Coolidge, Martha, 135
Cooper, Gary, 106, 130
Cooper, Merian, 112
Coppola, Carmine, 121
Coppola, Francis Ford, 4, 22, 23, 24, 35, 52–53, 64, 85, 97, 99, 127, 222
Cosmatos, George, 152
Costa-Gavras, Constantin, 162
Costner, Kevin, 74, 92
Cotten, Joseph, 80, 82, 151
Cotton Club, The, 85, 222
Court Jester, The, 85
Courtney, Tom, 89
Coward, Noel, 108, 151
Crichton, Charles, 114
Cro-Magnons, 192, 197
Crowther, Bosley, 57
Cruise, Tom, 85, 92
Crying Game, The, 85
Cukor, George, 100
Curtis, Tony, 146
Curtiz, Michael, 24, 32, 60, 76, 78, 162, 222
Cyrano de Bergerac, 85, 113

D

DaCosta, Morton, 66
Dalio, Marcel, 103
Dalva, Robert, 71
"Dance Chinoise," 91
Daniels, Jeff, 97, 132
"Danny Boy," 120
D'Antonio, Philip, 47
Darwell, Jane, 103

Index

Darwin, Charles, 173, 175, 188
da Vinci, Leonardo, 39
Davis, Andrew, 29, 96
Davis, Bette, 116
Davis, Brad, 35
Dawn, Marpessa, 71
Day for Night, 85–86, 227
Dean, James, 97
Dearden, James, 126
Death in Venice, 86
Death of a Salesman, 44
de Broca, Philippe, 112
Dee, Frances, 110
Deer Hunter, The, 86
Deliverance, 86
de Mille, Cecil B., 112, 150
Demme, Jonathan, 143
De Niro, Robert, 21, 76, 86, 99, 124, 134, 149–150
De Palma, Brian, 138, 158
Depardieu, Gérard, 85
Dern, Laura, 135
Descartes, René, 173
Deschanel, Caleb, 71, 121
De Sica, Vittorio, 24, 70, 143, 158, 223
Devil and Daniel Webster, The. See: All That Money Can Buy
Devil in the Flesh, 86
De Vito, Danny, 125
de Wilde, Brandon, 142
Diabolique, 87
Dieterle, William, 62, 111
Dirac, Pail, 202
Disney, Walt, 24, 91, 223
Dixon, Ivan, 123
Dr. Strangelove or, How I Learned to Stop Worrying and Love the Bomb, 20, 21, 35, 87, 225
Doctor Zhivago, 33, 40, 87–88, 225
Dodsworth, 88, 228
Donaldson, Roger, 123
Donat, Robert, 102, 151
Donen, Stanley, 51, 138, 144
Donner, Richard, 115, 116
Don't Look Now, 88
Do the Right Thing, 88
Double Indemnity, 37, 88, 227
Downhill Racer, 88
Dresser, The, 89

Dru, Joanne, 136
Dryopithecus, 177, 178, 180
Duck Soup, 89, 225
Dumont, Margaret, 122
Dunaway, Faye, 80, 151
Dunne, Irene, 66
Durante, Jimmy, 109
Duvall, Robert, 64–65
Duvall, Shelly, 142–143
Dwan, Allan, 137
Dymtryk, Edward, 76

E

East of Eden, 89
Eastwood, Clint, 108, 158, 175, 212
Echevarria, Nicholás, 75
Edwards, Blake, 24, 128, 138, 143, 159, 223
8½, 34, 89, 223
Eisenstein, Sergei, 24, 49–50, 60–61, 68, 109, 159, 223
Ekman, Paul, 201
Elam, Jack, 124
Electric Dreams, 89–90
Elephant Man, The, 33, 90
Eliot, T. S., 52
Elvira Madigan, 90
Empire of the Sun, 90, 226
Empire Strikes Back, The, 90
E.T., the Extra-Terrestrial, 20, 90–91, 226
Etcoff, Nancy L., 204
"Everybody Comes to Rick's," 58
Expression of Emotions in Man and Animals, The, 188

F

Fairbanks, Douglas, 105, 137
Falk, Peter, 130
Fantasia, 91, 223
Farrow, Mia, 133
Faulkner, William, 70
Feet First, 91–92
Fellini, Federico, 24, 34, 63, 89, 92, 112, 122, 223
Fellini's Roma, 92, 223
Few Good Men, A, 92, 226
Field of Dreams, 92
Fields, W. C., 109

Finch, Peter, 121
Finney, Albert, 41, 89, 152
Fisher King, The, 92
Fitzcarraldo, 92
Five Easy Pieces, 20, 92–93
Flaherty, Robert, 137
Fleming, Victor, 100, 161
Flynn, Errol, 60
Fonda, Henry, 103, 112, 117, 126
Fontaine, Joan, 105
Footlight Parade, 93
Forbidden Games, 93
Forbidden Planet, 93
Ford, Harrison, 29, 96, 161
Ford, John, 4, 23, 24, 103, 107, 108, 118, 133, 140–141, 142, 146, 212, 223
Foreign Correspondent, 93, 224
Forman, Milos, 63, 124
For Whom the Bell Tolls, 37, 93–94
Fosse, Bob, 62, 75
Foster, Jodie, 144
Foster, Lewis, 72
400 Blows, The, 94, 227
Frank, Melvin, 85
Frankenstein, 94
Frazer, James, 52
Frears, Stephen, 105
Freed, Arthur, 50
French Can-Can, 94, 226
French Connection, The, 3, 18, 20, 47–48, 94–95, 163
Fresnay, Pierre, 103
Freund, Karl, 120
Friedkin, William, 47–48, 94
From Here to Eternity, 95
Front Page, 95–96
Fugitive, The, 18, 19, 20, 29, 96

G

Gabin, Jean, 103
Gable, Clark, 162–163
Gallipoli, 96
Gance, Abel, 121
Gandhi, 96, 221
Garland, Judy, 33
Garson, Greer, 120
General, The, 97
Geronimi, Clyde, 113
Gershwin, George, 118

237

Gettysburg, 97
Giannini, Giancarlo, 141
Giant, 97, 227
Gibson, Mel, 137
Gilda, 97
Gilliam, Terry, 72, 92
Girl Can't Help It, The, 110
Gish, Dorothy, 125
Gish, Lillian, 125, 159
Glory, 97
Go-Between, The, 97
Godard, Jean-Luc, 93, 154
Godfather, The, 3, 21, 22, 32, 35, 97–99, 162, 222
Godfather II, 99, 222
Godfather III, 99
Gold Rush, The, 18, 20, 21, 22, 99–100, 154, 222
Gone with the Wind, 3, 19, 20, 21, 22, 100–102, 111
Goodbye Mr. Chips, 102
Good Fellas, 19, 22, 102, 226
"Good Morning," 145
Goulding, Edward, 135
Graduate, The, 102–103
Grand Illusion, 103, 226
Grant, Cary, 60, 66, 105, 122–123
Grapes of Wrath, The, 103–104, 223
Great Dictator, The, 20, 34, 104, 222
Great Expectations, 104, 225
Great Gatsby, The, 104
Greed, 105
Greenberg, Jerry, 46
Greenstreet, Sydney, 35, 117
Greer, Jane, 126
Grey, Joel, 75
Griffith, D. W., 71, 125, 159
Grifters, The, 105
Guinness, Alec, 21, 73
Gunga Din, 105, 227
Gwynne, Fred, 85

H

Haas, Lukas, 135
Hackman, Gene, 47–48, 72, 95, 123
Hamer, Robert, 112
Hamlet, 39, 105
Hancock, John, 67
Hand, David, 67
Hanussen, 105

Hardy, Oliver, 71
Harlin, Renny, 84
Haunting, The, 105, 228
Hawks, Howard, 24, 70, 136, 224
Heart of Darkness, 46, 52
Hedron, Tippi, 70
Heflin, Van, 142
Hemmings, David, 71
Henreid, Paul, 76, 79
Henry V, 21, 106
Hepburn, Audrey, 137
Hepburn, Katherine, 60, 148, 163
Herzog, Werner, 60, 92
Hess, Dame Myra, 116
Heston, Charlton, 42, 69, 150
"He Walks with Me," 129
High Noon, 21, 106
High Sierra, 106
Hill, George Roy, 74, 148
Hiroshima Mon Amour, 20, 106–107, 226
Hitchcock, Alfred, 2, 4, 22, 24, 27, 29, 54–56, 70, 93, 113, 122–123, 131, 135, 137, 138, 148, 151, 159, 170–171, 212, 224
Hoffman, Dustin, 29, 35, 102–103, 119, 153
Hoffman, John, 138
Holden, William, 73, 128
Holt, Tim, 29, 117, 154–155
Hominoidea, 177
Homo erectus, 178, 180, 182–185, 187, 191
Homo habilis, 178, 180–186, 191
Homo sapiens, 179, 180, 185, 191–194, 197
Homo sapiens sapiens, 179, 193–194, 196–197
Hopkins, Anthony, 21, 33, 90, 136, 142, 143–144
Hopper, Dennis, 72
Hopper, Tobe, 130
Hoskins, Bob, 85
How Green Was My Valley, 107, 223
Hudson, Hugh, 80
Hunter, Holly, 21, 127
Hunter, Jeffrey, 140
Hurricane, The, 107, 223
Hurt, Bill, 72

Hurt, John, 33, 90
Husbands and Wives, 107, 221
Huston, Angelica, 42, 105
Huston, John, 24, 29, 60, 111, 117, 118, 154, 224
Huston, Walter, 29, 62, 154–155

I

I Am a Fugitive from a Chain Gang, 107
Iceman, 174
Imitation of Life, 107
In Cold Blood, 108
Indiana Jones and the Last Crusade, 108, 226
Indiana Jones and the Temple of Doom, 108, 227
Informer, The, 108, 223
Ingram, Rex, 118
In the Line of Fire, 108
In the Name of the Father, 108
Invasion of the Body Snatchers, 32, 108
In Which We Serve, 108, 225
Isabel, 109
It Happened One Night, 109, 222
It's a Gift, 109
It's a Mad, Mad, Mad, Mad World, 109
It's a Wonderful Life, 109, 222
Ivan the Terrible, 109–110, 223
Ivory, James, 136
I Walked With a Zombie, 110
I Want to Live, 110, 228

J

Jackson, Wilfred, 112
Jaglom, Henry, 212
Jailhouse Rock, 110
Jamusch, Jim, 122
Jaws, 21, 110–111, 227
Jennings, Humphrey, 116
Jeux Interdits. See: Forbidden Games
Jewison, Norman, 125, 151
Jezebel, 111, 228
Joffe, Roland, 112
Jones, Tommy Lee, 29, 96
Jordan, Neil, 85

Index

"J. R.," 110
Juarez, 37, 111
Jules and Jim, 111, 227
Jurassic Park, 111, 227

K

Kadar, Jan, 143
Kagemusha, 111, 225
Kasdan, Lawrence, 72
Katzin, Lee, 115
Kaufman, Philip, 136
Kaye, Danny, 85
Kazan, Elia, 24, 44, 89, 124–125, 148, 159, 224
Keaton, Buster, 97
Keaton, Diane, 35, 63
Keighley, William, 60
Kelly, Gene, 18, 29, 50–52, 63, 144–145
Kelly, Grace, 135
Kerr, Deborah, 60, 95
Kershner, Irvin, 90
Key Largo, 111, 224
Kid, The, 111, 222
Killing, The, 111, 154, 225
Killing Fields, The, 112
Kilmer, Val, 152
Kind Hearts and Coronets, 112
King and I, The, 112
King Kong, 112
King of Hearts, 112
King of Kings, 112
King Solomon's Mines, 112
Kingsley, Ben, 126, 140
Kinski, Klaus, 60
Klein, Richard, 194
Klos, Elmo, 143
Koch, Howard, 58, 116
Kramer, Stanley, 109
Kubrick, Stanley, 4, 22, 24, 29, 35, 84, 87, 111, 126, 142, 156, 225
Kurosawa's Dreams, 112
Kurosawa, Akira, 24, 111, 112, 135, 141, 151, 225

L

Ladd, Alan, 142
La Dolce Vita, 112–113, 223
Lady and the Tramp, 113, 223
Lady Eve, The, 113
Lady from Shanghai, 113, 227

Lady Vanishes, The, 113, 224
La Femme Nikita, 113
Lamar, Hedy, 56
LaMotta, Jake, 133
Lancaster, Burt, 95
Landers, Lew, 67
Lang, Fritz, 116, 119
Lang, Walter, 112
La Régle du Jeu. See: Rules of the Game, The
Last Emperor, The, 113, 222
Last of the Mohicans, The, 113
Last Tango in Paris, 114, 222
Laughlin, Tom, 70
Laurel, Stan, 71
Lavender Hill Mob, The, 114
Lawrence of Arabia, 3, 18, 19, 21, 22, 40–41, 114–115, 225
Lean, David, 4, 23, 24, 40, 73, 74, 87, 104, 108, 114, 151, 225
Le Diable au Corps. See: Devil in the Flesh
Lee, Spike, 88
Leigh, Janet, 42, 54–56, 131–132
Leigh, Vivian, 76
"Le Jazz Hot," 159
Lelouch, Claude, 117
Le Mans, 115
"Le Marseillaise," 79
Lemmon, Jack, 146
Leone, Sergio, 124
Le Roy, Mervyn, 107, 133
Les Diabolique. See: Diabolique
Les Enfants du Paradis. See: Children of Paradise
Le Souffle au Coeur. See: Murmur of the Heart
Lethal Weapon, 115
Lethal Weapon 2
Letter, The, 116, 228
Levinson, Barry, 121
Lewin, Albert, 128
Lewis, Juliette, 76
Lewton, Val, 110
Like Water for Chocolate, 116
Liotta, Ray, 19, 92
Listen to Britain, 116
Little Big Man, 116
Little Foxes, The, 116, 228

Little Richard, 110
Livingston, Jennie, 126
Logan, Joshua, 128
Lonesome Cowboys, 116
Lord Jim, 46
Loren, Sophia, 158
Lorre, Peter, 116
Losey, Joseph, 97
Louisiana Story. See: River, The
Love and Death, 116, 221
Loy, Myrna, 70, 150
Lubin, Arthur, 127
Lucas, George, 146
Lumet, Sidney, 24, 121, 127, 141, 225
Lupino, Ida, 106
Luske, Hamilton, 113
Lynch, David, 33, 72, 90

M

M., 116
MacDonald, Jeannette, 138
Mad Max 2. See: Road Warrior, The
Magnificent Ambersons, The, 117, 227
Mahler, Gustav, 86
"Make 'em Laugh," 145
Malden, Karl, 43
Male Animal, The, 117
Malkovich, John, 108
Malle, Louis, 66, 120
Maltese Falcon, The, 35, 117, 224
Man and a Woman, A, 117
Man Who Shot Liberty Valance, The, 118, 223
Man Who Would Be King, The, 118, 224
Manhattan, 21, 37, 117–118, 221
Mankiewicz, Joseph, 46–47, 62, 83
Mann, Michael, 113
Mansfield, Jayne, 110
March, Frederick, 69–70
Mare Nostrum, 118
Marshall, Garry, 130
Marshall, Penny, 70
Marton, Andrew, 69
Marvin, Lee, 67
Marx, Groucho, 122
Marx Brothers, 89, 122

Maury, Nicole, 72
Maxwell, Ronald, 97
McBride, James, 73
McCabe and Mrs. Miller, 118–119, 221
McCarey, Leo, 24, 60, 66, 225
McCrea, Joel, 148
McGillis, Kelly, 161
McLaglen, Victor, 105, 108, 133
McLeod, Norman, 109
McLuhan, Marshall, 63
McQueen, Steve, 138, 151
Mead, Margaret, 201–202
Medium Cool, 119
Mello, Breno, 71
Menjou, Adolph, 95, 148
Menzies, William, 150
Merrick, John, 90
Metropolis, 119
Michael Strogoff, 119
Michelangelo, 39, 166, 167, 168, 203
Midnight Cowboy, 36, 119
Midnight Express, 35, 119
Mifune, Toshiro, 151
Milestone, Lewis, 62, 95
Miller, George, 137
Miller's Crossing, 120
Minghella, Anthony, 156
Minnelli, Vincente, 63
Mississippi Mermaid, 120, 227
Mrs. Miniver, 120, 228
Mr. Smith Goes to Washington, 120, 222
Mitchum, Robert, 126
Modern Jazz Quartet, 94
Modern Times, 120, 222
Mon Oncle, 120
Monroe, Marilyn, 62
"Moonglow," 128
Moore, Robin, 47
Moorehead, Agnes, 117
Morrissey, Paul, 116
"Moses Supposes," 144
Mulligan, Robert, 152
Mumau, F. W., 123, 148
Mummy, The, 120
Muni, Paul, 37, 107, 111
Murmur of the Heart, 120–121
Murray, Bill, 76
Mutiny on the Bounty, 41

N

Napoleon, 121
Nashville, 121, 221
Natural, The, 121
Neanderthals, 179, 187, 191
Nelson, Ralph, 136
Network, 121, 225
"Never Gonna Dance," 149
Newman, Paul, 85, 148
Niblo, Fred, 69
Nicholls, George, Jr., 119
Nichols, Mike, 76, 102
Nicholson, Jack, 76, 80, 92–93, 124
Nietzsche, Fredrich, 52
"Night on Bald Mountain," 91
Night and Fog, 121, 226
Night at the Opera, A, 21, 122
Night on Earth, 122
Nights of Cabiria, 122, 223
"Nobody's Perfect," 145–146
Nolte, Nick, 42
North by Northwest, 122–123, 224
Nosferatu, 123
Nothing But a Man, 123
Nothing Sacred, 123, 227
Notorious, 123, 224
Novak, Kim, 128, 159
No Way Out, 123
Nugent, Elliott, 117
Nutcracker Suite, 91

O

O'Connor, Donald, 51, 145
O'Donnell, Cathy, 70
Official Story, The, 123
Official Version, The. See: Official Story, The
O'Hara, Maureen, 133
Olivier, Laurence, 21, 105, 106
Once Upon a Time in America, 124
Once Upon a Time in the West, 124
One Flew Over the Cuckoo's Nest, 124
On the Waterfront, 3, 18, 19, 20, 21, 22, 28, 35, 43–44, 124–125, 224

Origin of the Species, The, 173
Ornstein, Robert, 190
Orphans of the Storm, 125
Ossessione, 125
Other People's Money, 125
O'Toole, Peter, 40–41, 114–115
Our Daily Bread, 125
"Our Love is Here to Stay," 63
Out of Africa, 125
Out of the Past, 126
Ox-Bow Incident, The, 126, 227

P

Pacino, Al, 98, 212
Pakula, Alan, 146
Palance, Jack, 142
Panama, Norman, 85
Paradjanov, Sergo, 142
Paris Is Burning, 126
Parker, Alan, 119
Parsifal, 126
Pascal, Gabrie, 76l
Pascali's Island, 36, 126
Paths of Glory, 126, 225
Patton, 127
Pawnbroker, The, 127, 225
Peck, Gregory, 125, 137
Peckinpah, Sam, 160
Pedestrian, The, 127
Peeping Tom, 127
Penn, Arthur, 116
Perkins, Anthony, 54–55, 132
Persona, 127, 222
Pert, Candace B., 198–201
Pesci, Joe, 102
Petersen, Wolfgang, 108
Pfeiffer, Michelle, 212
Phantom of the Opera, 32, 127
Piano, The, 21, 127–128
Pickens, Slim, 20, 35, 87
Picnic, 128
"Picnic" theme, 128
Picture of Dorian Gray, 128
Pidgeon, Walter, 120
Pietà, 39, 203
Pink Flamingos, 128
Pink Panther, 128, 223
Pinker, Steven, 175, 187, 189, 201, 204, 206
Pinter, Harold, 97

Index

Pixote, 36, 128
Place in the Sun, A, 21, 33, 128–129, 227
Places in the Heart, 129
Plan 9 from Outer Space, 129
Plato, 201
Platoon, 129
Player, The, 3, 18, 19, 20, 22, 28, 41–45, 129–130, 166, 221
Polanski, Roman, 24, 80, 136, 150
Pollack, Jackson, 165
Pollack, Sydney, 27, 107, 125, 153
Poltergeist, 130
Porter, Cole, 74
Powell, Eleanor, 74
Powell, Michael, 127
Powell, William, 150
Presley, Elvis, 110
Pretty Woman, 130
Pride of the Yankees, 130
Princess Bride, The, 130, 226
Producers, The, 130
Prokofiev, Sergei, 61
Psycho, 2, 3, 18, 20, 22, 29, 30, 32, 53–56, 131–132, 170–171, 224
Public Enemy, The, 33, 132, 227
Puccini, Giacomo, 84
Puenzo, Luis, 123
Pumpkin Eater, The, 132
Purple Rose of Cairo, 132–133, 221
"Puttin' on the Ritz," 162

Q

Quest for Fire, 174–175
Quiet Man, The, 133, 224
Quinn, Anthony, 126
Quo Vadis, 133

R

Radio Days, 133, 221
Rafaelson, Bob, 92
Raft, George, 56
Raging Bull, 18, 133–134, 226
Raiders of the Lost Ark, 134–135, 227
"Raindrops Keep Falling on My Head," 75

Rains, Claude, 58, 76–78, 120, 123
Rambling Rose, 135
Ramis, Harold, 76
Ran, 135, 225
Rappeneau, Jean-Paul, 85
Rashomon, 135, 225
Ratoff, Greg, 62
Razor's Edge, The, 135
"Ready Teddy," 110
Reagan, Ronald, 56
Rear Window, 135, 224
Rebecca, 135, 224
Redford, Robert, 75, 121, 148
Redgrave, Michael, 74
Redgrave, Vanessa, 71
Red River, 136, 224
Reed, Carol, 150–151
Reiner, Rob, 24, 92, 130, 160, 226
Remains of the Day, The, 136
Rembrandt van Rijn, 169
Renoir, Jean, 24, 94, 138, 226
Repulsion, 136, 226
Requiem for a Heavyweight, 136
Resnais, Alain, 24, 106, 121, 148, 226
Reversal of Fortune, 136
Reynolds, Debbie, 51
Reza, Jasmina, 165
Richardson, Tony, 149, 152
"Ride of the Valkyries," 18, 20, 30, 53, 64–65
Riefenstahl, Leni, 155
Right Stuff, The, 136
Ritchie, Michael, 88
"Rite of Spring, The," 91
River, The, 137
Road Warrior, The, 137
Robbins, Jerome, 160
Robbins, Tim, 43, 130
Roberts, Julia, 42, 130
Robin Hood, 137
Robinson, Edward G., 88, 111
Robinson, Phil Alden, 92
Robinson, Sugar Ray, 134
Robson, Mark, 73
Rocky, 137
Roeg, Nicholas, 88
Roemer, Michael, 123
Rogers, Buddy, 161
Rogers, Ginger, 149, 153

Rogers, Mimi, 146
Roma. See: *Fellini's Roma*
Roman Holiday, 137, 228
Romeo & Juliet, 137
Rope, 137, 224
Rose Marie, 138
Ross, Katharine, 75
Rossellini, Isabella, 72
Royal Wedding, 138
Rules of the Game, The, 138, 226
Russell, Harold, 70
Russell, Roz, 66
Ryan, Meg, 160
Ryan, Robert, 67
Ryan's Daughter, 40

S

Saboteur, 138, 224
Saint, Eva Marie, 43–44, 124
Sand Pebbles, The, 138, 228
Sanders, George, 62
Sandrich, Mark, 153
San Francisco, 138, 163
"San Francisco," 138
Sardi, Phillipe, 150
Satyricon, 138, 223
Savage-Rumbaugh, Sue, 174
Scarface, 138
Scent of a Woman, 139
Scheider, Roy, 146
Schell, Maxmillian, 127
Schindler's List, 3, 21, 22, 139–140, 227
Schlesinger, John, 119
Schoedsack, Ernest, 112
Schroeder, Barbet, 136
Schulberg, Budd, 43
Scorsese, Martin, 24, 40, 76, 85, 102, 133–134, 149, 226
Scott, Ridley, 24, 61, 146, 150, 226
Searchers, The, 141–141, 224
Sellers, Peter, 21, 69, 87
Serpico, 141, 225
Seven Beauties, 141
Seven Samurai, 141, 225
Seventh Seal, The, 141, 222
Shadowlands, 142, 221
Shadows of Forgotten Ancestors, 142
Shaffner, Franklin, 127

241

Directors' Choice

Shakespeare, William, 39
Shane, 142, 227
Sharif, Omar, 3, 18, 19, 20, 40–41, 88, 114
Sharpsteen, Ben, 91
Shaw, George B., 76
Shaw, Robert, 21, 110
She Wore a Yellow Ribbon, 142, 224
Sheen, Martin, 52, 66
Shelton, Ron, 74
Sheridan, Ann, 56
Sheridan, Jim, 108
Shining, The, 142–143, 225
Shoeshine, 143, 223
Shop on Main Street, The, 143
Short Cuts, 143, 221
Shostakovich, Dmitry, 109
Shot in the Dark, A, 143, 223
Sidney, George, 75
Siegel, Don, 80, 108
Silence of the Lambs, The, 21, 143–144
Sinatra, Frank, 44
Singin' in the Rain, 3, 18, 19, 22, 28, 29, 50–52, 144–145, 169
"Singin' in the Rain," 51, 84, 144–145
Sleeper, 145, 221
S.O.B., 145, 223
Soldier and the Lady, The. See: Michael Strogoff
Some Like It Hot, 145–146, 227
Someone to Watch Over Me, 146, 226
Sophie's Choice, 146
Sorcerer, 146
Sound of Music, The, 146, 228
"Sounds of Silence," 103
Spiegel, Sam, 40–41, 44
Spielberg, Stephen, 2, 4, 22, 24, 41, 84, 90, 108, 110, 111, 134, 139, 226
Stagecoach, 146, 224
Stahl, John, 107
Stanwyck, Barbara, 37, 88, 113
Starman, 146
Star Wars, 146–147
State of the Union, 148, 222
Stavisky, 148, 226
Steiger, Rod, 18, 43–44, 124–125, 127

Stephenson, James, 116
Stevens, George, 24, 97, 105, 128, 142, 149, 227
Stevenson, Robert, 112
Stewart, Jimmy, 118, 120, 135, 159
Sting, The, 148
Stoller, Shirley, 141
Stone, George E., 95
Stone, Oliver, 129
Strangers on a Train, 148, 224
Strauss, Richard, 157
Streep, Meryl, 146, 212
Streetcar Named Desire, A, 44, 148, 224
Streisand, Barbra, 162
Sturges, John, 67
Sturges, Preston, 113, 148
Sullivan's Travels, 148
Sunrise, 148
Sunset Boulevard, 36, 148–149, 227
Sutherland, Donald, 88
Swing Time, 149, 227
Syberberg, Hans Jürgen, 126
Szabó, István, 105

T

Tale of Two Cities, A, 149
Tamiroff, Akim, 34
Tarzan, 174
Tashlin, Frank, 110
Taste of Honey, A, 149
Tati, Jacques, 120, 154
Tattersall, Ian, 197
Taurog, Norman, 74
Taxi Driver, 21, 149–150, 226
Taylor, Elizabeth, 21, 33, 128–129
Ten Commandments, The, 21, 150
Tenant, The, 150, 226
Teshigahara, Hiroshi, 162
Test Pilot, 163
Thelma and Louise, 150, 226
Things to Come, 150
Thin Man, The, 150
Third Man, The, 150–151
39 Steps, The, 151, 224
This Happy Breed, 151, 225
Thomas Crown Affair, The, 151
Thompson. Emma, 136
Thorpe, Richard, 110

Throne of Blood, 151–152, 225
"Thus Spake Zarathustra," 157
Tierney, Gene, 135
To Kill a Mockingbird, 152
Toland, Greg, 45
Tombstone, 152
Tom Jones, 152–153
"Tonight/Rumble," 160
Tootsie, 29, 153
Top Hat, 153
Tornatore, Guiseppe, 80
Touch of Evil, 19, 21, 22, 34, 42–43, 129, 153–154, 227
Tournuer, Jacques, 110, 126
Tracy, Spencer, 67, 163
Traffic, 154
Tramp, The, 154, 222
Treasure of the Sierra Madre, The, 21, 22, 29, 154–155, 224
Trial, The, 155, 227
Trintignant, Jean-Louis, 85
Triumph of the Will, 155
Trousdale, Gary, 69
Truffaut, François, 24, 45, 47, 85, 94, 111, 120, 227
Truly, Madly, Deeply, 156
Turner, Kathleen, 72
Tushingham, Rita, 149
2001: A Space Odyssey, 3, 18, 20, 21, 22, 29, 156–158, 225
Two Women, 158, 223

U

Umberto D, 158, 223
Un Chien Andelou, 158
Unforgiven, 158
Untouchables, The, 158–159

V

Van Dyke, W. S., 138, 150
Vermeer, Jan, 166, 167, 196
Vertigo, 159, 224
Victor/Victoria, 159, 223
Vidal, Gore, 172, 212
Vidor, Charles, 97
Vidor, King, 125
Vigo, Juan, 162
Visconti, Luchino, 86, 125
Viva Zapata!, 159, 224

Index

Voight, Jon, 119
Von Stroheim, Erich, 103, 105
Vorkapich, Slavko, 138

W

Wadleigh, Michael, 161
Wages of Fear, 159
Wagner, Richard, 30, 53, 65, 171
Wallis, Hal B., 58
Walsh, Raoul, 106, 160
Warden, Jack, 69
Washington, Freda, 107
Waters, John, 128
Way Down East, 159
Wayne, John, 118, 133, 140–141
Weaver, Sigourney, 61–62
Weir, Peter, 96, 161
Welles, Orson, 4, 23, 24, 34, 42–43, 45–47, 80–81, 113, 117, 151, 153, 155, 165, 227
Wellman, William, 24, 123, 126, 132, 161, 227
Wertmuller, Lina, 141
Weston, Jessie, 52
West Side Story, 160, 228
Wexler, Haskell, 119
Whale, James, 94

What Ever Happened to Baby Jane?, 160
What's Up, Doc?, 160
When Harry Met Sally, 160, 226
White Heat, 160
Whitty, Dame May, 113
Who Framed Roger Rabbit?, 160
"Who Put the Blame on Mame?" 97
Widerberg, Bo, 90
Wilcox, Fred, 93
Wild Bunch, The, 65, 160–161
Wilder, Billy, 24, 63–64, 88, 145, 148, 227
Wild Strawberries, 161, 222
Willis, Bruce, 42
Wilson, Edward O., 172–173, 174, 188, 189, 197, 204, 206, 207
Winger, Debra, 142
Wings, 161, 227
Winters, Shelly, 109
Wise, Kirk, 69
Wise, Robert, 24, 105, 110, 145, 146, 160, 228
Witness, 161
Wizard of Oz, The, 33, 161
Wolfen, 33, 161–162
Woman of the Dunes, 162

Women on the Verge of a Nervous Breakdown, 162
Wood, Edward, 129
Wood, Natalie, 140
Wood, Sam, 93, 100, 102, 122, 130
Woodward, Joanne, 132
Wray, Faye, 112
Wuthering Heights, 162, 228
Wyler, William, 4, 23, 24, 69, 88, 111, 116, 120, 137, 162, 228

Y

Yankee Doodle Dandy, 162, 222
Yates, Peter, 89
Yentl, 162
Young Frankenstein, 162

Z

Z, 162
Zeffirelli, Franco, 137
Zelig, 162, 221
Zemeckis, Robert, 160
Zero de Conduite, 162
Zinnemann, Fred, 95, 106
Zucker, David, 60
Zucker, Jerry, 60
Zwick, Edward, 97